Conversations

Freedom Is Everything & Love Is All the Rest

Dr. Richard Bandler & Owen Fitzpatrick

Health Communications, Inc.
Deerfield Beach, Florida

www.hcibooks.com

First published in 2005 by Mysterious Publications.

Library of Congress Cataloging-in-Publication Data

Bandler, Richard.
    Conversations / Richard Bandler and Owen Fitzpatrick.
      p. cm.
    "First published in 2005 by Mysterious Publications."
    ISBN-13: 978-0-7573-1381-3
    ISBN-10: 0-7573-1381-7
    1. Autonomy (Psychology)   2. Change (Psychology)
  3. Neurolinguistic programming.   I. Fitzpatrick, Owen.   II. Title.
  BF575.A88B36 2009
  158'.9—dc22

                               2009019875

Publisher: Health Communications, Inc.
          3201 S.W. 15th Street
          Deerfield Beach, FL 33442–8190

Cover photograph ©James Steidl, Fotolia.com
Cover design by Larissa Hise Henoch
Interior design and formatting by Lawna Patterson Oldfield

To Paula Bandler
The most beautiful soul that ever lived.
The loveliest being that exists.
The sweetest spirit that will be forever.
With love.

&

To Robert Anton Wilson . . .
the smartest man I know.

Warning to Readers

Warning to "Ex-Spurts"

This book is only for those who are interested in improving their quality of life, becoming happier and more delighted with life. Do not read this book and absorb the ideas within if you are not prepared to open up and enjoy how simple ideas really can be presented simply. Those who are interested in remaining in the chains of the free—this book could make you remember to forget what isn't important. Reading this book might open your real eyes, which can help you to see through the real lies of limitations, sadness, and fear and show you the world is full of rare and unprecedented opportunities to find an unexplainable sense of well-being.

Warning to Everyone Else

This book is full of ideas, suggestions, and techniques that can make your life better. Although Neuro-Linguistic Programming (NLP) is a technology that is becoming more and more popular across the planet, simply because someone practices as an NLP practitioner does not mean that he or she is adequately skilled. We highly suggest that if you are interested in learning to use NLP you complete a course with a trainer licensed directly by Dr. Richard Bandler.

Contents

Part III: The Keys to Changing Your Life

Part IV: Breaking the Chains of the Self

Part V: The Art of Loving Freedom

Part VI: The Art of Spiritual Freedom

Acknowledgments

From Both Authors

These are the people who have made our lives better. We count them as both colleagues and as friends. Thanks to: John and Kathleen LaValle, Paul McKenna, Kate Benson, and Gabe and Barbara Guerrero.

From Richard

To Jay, Elizabeth, Jayson, and, of course, Polly
To my mother, Ruby, and my sister, Pam
To Dr. John O'Dea and Debra
To Sean and Maura Flannagan
To M. Gerald Schwartzbach
And to all those lovely clients, without whose difficulties I would have had nothing to learn.

From Owen

I want to thank the following who have had a profound impact on my life and my acquisition of freedom and love.

My family

My parents, Marjorie and Brian, for everything. You are the best parents one could wish to have, and I love you more that you could know. Emer, for being a great sister. My Granny for loving me, and my heroic uncle Shea.

Granny Packie, Aunty Joe, Granda, Great Aunt Peggy, and Uncle Tony for their love when they were alive. My bigger family including Brendan, Michael K., Aisling, Sinead, Orla, Donal, Oisin, Lucy, Michael G., Robert, Pat, Bob, Mat, Kelly, Maureen, and Bill, and all the rest. I am very proud to be related to all of you. My training partner, Brian, for being such a fantastic partner and dear friend, and his family who feel like mine, Theresa, Cian, and Dylan.

Those Who Helped Directly with the Book

My amazing friends like gorgeous Gillian McNamara-Fowley, Michael Connolly, Aoife Ni Bhreachain Curran, and Barry Holden for all the brilliant help with the book. Richie Collins, my friend, for his transcription work and making me laugh. Claire Rourke, who has been of immense help in the editing of this book.

Mentors and Teachers

Eric Robbie for all his wisdom, insight, and creativity. Frank Farrelly for making me laugh out loud. David Northrop for his great friendship and advice. Joe Keaney, the Dalai Lama, Michael Breen, Liz Dunne, and the other teachers I've had from whom I've learned much.

Friends

To Ali: TQ. My "homies": Eddie, Davee, and Shane for making me smile, laugh, and feel loved. My other good friends: Joe Higgins, Lauren, Kevin, Niall, Cindy, Tamir, Steve, Lynda, Mark D., Brian F., Ruth, Lizzy, Audrey, Joe, Annette, Ciaran, Eileen, Baggo, Nevvy, Stevee, Susan, Mark, Martin, Car, Rob, Cliona, and Colm. My college friends: Ruarai, Maire, Caoilte, Karl, Paul, Aleisha, Darragh, Tommy, Mick K., Gary, Martin, John, Sean, Alan C., Niamh, Fiona, Siobhan D., Helen, Rob, J.P., Martina, Olga, Anne Marie, Murissa, Mick H., Carolyn, Catherine, Martin, and

Gerrie. Roisin the angel, Ben for making me proud, and Number 6 for making me grin. Rab and Michelle for their wonderful generosity, friendship, and inspiration. Siobhan Mac for an experience worth having. My love and sincerest thanks to all of you.

Colleagues and Friends

Alessio, Hugh, Thomas, Anton, Zana, Morag, Niamh, Allison, Anna, John, Rachel, Steve, Gabrielle, Ed Percival, Deirdra, Rachel, Cora, Judymay, Cathy, Gail, DP, Maurice, Fergal, Lynda, Kay, Bryan, Phillipe, Gerry, Rob, Laura, Harry, the John B's, Colin, Mahboob, Mark, Ron, Edie, Phil, Jackie, Lenny, Peta Heskall, Pete Cohen, Clay, Jag, Kier, Maria O'M, Michelle, John S. LaValle, Neill, Uwe, Yvonne, Jamie, Derek, James, Mark, Dave, Holly, Reeney, Omar, Liopi, Javier, Eduardo, Gaby, Sergio, Olga, Edgar, Reed and all the rest for their advice and help. Sabrina Hussain, Jan, Van, Dan, Sajani, Ashlesh, Monica, Hemant, and all the rest of my very special friends in India. Thank you all for your wonderful hospitality and friendship.

Other Acknowledgments

My trainees, clients, and students who taught me as much as I taught them. My true love, Glasgow Celtic FC, for making me happy. Martin O'Neill, Henrik Larson, U2, Morrissey, Eminem, Ricky Gervais, Billy Connolly, Eddie Izzard, Bill Hicks, Cecilia Ahern, Tommy Tiernan, and Karl Spain for inspiring me with their brilliance. God (every different version) for being good to me.

Preface

Over the past thirty-five years I've written prefaces and forewords to not just my own books but to books that many of my students have written. However, here my preface is to a book that I participated in creating. It's based on conversations I had with Owen Fitzpatrick about my perspective on the field of Neuro-Linguistic Programming (NLP), which is actually much bigger than simply the techniques of NLP itself.

This book also includes ideas from the fields of Neuro-Hypnotic Repatterning and Design Human Engineering, but it is very different from other books I have written on these subjects. Most of the books I have published over the years have included case histories and methodical, step-by-step techniques by which readers could improve the odds of overcoming such things as phobias. By reading them, you could study language patterns and increase your skills in asking questions or in creating sentences that help you to persuade people powerfully and change their beliefs.

This book is designed to do something entirely different. It's designed to change your perspective about what freedom is. To me, freedom is the single most important experience that human beings can have. It is the act of creation itself—not just creating great things, like art and music, but creating the moments of your life.

Most people have difficulties and limit how much joy they have in their lives because they don't grasp opportunities available to them or maximize their resources. The very way people think about things and the very beliefs they have prevent them from being able to achieve the best that life has to offer. The byproduct of these limitations manifest themselves in many ways—from schizophrenia to depression to all kinds of ludicrous self-defeating behaviors.

To me, people who make life more miserable than it needs to be are chaining themselves to the belief that life is suffering. They forget that life is not about remembering and reliving unpleasantness from their past, but about going forward to look at life as the adventure it can be. They're supposed to ask themselves more challenging questions, such as "How can I enjoy myself?" "How can I make this easier?" "How can I make this fun?"

However, today we can go one step further. We have techniques that can help make you feel really good for no reason, so that when you actually do have a reason, you'll feel even better. This has become the foundation of my work over the past thirty-five years—the art of enabling people to alter their state of consciousness, the very chemical state in which they exist. To me, the use of words is about helping people to get to a happier future more effectively.

So if you're learning to do something, you can learn it more quickly, more easily, and better than before. If you're just trying to strip yourself of your difficulties, you'll have all this spare time, and you may end up finding new difficulties to fill the gap they left. This book will ensure that you learn skills that can not only help you overcome challenges but can also provide you with better things to do instead. You'll start to ask different questions such as: How much fun can I stand? How much pleasure can I have?

The process of writing this book was a pleasure, as I enjoy Owen's company. We agreed to create this book through recording our conversations. I told him that he'd have the chance to ask me whatever he wanted, and then he could organize my responses and fit them with his own experience.

Over the years I've referred many clients to Owen, and never once has he come back and told me that they were stuck in the same old rut. He has always found a way of getting people through their difficulties because, in one sense, he comes from the first real generation of Neuro-Linguistic Programmers. They are the people who see NLP as an attitude and methodology to become happier and more effective. They weren't people trying to get out of the therapy business or buying into the ideas that were intrinsic in the field of psychology about how broken things were.

Owen started out with me, and he went on learning the techniques that I was using at that time. As I changed, he changed with me—and he has gone on to develop some techniques of his own. The stories about his own clients, the techniques used, and his own perspective about what questions he asked me, as well as the questions he answered himself, became an important part of the process of writing this book.

I've cowritten books with lots of people over the years. I've written books with John Grinder. I've written books with John LaValle. Right now, I'm coauthoring books with three different people, and every time you write with somebody it's a different process.

This particular process has more life to it because we were not trying to fill in a previously defined outline. What we were trying to do was open up the rules so that readers could open up their beliefs and have a broader sense of choice—so that you can look at the vastness of the universe with excitement rather than look at it as a burden. This is your chance to have some fun and to get some new ideas. More important, this is your chance to gain some new directions and some new perspectives. Take a chance.

Dr. Richard Bandler

Note for the Readers

Conversations recounts extensive conversations between myself, Owen Fitzpatrick, and Dr. Richard Bandler, the cofounder of a personal development field known as Neuro-Linguistic Programming (NLP). Richard is my teacher, my mentor, and my friend, and he is regarded by many all over the world as a living genius. This book came about as a result of conversations that took place in different parts of the world from 2002 to 2005. During 2003, I traveled for a few months around the world, and experiences from my travels, as well as those with clients, also contribute to this book.

Richard is the creative artist behind the ideas that have revolutionized modern psychology, business, and the fields of coaching, self-help, and self-improvement. His insights into the human mind have had a huge impact upon the world—every corner bookshop has books on NLP.

I sincerely hope that one day due credit will be awarded to Richard for all that he has achieved. Until then, I offer this book as my tribute to his life's work. I hope that it can shine the same delight on readers that has affected so many souls over the years since he first began teaching people how to become happy and free over thirty five years ago. The conversations we had were often one-sided, due to my efforts to utilize the time with Richard in the best possible way. At Richard's suggestion, many of my own stories, perspectives, and examples have been included as well. And, from all of this, a book was born. In retelling case histories and personal anecdotes to help explain the ideas we present, names have been changed or concealed to protect the identity of those involved. Some people have given permission to use their real names.

We have omitted most of the expletives from the conversations related here; however, in particular cases when they served an important purpose, we have left them in.

From time to time, it may seem that some sentences are not grammatically correct, but these are written for a purpose, as NLP and conventional grammar do not necessarily share the same structure. Many people who have had the pleasure of attending a workshop with Dr. Bandler will understand that, somehow, you leave the workshop and find yourself engaging in new behaviors with new skills and a different attitude. When you have finished this book, you will have a similar experience. There is a specific reason for this.

In this book, the terms "conscious" and "unconscious" will be used to convey aspects of the mind. By "conscious" we mean that part of your mind that thinks critically, rationally, and logically. By "unconscious" we mean that part of your mind that is responsible for your feelings and creativity and contains all your memory, wisdom, and perceptions.

Your unconscious is the part of your mind that controls your habits and habitual ways of thinking. The key to changing your life is to learn to use your unconscious in more effective ways.

So many books attempting to teach NLP are written in a complicated way. This book is different. Here, we have used a sophisticated system of nesting information, ideas, and suggestions inside layers of stories and examples to help the reader unconsciously develop new ways of thinking and feeling.

We hope that those of you proficient in NLP will enjoy studying the text in more detail and learning more about the patterns we have used in tailoring the book to both the conscious and unconscious mind. There are many, many examples of language patterns, nested stories, and multilevel metaphors that make this book much more effective in its impact on the reader.

For those of you with little or no experience in NLP, despite the sophistication that has gone into the multilevel communication in this book, we hope that you find the ideas as inherent and simple as they truly are. Personal freedom is an easy thing to understand, learn about, and develop once you know how. Please do not be too surprised at how quickly you find yourself feeling happier and developing new, more liberating attitudes and perspectives as you read. Remember, most of it is done through simple psychology—the art of unconscious suggestion.

This book is divided into a number of sections:

- Part I explains more about how this book came about and the concept known as NLP.
- The conversations with Richard begin in Part II, where we discuss the notion of personal freedom.
- In Part III we explore the process of how long-lasting, permanent change occurs and what are the keys to changing anything in your life.
- In Part IV, we examine how to deal successfully with the problems people have with themselves and their lives.
- In Part V, we explore how to improve your relationships with others.
- And finally, in Part VI, we discuss how you can best develop yourself spiritually and connect more usefully with your universe.

We also include a random ramblings chapter between each section. These chapters are simply random excerpts that we wanted to include but for which we could find no other specific place within the book. They, too, have their own functions.

Some chapters include a number of exercises or tasks that will help you master the new attitudes, understandings, and skills that you have learned. DO THEM. It's so important that you gain the experiences they provide so that you can fully understand how things fit together. Tasks are provided for you to get into the habit of engaging in specific disciplines. Following the instructions will have a remarkable impact upon your life.

As with any book, this will have its critics, and we accept that we can never please everyone. We can never "make" anyone free. We can only teach people how to open the door—but they must walk through. All we hope and encourage you to discover is that your prison is not as strong as your desire for the unknown, yet wonderful, world of liberation, inner peace, and happiness. People who want to change sometimes resist with excuses, skepticism, hesitation, or laziness. We ask you to commit your efforts toward reading and using this book to improve your life. This is why it was written.

Introduction:
Adventures in Personal Freedom

Many years ago, the same word "freogan" denoted the verbs "to free" and "to love."

Freedom and love were once the same.
Somewhere along the way they got separated.
This is the story of how they got back together.

Every so often, a moment can just grab you. It can arrive out of nowhere. You could simply be minding your own business, dwelling on some incessant worry, and then suddenly it hits you. You could be moping about your past, sick of living, and then, without warning, it just turns your life upside down. You could be absorbed in your everyday problems, and then, out of the blue, it seizes you by the scruff of the neck and shows you something you have never seen before.

We live in a really weird world. Think about it. You wake up, you do some kind of work, you eat, you hopefully spend some time with your loved ones, and then you go to sleep. You wait around for the next good feeling. Maybe it'll come in a bar of chocolate or a program on television. Maybe it'll be a party on the weekend, a dinner in a couple of weeks, or a vacation once a year. Maybe it's a new house, a new car, a new computer, a stereo, a digital television, a DVD, an iPod, or a new dog. Whatever it is, you wait in the hope that it will happen. Then, if you get it, you wait for the next thing to happen to make you feel good.

Maybe you have not been that lucky. Maybe you have been finding life a bit of a struggle. Maybe you have been feeling lonely or frustrated, stressed or depressed. Maybe your greatest desire is to find out who you really are and to become happy with yourself.

No matter who you are, wouldn't it be nice not to have to wait to feel good? Wouldn't it be nice to just feel great now for no reason? Wouldn't it be nice to feel happy about yourself, your prospects, your relationships, and your reason to "be" in this world?

Yes, of course, it would. Unfortunately, so many people are imprisoned by what Dr. Richard Bandler calls the "chains of the free." Many people fill their lives with moments of fear, sadness, apathy, disgust, despair, anxiety, worry, stress, anger, and stupidity. I imprisoned myself in many of these chains for many years—but I don't any longer. I truly feel free.

When I say the word "free," I do not mean that I have no problems or times when I make mistakes. By "free," I mean the sense that I have control over my own life, my own destiny. I do not need to know exactly what my future has in store, because I feel capable of dealing with anything and making every moment of my life wonderful.

When I was younger, I dreamt about becoming a famous soccer player. I dreamt about beating up bad guys and becoming a hero. I spent much of my childhood hanging out in pool halls and planning how I would win the world snooker championship. These were the dreams of my childhood. I never did turn out exactly as I planned all those years ago, but I did fulfill one dream. When I was just a boy, I also dreamt about being so strong that no monster and no evil could ever get me. Now, in this moment, I realize that I am strong enough to tackle any monster and overcome any evil. The evil monsters that exist in this world come in the form of sadness, fear, anger, hate, and despair. When you can face them all and know you will succeed, you are free.

As you turn each page of this book, I want to introduce you to my world and my adventures in personal freedom with Dr. Richard Bandler. I want to tell you the story of my conversations with a genius, in which I learned what real personal freedom is all about and how it is possible for anyone to become free. I want to take you on a journey through some of my own stories and real-life experiences and help you gain more useful perspectives and ways of seeing the world.

Talking with Richard one on one is completely different from going to see him present a workshop, watching him with a client, or reading his books—but equally entertaining and enlightening. From time to time, Richard would answer questions I had in my own life, when I had actually asked him about something else. Sometimes he would seem to magically read my thoughts, and during each conversation, regardless of how many months passed in between, Richard would manage to pick up from where he left off.

I have written this book from a personal perspective. I hope that as you take the time to understand my perspective, you gain a new understanding of some of the things that have troubled you. I have always found other people's experiences immensely helpful. I hope that you can relate to my personal narratives, too. In this book, I present to you what I learned and how I changed as I wrote it. You'll learn how I use NLP to deal with life in the most effective way.

One of the moments that really grabbed me happened as I reflected on the book you are reading. In my apartment, I read over some of the draft chapters and listened again to the tapes of my conversations with Richard. I thought about my fantastic journey over the past couple of years. I remembered our different conversations—at the kitchen table of his home, as well as on trips to Edinburgh, London, and Puerto Vallarta in Mexico. So much had happened. I stood up to take a break. It was during that break that I felt an incredible sense of liberation. I knew from that moment I would never look back.

PART I

Escaping from a Miserable Prison

CHAPTER 1

A Moment of Clarity

THE RAIN POURED DOWN heavily as I looked out of my apartment window. It was about two o'clock on a Monday afternoon in a southwestern suburb of Dublin. I was taking a break from reading some draft chapters of this book, and as the thunder rumbled in the sky, I sang along to a song I just put on. The music blared in my apartment, but it would have been inaudible outside because of the sound of the storm. I was fully absorbed in the moment as I looked at the colors of the world. I noticed the reds, the blues, and the greens of the buildings and parks in the distance. I listened to the sounds of the world, and I heard, beyond the melodies of the music, the constant sound of heavy rain. The clouds were gray and dark. I saw a crackle of lightening as the sky lit up. I pressed my face gently against the window.

I was simply appreciating the moment. As I stood there, time seemed to go by so slowly. I thought about my life. I recalled my mistakes, my hard times, and my heartbreaks. I recalled the times I was prepared to give up everything I had because of the agonizing pain I was going through. And I remembered my greatest achievements, the best successes, the moments of inspiration that affected me. I remembered the feelings of elation.

I realized right there and then that I had as many problems as I'd ever had, and yet none of them really bothered me. I was going to deal with them, and that was that.

I just wouldn't tolerate the bad feelings like I used to. It was so liberating. Finally, I was feeling free.

We are imprisoned by how we experience the world. You experience your world through the limitations of your thoughts. Many people learn to think of the world in terms of black and white. They never realize that there are many ways to experience the same event.

A great time to discover this is when you are asleep. When you sleep, you can reach heights of bliss and freedom. Your dreams can provide you with a gorgeous sense of happiness. They show you the world in a different way. You can see it from many different perspectives: time and space are not limiting, your logic is not restricted, a figure can be more than one person at the same time, and you can be doing more than one thing at a time. Life can be lived without the rules you have learned.

In this moment at the window, I finally got it. If you want to become free or if you want to bring more joy into your life, you must choose to change in certain ways. You must choose to learn about freedom. You must choose to learn about change. You must choose to change how you experience your problems. You must choose how you experience your relationships. You must choose how you understand the universe. You must choose how you act, how you think, and how you live.

You must do so keeping in mind that there is always more than one way to look at a situation and that there is always another way to think about it. When you think differently, you will feel different. Once you feel different, the chemistry of your brain will literally alter. Your brain is made up of lots of chemical cocktails and electrical connections. When you think in useful, positive, and productive ways and you feel good, your brain will start working well for you. You will find it producing the most optimal environment for the best thoughts and feelings. Once you choose what is useful, you gain freedom. I made my choice. I felt free.

My body tingled and a shiver ran up and down my spine. I opened the window and let the spray from the storm bounce in. I put my head out into the wet wind and took a deep breath as I closed my eyes. When I opened them again, the world was so beautiful. I wondered what took me so long to really see it.

So how do you choose this freedom?

When I was twenty-four, I decided I wanted to write a book. I wanted to write a book that would help people change their lives and become happier. I wanted to write a book that would inspire those already doing well to do even better. I wanted to write a book that would make the world, literally, a better place to live. It was then, at this stage in my life, that I got one of those lucky breaks.

CHAPTER 2

The Opportunity of a Lifetime

SOMETIMES YOU JUST GET LUCKY. There I was just a young bloke from Dublin, and suddenly I get the opportunity of a lifetime: I get to ask any questions to one of the smartest men on the planet and put them in a book to share with the world. As I studied the field of Neuro-Linguistic Programming, I began to get to know Dr. Richard Bandler. Richard had cocreated NLP with John Grinder in the mid-1970s. One December evening in 2002, Richard suggested we write a book together. The book you are reading is the product of that suggestion.

Richard has taught millions of people across the world to become happy and free from fears and doubts, stress and depression. He has done what so many philosophers and psychologists have tried to accomplish over the centuries: he has discovered secrets to happiness, freedom, and love. I can testify to that because I found these answers and secrets in both my dialogues with Richard and in experiences in my own life. Books are written to inspire, to educate, and to entertain. They are written with the hope that the reader will gain inspiration, knowledge, and enjoyment from them. They are written to stand as timeless elements of wisdom, to share their words for eternity.

Richard giving "that look."

Words enable us to transfer ideas to other people. Ideas can inspire different ways of thinking, different attitudes, and different behaviors and have a power inside them that is released when they are acted upon.

The power of ideas within this book will help you transform your entire world. Read. React. The mere act of reading this book will automatically start you thinking differently about things. Once you have been exposed to the ideas of freedom and love, life will take on a new meaning for you.

I remember working with my very first client. I remember having a plan and soon realizing that plans never work out exactly. Over the years, I've helped suicidal people, those who thought they were superheroes, sociopaths, and those who thought they had gone mad. I've treated people for everything from serious depression, stress, and panic to addictions and relationship problems—from top business executives and celebrities to athletes and children. My role has been to help people succeed more in their lives, and throughout all of this, I've found NLP incredibly useful.

My approach is not always conventional. From taking clients out into shopping centers and bars to sparring in the boxing ring with them while testing the work, I've experimented plenty. Mostly, though, I just help people change the way they think and feel. I teach people how to feel better about their problems and to laugh at them.

Richard Bandler is a unique individual. He is provocative, hilarious, and highly inventive. For all those who see him present workshops, he is not only a mind full of wisdom but a captivating storyteller as well.

Sometimes, all that is needed for a life to turn around is for a person to act upon a set of ideas. You, too, can experience true personal freedom. If you don't act, you could find yourself living in the chains of the free and exist in the most awful tragedy this planet has ever known. This tragedy is what I call the "source of human misery."

CHAPTER 3

The Source of Human Misery

IT WAS ONE OF THE greatest tragedies ever. They were imprisoned for a crime they did not commit. Their captors would not reveal what the supposed crime was but held them prisoners anyway. They were given their basic needs, but their lives were hell. Most moments of every day they were tormented and treated horribly. They were insulted constantly and told they were no good.

They were filled with fears and worries about everything and anything. They were victimized and given so many conflicting messages that they became insecure and unsure of who they were and what they could do. Some were isolated from others, while some were kept in bad company with those who constantly pushed their buttons and goaded them. Some wanted to die. Some carried on struggling with life. Everyone was held captive to some degree—some more than others.

They were constantly criticized about what they did. They were made to feel horrible each time they made a mistake. They were held back from everything that they ever wanted. They grew more disappointed and more hopeless every day. They pitied themselves and took their frustration out on each other. Meanwhile their captors made things worse, and the prisoners wondered if it would ever end. They were overwhelmed with everything they were forced to do. They suffered and were helpless.

They were given moments of freedom, but it was not really freedom. Deep down they knew they would have to endure the pain from their captors again soon, and the brief reprieves meant nothing. They suffered most of the time. Their health waned from the bad treatment. Many of them could not go to sleep. Their lives became devoid of any meaning, which had existed once. They walked around depressed, anxious, fearful, stressed, and frustrated with everything. They longed for freedom.

So who were they? Who were their captors?

"They" were the human race, and their captors were their minds.

Since your birth, you have picked up habitual ways of thinking, feeling, and behaving. Many of these habits imprison you in unhappiness, loneliness, self-doubt, self-pity, fear, and hatred. These feelings in turn, affect your health, your relationships, and your life.

We all want to be happy, don't we? We all want a meaningful existence. We all want to feel connected to someone, to something. We all want to share our lives with loved ones. We want to live our lives with freedom to do what we want.

At some point in the past, you were put upon this earth. You were born. At some point in the future, you will be taken from this earth. You will die. Maybe you'll go to heaven, maybe you'll be reborn in a new life, or maybe there's nothing after this life.

Regardless, the clock is ticking. Every moment that passes you cannot have back. You have a certain amount of time in the life you are living now. This life will involve many moments of triumph and delight, sadness and despair. It will lead you into dark times and out to brighter days. You will encounter opportunities and problems. This is your life.

You will meet certain characters along the way. These characters will be around you at different times. There will be those who love you, those who like you, those who dislike you, and those who are indifferent to you. Sometimes they will treat you well, and sometimes they will treat you badly. Sometimes they will enter your life and sometimes leave. Sometimes they will be the object of your uncontrollable, undying love and sometimes the source of your devastatingly cruel heartbreak. This is your life.

You will experience many events during your time here. Some will be good, and some will be bad. All will teach you. You will learn many things. Some will be useful to you and some will not. You will forget many things. Some will be important, some will not. Sometimes you will fail. Sometimes you will succeed. Some people will be born with fortune, some without. You will have moments of hope and bliss and moments of disappointment and devastation. This is your life.

These stand as the inevitable truths of life. While you live on this planet, you have one major choice. This choice comes down simply to this: how do you want to live?

Some live free; some don't. To me, living free means living happily, being successful, connecting wonderfully with others, and making a real difference in the world. To me, being happy is about regularly creating, in ourselves, good feelings so that we can enjoy what we do more and think in more positive and useful ways. To me, being successful is about achieving whatever the goals are that we set for ourselves, whether they are material, spiritual, or simply living a better life. To me, connecting wonderfully with others is about manifesting relationships and friendships with those around us and helping them to feel happy and to be successful, too. To me, making a real difference in the world is about creating, developing, improving, or refining something that will affect the world in a positive way.

The truths of life will occur over and over again for everyone the same way. The real question is, again: how will you live? Up to the very moment that you read this sentence, how have you been living? Have you been feeling happy and cheerful most of the time? Have you been doing what you want to do in a way that you enjoy? Have you made meaningful relationships and connections with people? Have you made a real difference to the world around you?

Human beings have achieved miracles. Consider all the inventions over the centuries. We started with just natural resources, and now we have built an entire world. We have accomplished immense creation with the barest essentials. You have to stop and become aware of all the things we can do now that we could not do 150 years ago. All of these amazing inventions started in the minds of human beings. Yet the one machine we have, as yet, failed to master, is our own minds. All progress of mankind is based upon fulfilling our needs and making us happier and more successful. The kind of progress we offer here is progress inherent in learning to master our minds.

We all want freedom from our problems. We all want to feel and experience love that lasts unconditionally and forever. We all want to live life as well as we can and be as happy as we can.

You have the same number of problems in your life whether you are happy and content or sad and miserable. The difference is how free you are from being affected negatively by those problems. The types of people you meet are the same whether you are building relationships successfully or destroying relationships. When you are spiritually delighted and free, there are still as many good and bad things happening in the world. Your choice is to be free in this world regardless of the circumstances or to be overwhelmed by the problems and imprison yourself in the painful torture chambers of your own mind.

The source of human misery is the way we have learned to limit ourselves through our minds. It is the way we have learned to think about and treat ourselves and other people. Becoming free from this misery involves taking charge of our minds again and choosing joy over misery, freedom over the chains that limit us, and love over the hate and fear that suffocates us. It is then that we will discover the true source of human joy.

Freedom is not simply an ideal we all strive for—it is everything wonderful we can be. It is not fear, sadness, loneliness, despair, regret, disappointment, anger, or pain. Freedom is hope. It is wisdom. It is happiness. It is enlightenment. It is friendship. It is humor. Most of all, it is love.

There are lots of people striving all of the time to make their lives better. Whether you are depressed or stressed out, fearful or stuck in a rut, unsure of your life's path or simply looking to excel in an area of your life, essentially we are all on the same journey. We all want to do even better, become even better, and feel even happier.

Think of this as a guidebook. You can use it to explore the adventure of life and learn how to deal with that adventure more successfully. You will learn about transformation and change. You will understand how you can use your brain in the most effective way. This book will discuss the meaning of living, the achievement of happiness and success. It will bring you to the steps of improving your relationships, making more friends, and communicating more influentially in your life. It will enable you to master your use of time, relax when you used to be stressed, and motivate yourself. It provides the keys to overcoming most of the problems you face in life and offers you a powerful transformational understanding and perspective on spirituality and your connection with the universe.

Wouldn't it be nice to learn how to put more smiles on more faces, put more happiness in more hearts, and make a contribution that improves the quality of living for other people in the world?

Allow us to help you understand some things you've probably never realized before. Let us take your entire perspective on life and change it so that you begin to use your brain, use your body, and live your life in a way that enables you to experience more love, more freedom, more happiness.

Many of the ideas that lie in these pages come from the human technology known as Neuro-Linguistic Programming (NLP). In the next chapter, we will explain a little more about this transformational, personal enhancement tool.

CHAPTER 4

NLP: A Story of the Technology of Success

BECAUSE A LARGE AMOUNT of this book relates to developments that have emerged from the field of NLP, it is necessary to explain a bit about this field of work. There are many different accounts given of the exact events that brought about the field of NLP. What we know for certain is that, in the early 1970s, Richard Bandler began to study the most successful therapists he could find. He soon collaborated with John Grinder, and they founded the field of Neuro-Linguistic Programming (NLP). They studied Virginia Satir (a pioneer of family therapy), Fritz Perls (a Gestalt therapist), and Milton Erickson (a clinical hypnotherapist) to start with and were guided by the advice of a famous anthropologist, Gregory Bateson.

NLP soon became one of the most popular, respected, and powerful technologies of the self-improvement movement. Today, it is used by millions throughout the world, although it is known by many different names, and it offers some of the most effective and efficient change techniques and ideas.

NLP studies the way we represent our experience through our neurology (neuro), how we communicate with ourselves and others (linguistic), and how we can change our habitual ways of thinking, communicating, and behaving (programming). NLP is the process of learning about how we think, communicate, and act so that we can start thinking, communicating, and acting more usefully and fluently.

NLP is described as an "attitude," "methodology," and "technology." It is an attitude that enables you to live life in a happy, productive, and successful way. It is a methodology that enables you to usefully model successful people in different areas, such as education, medicine, and business. It is based on the principle that no matter what someone else can do, you can learn how to do the same thing once you understand what that person did in the way they thought as well as in action or behavior. It is a technology that contains within it systems and skills that enable you improve the quality of your life.

Having been trained by both cofounders of NLP as well as by many other well-known trainers in the field, I discovered that there was a great difference in skill between presenters. Like methodologies in any field, NLP has been taught both brilliantly and badly. It has been abused by some and used wonderfully by others. NLP was originally a reaction to the field of psychology, which failed to present effective ideas to help people change.

NLP represents a different approach to the medical model of labeling and categorizing people. It works from a basis of understanding that people are not their behaviors or thoughts, and, therefore, when they learn to change the way they think and behave, they change their lives.

Unfortunately, some people do not use NLP in the ways the cofounders originally intended. Instead of sharing ideas with others to help improve the quality of life on this planet, some use it in an attempt to be revered or to style themselves as a guru. They take the simple ideas and make them complicated. Some have tried to claim that their techniques are creative models or new fields, but they are not—they are just techniques made up of the skills that were already developed by Richard and his colleague at the time, John Grinder.

But there are also many people who have become interested in NLP who have taken the skills it offers and attempted to improve the quality of life on this planet. It is time to focus on how we can best use all the developments of the last thirty-five years with integrity to bring about wonderful change to the world.

To me, this wonderful change will not be brought about by explaining NLP in convoluted, prestige-seeking academic language. It will not be brought about by taking one part of NLP and trying to turn it into another field in an attempt to gain status or become a revered guru. It will not be brought about by trying to explain NLP sequentially, as if it were a subject in school.

The best way we can bring about such a change is to focus on making NLP as simple and as available as possible to as many people as possible, to give credit where credit is due, and to use NLP to teach NLP. In this way we help people to become immersed within an NLP world where they can master the attitude that exists within them.

Richard has since developed two further technologies that are innovations beyond NLP. Design Human Engineering (DHE) and Neuro-Hypnotic Repatterning (NHR) focus on making personal change, evolution, and improvement faster, easier, and better. DHE is about learning to create a more powerful mind by imagining building machines inside your mind that can help you evolve further. NHR is about repatterning your habitual ways of thinking, feeling, and behaving by hypnotically altering your neurochemistry. (Of course, these are simply my brief definitions and do not completely and adequately describe these fields in full.)

What these three technologies really all come down to is helping people to change the way they think about the world and feel inside their bodies so that they can change their behaviors and enhance the quality of their lives.

When I got that "moment of clarity" at my window, what I really mean is that I began to put all these different ideas together into a single philosophy about a more useful way to live. Now it's time to take you on the journey that began during a meeting between Dr. Richard Bandler the "Einstein of the mind" and myself one afternoon a few years ago.

CHAPTER 5

Random Ramblings 1: The Secret Code of Freedom

EVERY CHAPTER IN this book is designed to teach you specific things that will help you, as well as to communicate with you on an unconscious level to assist you in developing a new way of thinking about your problems. Although these random ramblings chapters may not seem to connect directly with the rest of the text, they do have their own specific functions at the end of each section. Along with plenty of information coded for your unconscious mind to get, we have also provided a task for those of you interested in figuring out codes.

During the nine years I spent learning from Richard, I heard him mention the six main problems that most people have. However, I never heard him mention more than one or two of them in any one workshop. In this book, these problems are revealed for those of you who are prepared to read a little deeper into the text.

Inside these chapters, we have hidden these six problems. I first heard Richard begin to describe them on a CD set of his work in the 1990s. In each of the ramblings chapters we will reveal another of the problems. Once you have found all six problems, the key is to discover how you can use the ideas you've learned from this book to apply them to solve these problems.

Somewhere in this book a date is given in full. This date has four numbers above zero in it. Each of the four numbers represents a paragraph in a different random ramblings chapter. For example, if the date were March 1, 2001, the code would be the *first* day of the *third* month in the year *two* thousand and *one*. So, the corresponding paragraphs would be paragraph 1, paragraph 3, paragraph 2, and paragraph 1. The first problem will be mentioned in this chapter and, from then on, the code will follow the date mentioned in the book. The sixth problem will not be mentioned in any of the random ramblings chapters but instead is revealed elsewhere in the book.

The first of the six main problems that Richard says human beings have is the problem of hesitation. Unfortunately, people hesitate and do not take the action that could enable them to achieve their goals. Many people hold themselves back in case the action they are thinking of taking is not the "right" action. Unfortunately, while they sit there and do nothing, the world goes on without them. However, the one thing that people rarely hesitate about is fear. Fear is something that you *do*—the act of fearing.

> *"Fear doesn't come from nowhere.*
> *You have to do something to be afraid."*
>
> —RICHARD BANDLER

It's like the idea of freedom. With the governments of the world throwing the term "freedom" around so flippantly, it is hard to give back to the term the wonderful feelings that were once emitted by the very mention of the word. The kind of freedom we talk about here is different, however. It, again, is something you can do. You can free yourself.

In the 1970s, Richard believed anything was possible. He believed that he could help anyone change. The greatest example in his belief in human beings was his continuous work in mental hospitals, where he worked with patients who had been dismissed by traditional psychologists and psychiatrists as being "chronic" or "permanently mentally ill." Richard went in, and using wacky and "off the wall" yet incredibly effective methods, enabled these patients to become free from both the hospitals and the misery that once bound them. He became known for joining schizophrenics in their reality and then changing it. Richard's experiences with these patients offer great examples of the true attitude that drives NLP.

Today, he still works as a "freedom fighter" on behalf of all those imprisoned by their own minds, and he has taught millions of people to free their minds. I don't believe it is "freedom fighting," however. I believe it is "freedom designing." To everyone in the world who feels trapped, slaves to their environment, in chains of a negative world, there is always hope, and there is always freedom, and once you grasp it, you can change the world. It's like Richard says: "Act as if you are the controlling element in your life."

When you do this, you will be.

PART II

The Art of
Personal Freedom

CHAPTER 6

The Adventure Begins

MY ADVENTURE IN WRITING this book began one drizzling winter's evening when I visited Richard Bandler and his lovely wife, Paula. It was only four o'clock, but darkness was already approaching, it was freezing, and the sky was painted a deep blue-gray and, as the sun set, a powerful red. The clouds above parted as I drove up to the house and parked outside. I looked around and surveyed the marvelous hill to one side, the gorgeous grassy fields that surrounded the house, and the beautiful glistening ocean almost a stone's throw away. The sun was being swallowed by the water as the birds soared majestically through the sky on their way to somewhere they called home.

Despite the rain and the impending darkness, it was magically beautiful. It was escape from the constant rush of modern-day society. I turned off my phone before getting out of the car. I could hear the distant lapping of the foamy waves on the seashore. It was the gentle pitter-patter of the random raindrops upon my car and the sound of each step I took on the stony path that led to the house that captured my attention—that and the other sounds of nature that drowned out everything else. No traffic, no crowds of people, just the odd moo from a cow in a field hundreds of yards away. Except for the meditative sounds of nature, it was quiet, just completely quiet. I glanced at the house. I was about to see a wizard.

It was that night that Richard and I first discussed writing a book together. We sat at the kitchen table in one of our usual conversations—the topics of which were unlimited, covering anything and everything. Visiting the Bandlers is always the kind of refreshing break that feels terrific. On this evening, when I first began to talk with Richard, I asked him questions. What sort of a book do people want to read? What sort of book can really transfer the ideas we have to give on living a happier and more fulfilling life? What sort of book can turn lives around?

I wanted to put so many ideas in the book, and because Richard wrote his last books in the 1990s, there is so much more he has to share. We decided it would have to be a broad-ranging book, which simply and easily taught the principles and ideas that Richard taught me and that I teach throughout the world. It would have to provide examples from our client work and trainings, from our travels, and it would have to include his classic work and latest work and my own ideas and applications from NLP.

So with the small cassette recorder Richard lent me, some batteries, and a blank tape freshly bought from the nearby shops, I set out to explore the wisdom of a genius. We would talk about the keys to freedom and the keys to love, and we would offer these keys to the world through our words. I tore away the wrapping on the tape and carefully placed it in the recorder. I pressed record.

CHAPTER 7

Defining Personal Freedom

"OUCH."

I began to think that I made a mistake trying on my new hiking boots for the first time as I began to trek up the mountain. They fit fairly well, and they seemed okay for the first couple of days, but now they were beginning to hurt. I looked around me, and as I looked at the most amazing sight I have ever witnessed, I forgot the pain. I was standing at 11,000 feet overlooking the valleys and peaks of Mount Everest.

My guide was called Chabbi, and he was Nepalese. Like many people I met there, he ate the exact same meal every single day of his life: dal bhat. It included all the nutrients he needed, and it tasted okay, but I could never figure out how he managed to do it every single day. I fed myself, as we traveled up, on plenty of pancakes and muesli from the various small cottages that we stayed in each night.

What I discovered, however, was that the experience of traveling from place to place far away from problems back home was not freedom. I realized that the things in your life come with you in your mind and that you can never escape from them. As I traveled around the world for those few months, my mind was often at home. No matter what I did, my thoughts were still on my family, girlfriend, and friends, all of whom I missed dearly, and my business, which Brian, my business partner and friend, was looking after. You can distract yourself, for sure, but I wondered whether anyone could ever be really "free."

One hiking boot, one sneaker—my Everest trek.

It was interesting. Regardless of how far up we were, my mind was still on things back home. I couldn't wait to share my experiences with my friends. I also pondered everything else in my life. I always thought that a trip around the world would make me feel free.

The more I traveled, the more I understood personal freedom was much different from what I had thought it was. Some people seemed to be freer than others. I had even gotten this feeling from my clients over the years. What was the difference between someone who was a prisoner of his or her own mind and someone who lived happily and freely? In my travels, I experienced moments of freedom, but just as Richard explained to me, what I was looking for could only be gained by me, from me.

Before the amazing experience in the Himalayas, on that very first night when I began to talk to Richard about the book at the kitchen table, we began with this theme of personal freedom. I heard him mention the concept often. I wondered what exactly he meant by it. So we began.

OF: Richard, can you begin by explaining how you define personal freedom?

RB: Sure. Personal freedom is the ability to feel what you want so that the "chains of the free"—of fear, sadness, and hate—are broken. Real personal freedom is about being able to go through and break as many of these chains as you possibly can. These chains are made up of negative feelings, limiting beliefs, and destructive behaviors. It's about being able to build the kinds of internal states that take people to good places through curiosity.

Instead of being a victim to these chains, you can become curious about new things, or even become disinterested; that's your choice. If people were more curious about other cultures there wouldn't be so much hate on this planet. For some people, the only response that they could have when they face a different culture is fear or anger. As far as I'm concerned, these feelings are just rampant forms of stupidity.

I mean, being afraid of a poisonous snake or tiger that could kill you is a good choice, but being afraid of people because they are a different color or religion or because you don't understand their culture is ridiculous. People who have tigers learn how to be around them without getting hurt.

I used to breed parrots that could kill you: huge, big, giant macaws. People would always say, "Do they bite?" and I would answer, "Yes, but they only bite people under certain circumstances—if you're too close, if you stick your finger out, if they don't know you, or if they are breeding (when no one can get near them)." You need to be smart about things. However, personal freedom goes one step further than just making good decisions. It's about learning how to think in such a way that you can make these decisions.

For example, anorexics and bulimics don't have freedom about food; they have to think about it and avoid it or think about it and throw it up. They either have to binge or starve, but they don't have the freedom to take it or leave it.

Personal freedom is about being able to choose one or the other and to do so to stay healthy.

OF: So there's a time to be afraid and a time to be okay. It's about being able to choose to respond intelligently in the right situation. Is that what personal freedom is about?

RB: Well, yes. It's also about being able to take the good internal states and the things that you are curious about and manifesting them in your life. That's going to be harder for someone who is born in a poor country, but not impossible. People have found ways out of horrible situations and made situations where they have become very wealthy.

Regardless, I don't think it requires a tremendous amount of money for people to have enough wealth to do most of the things they want to do in the world. Freedom enables you to find things like love, success, music, and art. You don't need to have a million dollars to find them.

OF: So personal freedom does not start with your circumstances then? It begins inside of you?

RB: Yes. Some people think that if they have a big car, house, or boat, then all of their problems will go away. That's not necessarily true. People should think through what's going to make them happy. Most of the time it doesn't require all of these trappings, and once people figure that out—it's funny because all the trappings seem to accumulate around you anyway.

I struggled a lot over the years with poverty and fought it tooth and nail and never got anywhere, but when I started doing something that fascinated me, where I wasn't worried about money, it suddenly started falling out of the sky.

Personal freedom gives you the ability that, when you decide to do something—when your neurology lines up to do it—you do it with all your heart and soul. That, whether it's taking a swallow of ice tea or exercising or drawing or writing or kissing, is what you are doing, and you're doing it 100 percent.

OF: Okay. So tell me more about the "chains of the free."

RB: The chains of the free are all of the reticence and all of the fears and all of the doubts that people have. A lot of this comes from bad training from childhood, from schools, from adults and religious leaders—and it also comes from the fact that people haven't sorted out their morals.

To be free you have to be moral, because then you won't have dilemmas about what's good and bad. If you are doing the right thing for the right reason, then every part of you will line up and do it perfectly. But if you are cheating on your wife, then you are never going to kiss her, or whomever you are cheating on her with, fully.

Freedom from these chains really comes from intelligence. Real freedom is not based on a personal inventory. It is based on bathing your neurology in other chemistry. Freedom is not about following rigid ideas. It is about going into a state where you find your own personal destiny. It is about having flexibility in your behavior, not rigidity. It is your ability to change your own internal state.

The ideas of being free from the constraints of your mind, free from the negativity that infects so many lives, free from the limitations imposed by cultures were all things that fascinated me. If freedom was achieved by intelligently controlling your own internal state so that you gained flexibility of behavior and were able to discover your own destiny and live it out—each moment fully, completely, and morally—then the art of personal freedom was to develop this kind of intelligence.

The concept of emotional intelligence is well known in the field of psychology. It deals with a form of intelligence related to controlling and using emotions: being emotionally aware and skilled and dealing with life's issues successfully. The concept of intelligence that we are talking about here is not simply emotional intelligence, however; it is spiritual intelligence; it is social intelligence; it is personal intelligence. We can refer to it as the intelligence of personal freedom.

The intelligence of personal freedom is about becoming aware of how you think and experience the world. It is about being pragmatically responsive to the world so that you allow things to inspire you, and you motivate yourself powerfully. It is about letting go of problems and thinking more about solutions. It is about feeling good most of the time. It is about dealing with the tough times you have and the difficult people you meet with grace and skill. It is about understanding where you fit into the universe spiritually.

Great artists learn the skills to paint well. The rest lies in their creative output—what do they want to draw and paint? What will inspire them? All that is left to decide to create beauty is the content of their masterpiece, and then they must let themselves go into the right state of mind and do what they have learned to do well.

Think of yourself as your own personal life artist. You are reading about the processes and skills, which enable you to paint your life wonderfully and fill it in with great feelings. Your life is the canvas, and your brain is the paint. It's a matter of you letting yourself decide where you want to go, what you want to paint. This is the art of personal freedom.

As humans, our greatest strength lies in our greatest weakness: our ability to choose. It is the great paradox of existence. We have that freedom, and yet we use it to imprison ourselves. We can choose to be great. We can choose to not be great. We have that choice. The trees have no choice. They grow as tall as they can.

As humans, however, we can be as good as we can be, or we can do nothing. We have that choice. As a strength, it gives us the power to be happy. As a weakness, it gives us the opportunity to be sad. As a strength, it gives us the power to live wonderfully. As a weakness, it gives us the opportunity to be lazy. The art of living wonderfully, for me, comes down to mastering choice and choosing well.

Consider the word "freedom." It is usually associated with coming from or going to somewhere. We need freedom from something and freedom to be able to do something. Freedom doesn't just exist. It is a process. To be free, we must free ourselves. You can't just *have* freedom; you can only *do* it. The techniques and exercises you can practice in this book represent what you can do to "free" yourself.

What's important to remember is what you are freeing yourself to do. It is one thing to free yourself, but it's also important that you do so to make your life happier and more successful and to improve the world in whatever way you can.

Back on the trek up Everest, I learned much about Chabbi and his family. At 11,000 feet, I found myself noticing the lack of oxygen as we reached our destination, Namche Bazaar. On the route up, we met an American woman, an Italian guy, and two porters who came with them. We all talked about our experiences and what our plans were in the future. We played card games, and I learned so much about Nepalese culture. I went with Chabbi out to the top of the hill to see if we could catch another glimpse of the peak of Everest. I stood there looking into the midmorning fog, higher up on this planet than I had ever been—we could actually look down at the clouds—and I felt the special serenity of this place; it seemed so far away from the world that I knew. Inside, however, my thoughts were still of the world back home. I didn't really find freedom there.

Chabbi lived with his wife, a young son, and a daughter in a one-room home outside Kathmandu. I could not imagine what it must be like. As we trekked up and down the highest mountain in the world, I talked to him about life, love, happiness, and freedom. I began to understand that freedom has nothing to do with wealth or knowledge. It has nothing to do with where you are or what you do. It has to do with having the right attitude and perspective.

In that first conversation, Richard had given me an extensive definition of personal freedom. I decided to work with that for the time being. This would be what the book would be about. I had a lot to think about, and my mind began to wander to the first time I met Richard.

CHAPTER 8

Developing Real Freedom

I FIRST MET RICHARD almost fifteen years ago while I was just a student. When I arrived at my first NLP workshop with Dr. Richard Bandler, I was in awe. At the end of the day, I walked up to Richard nervously. He was signing autographs only moments after he concluded the workshop. I was nervous around him as he seemed to possess so much personal power. He seemed so intimidating from where I had been sitting, down in the crowd.

As Richard signed autographs, music was playing in the background. There was still a bunch of people vying for his attention. He didn't seem concerned with being "exceptionally nice" to everyone; he was just being himself. Some of the comments he smiled at and retorted to, and some he had no reaction to whatsoever.

Eventually I reached the front of the line. I handed over my old, tattered version of *Using Your Brain for a Change* and tried to say something nice. "Eh, that was great." My voice shook as I spoke. He didn't look up, simply scrawled his name on my book and looked to the next person. As I stepped off the stage, I felt slightly dejected. I expected more, or more accurately, I hoped for more—maybe a smile, maybe a word of encouragement. I got nothing except his autograph. I felt disappointed.

It's funny, but when I think back on this experience, it helps me understand the difference between being impressed and being transformed. You see, I was impressed with the genius and the amazing stories of his experiences in discovering NLP. Walking up to him, being nervous, needing words of kindness from him, needing acknowledgment, and being disappointed: all reflected my insecurities, fears, and neediness.

More accurately, it reflected the way I created feelings of insecurity, fear, and neediness through the way I thought. You see, by focusing on how I came across to him I lost sight of what was truly important: feeling good. I was creating images of how I wanted him to react to me, and when he didn't even make eye contact, I was crushed. I planned my own disappointment.

There he was, teaching us to change the way we think and feel about the things that affect us—how disappointment required adequate planning and how to generate powerful states in ourselves so nobody could make us feel bad. And here I was feeling all these bad things based on my own expectations and his failure to comply with my ideals about receiving some sort of validation from him.

From then on, I noticed something each time I was in contact with Richard. When I was nervous around him, he never seemed particularly nice. When I was relaxed around him, he seemed really nice and kind. That is how things seemed to me. The bottom line was that I had been there the entire day, experiencing Richard Bandler, but I failed to really listen. Many of his ideas seeped through and affected the way I saw the world, but I still had some limitations because I missed the point of it all. The point is that you have to really take in things. As we present ideas in this book that can change your life, the key for the reader is to avoid getting caught up in the search for emulation or the search for the guru to change your life. It's about your life.

The fact that I felt disappointed and saddened because I didn't get the response I wanted meant that I had imprisoned myself in the most ridiculous of ways. Unfortunately, we are always doing this to ourselves. Instead, we must take the necessary steps to learn how to manifest more personal freedom in our lives.

I heard all sorts of things about Richard when I became interested in NLP. Many people who had never even seen him warned that he was "off the wall," "dangerous," and "unethical." What I realized is that those who had never seen him based their opinion on what they heard from those who felt intimidated by him. Some of the biggest names in the field of NLP, who were scared or provoked by Richard, made such comments about him.

I began to ask the question: how could people learn NLP so well and yet not realize what I had realized—that NLP should be used first to ensure that nobody could affect your emotional state in a negative way? We learned about how to control the way we interpret our experiences more usefully and respond to the world more effectively.

I soon learned that Richard was "off the wall," and that was one of the reasons he got such great results where other people couldn't. I also realized that he was "dangerous"—to those who wanted to hold on to their problems, as he was liable to rid people of them. He is the most ethical change worker I have ever experienced because he is actually focused on producing change and not on how many sessions he can arrange with his clients or about how much he can get the client to like him or be impressed by him.

When you become free in your mind and develop true personal freedom, no one else can control your state, either deliberately or not. No one and nothing can ruin your day or intimidate you. No problem can dominate your life. You gain control over the way you feel and the states you go into. You get to make good decisions and deal with challenges in smarter ways. You get to smile no matter what, and you get the peace of mind that comes from not relying on others to make you feel good.

The challenge I eventually succeeded in was having the ability to hold my own state regardless of who was in my space. If you let yourself feel intimidated by anyone, including the teacher who is training you, and let them control your state, you are not putting into practice what you have learned. Life is not like the inside of a seminar room or like the inside of a book. What you learn must be applied, but it must be applied first by you, to you. It must be used to look at your reality in a different way. Often what we think is real is far from true, and it is when this limits us that we need to gain a different perspective to give ourselves more options. More options help us to break the chains of the free.

CHAPTER 9

Breaking the Chains of the Free

Bernard was about twenty-two years old, a tallish, thin guy wearing a red sweatshirt and blue jeans. He sat in front of me and I started with the usual.

OF: What can I help you with?

He responded in an exhausted tone.

Bernard: Well, I shouldn't be here. I keep getting sent to people like you because everyone thinks I'm crazy. They just don't understand. You see, I have these special powers, and I was born to use these powers. But people just think I'm mad.

Sometimes, it's really hard not to laugh in therapy sessions. I pursed my lips tightly to stop myself, looked at him, smiled, and paused for a second.

OF: Bernard, you are crazy.

As I replied, he looked at me with an indignant expression on his face and anger in his eyes.

Bernard: You are just like everybody. . . .

I cut him short.

OF: You muppet. What sort of stuff have you been trying?

He answered defensively.

Bernard: I've been practicing lifting off from the ground and seeing through lead.

OF: Nobody has told you about the book, then, eh?

Bernard: What do you mean, book?

I had his curiosity.

OF: The book. The book. The guidebook for those with special human powers. Nobody has told you about it, have they?

Bernard: Eh, no. What is it? Where do you get it? What's it about?

OF: Well, I don't know where you get it, but I know someone who came to me before who had read it, and he explained a bit about it to me. You have been really mucking yourself up mate.

I smiled at him. He replied back.

Bernard: How do you mean? What are you talking about?

OF: Well, those who are born with these kinds of powers are supposed to practice the simple stuff first and work their way up after a few years to the other stuff. I can't believe nobody ever told you that.

Bernard: What? So you believe me?

OF: Of course. Why shouldn't I? Are you lying? ·

Bernard: No. It's just you're the first person to believe me. So what is the simple stuff, anyway?

I began to teach him various memory tricks where he could use his mind to remember things more easily, and I taught him how he could go into powerful resourceful states, like being confident or happy or relaxed by imagining himself at a time when he felt that way and creating a trigger for that state. He loved it all and was very excited to practice it all.

OF: Now, in the future, in a few years time when you've mastered all of these and more, you can practice the other stuff—always in safe environments. No jumping off buildings, okay?

He smiled.

Bernard: What do you think I am? Mad?

OF: One other thing, by the way. Why does Superman have Clark Kent? Why does Batman have Bruce Wayne? Why does Spider-Man have Peter Parker?

Bernard: Oh, they are secret identities in case people think they are freaks or going crazy or something.

I simply looked at him and raised my eyebrows. It eventually hit him. He sat back, sighed deeply, and smirked.

OF: So use your name, never mention the powers again, practice the powers you learned to use with me, and you'll have a lot less people on your back, won't you?

He nodded and agreed with a smile. I kept in touch with him, and he is still doing well, over two years later.

Richard had a theory of schizophrenia. He suggested that if schizophrenics aren't in touch with reality, then change reality to join them in theirs. So act like you believe them, and you will be in a position to help them.

I became quite used to doing that. What I discovered was that all of my clients—from the wackiest to the most sane—experienced different realities, as did I. In fact, the only difference was that the more "sane" people I knew had more agreeable and "normal" beliefs than those who were considered crazy.

To me, understanding the chains of the free is about understanding the similarities between all the problems that exist in the mind. Every problem comes from the beliefs you have, the attitudes you hold, the thoughts you think, the feelings you experience and the behaviors you engage in. When you can realize this, you can begin to ask the question: how can I take control over what I believe, my attitudes, what I think, what I feel, and what I do?

The chains of the free must be broken and released. The chains include sadness, fear, hate, doubt, stress, poverty, loneliness, hurt, bad relationships, difficult people, and the tough times.

There are ways to break each chain, and once they are all broken, you will experience a profound sense of personal freedom. You will find yourself automatically feeling really good for no reason. You will discover how wonderful it feels to be able to change things in your life with ease. You will feel relaxed and confident in yourself and what you do. You will earn more, organize your time more effectively, and connect with more people in more positive ways. You will deal with difficult people in the smartest way and get through the tough times with a stronger character.

The chains can reappear, however, so it is vital that you continue to maintain the freedom that is your birthright. What it is vital to realize is that, by applying the ideas in this book and using them in your life, the locks will be opened, and the chains will be removed.

Why do people become sad? Or scared? Why do people doubt themselves? Why do people hate each other? Why do people get stressed out? Why do people feel overwhelmed? Why do people feel lonely? Or hurt? Why are some people poor? Why do some people relate poorly to each other? Why are some people difficult to deal with? Why do people have to go through tough times?

The answer to these questions is because we were born, we grew up, and we have learned to think and act in particular ways. We form attachments and sometimes addictions to people, ideas, and objects. We learn to connect unrelated events together. We make decisions based on how we feel, and sometimes these decisions are not useful. Our behavior, both inside our minds and outside in the real world, determines how we experience this life. When we let the world control our behavior, we are at the mercy of luck, misfortune, and circumstance. When we take control over our behavior, we use our brains, make use of our intelligence, and make the best of our circumstances.

Before we can break out of the chains of the free, we must learn how we created them. We must understand how we enabled these chains to limit us and imprison us. Often we place responsibility with others and the world. We believe that we are the victims of chance or destiny—that this is our lot, and it is all we can do to survive the life we have been given. People become depressed because the world is an awful place for them. People become scared because a feeling comes inside of them in certain situations. People become hurt because others make them feel that way by treating them badly.

There is a different way of seeing all this. People become depressed because they make themselves feel that way. People become scared because they scare themselves. People become hurt because they allow themselves to be hurt.

I can hear the sounds and cries of all the victims shouting, "Rubbish! We don't choose to feel this way." However, I never said that people "choose" to feel that way. I said that they are the true source of it. Being the source of a feeling and being the blame for it are two different things.

Blame can be placed upon many different shoulders. To truly blame accurately, you would have to take every single event and influence in your life up to this moment and cite them all as causes. However, my question is: what is the point? Blame helps nobody, including you. Instead, let's move toward the idea of responsibility. If you choose to take responsibility, then you gain the power to control things. When you are responsible, you are "response able." You can respond as you decide to in the world.

You see, we cause ourselves problems, but often we are unaware of how we do it. That's because we are not aware of our natural habitual patterns of thinking and acting. We automatically engage in thought processes and behaviors that lead us into negative states and create problems for us. Once we can identify how we engage in these thought processes and act out these behaviors, we can gain the ability to change them.

The chains in which we imprison ourselves develop from our habitual ways of thinking, feeling, and doing. The key is not to try to consciously reason our way out of these habits. Instead, it's crucial to develop new unconscious habits. One way to do this is to take control over influencing the unconscious part of our minds. Another way is to become aware of how we do what we do, and then engage in disciplines that ensure that we do things differently.

One of the reasons psychology has failed to help us break these chains is that it has primarily focused on trying to understand why people do what they do. Unfortunately, the vast complexities that exist in attempting to explain the interrelationship of the human brain with millions of brain cells, and the impact of genetics and the environment and the infinitely large amount of potential influences on us, make this virtually impossible.

Instead, NLP focuses on helping people realize that it does not matter *why* they do something, it only matters *how*. Sigmund Freud got some things very, very wrong. It's not what happens to you; it's how you deal with it. The cause is not the event that happened. It is the way you think about it. Two individuals were abused. One is psychologically okay; one isn't. What is the reason for this difference? The reason is because of how each dealt with the experience.

A friend of mine, Helen, once gave me an example of the difference between why and how. If I fell into the river and couldn't swim, would you best help me by finding out why I fell in? Or would you better help me by jumping in, saving me, and teaching me to swim? To me, that's a lovely way to explain how people can learn to change. NLP teaches us so much about how people think and create feelings. Through using this model, we can discover how unconscious patterns work.

When we learn how these unconscious patterns work, we can make them conscious. When we make them conscious, we can change them. When we change them, we can make our new patterns unconscious. Thus, we can change the way our brains are programmed or wired and develop more useful habits of thinking and behaving. Only then will the chains of the free be broken! I know this from personal experience. Once upon a time, I was imprisoned in my own personal jail, a hell of feeling depressed, fearful, and stressed.

CHAPTER 10

My Own Personal Hell

Martin: I need to talk to Owen Fitzpatrick.

OF: Yeah, that's me.

I didn't recognize the voice, but he sounded troubled, very troubled.

Martin: I need your help. I was told you were the only one who could help me. I can't, I just can't go on any more. I hate it. I'm going to kill myself now. I can't take it any more. I'm going to take these pills that I have here. They don't know I have them. They can't help. All they do is give me pills. I've heard you can help. I need help.

The voice at the other end of the phone was rambling. It was another suicidal call. It was about 3:30 on a Tuesday afternoon. He had spoken to someone who recommended me. So I talked with him. I knew what to say. It had become instinct.

When I was a young teenager, I first read a book on hypnosis that introduced me to the field of NLP. NLP soon became my hobby, my passion, and my career. A friend of mine once asked me, "If you never got involved in NLP, what do you think your life would be like now?" I always wanted to be someone who saved people and positively impacted their lives: a cop, a fireman, a doctor. I always wanted to be the hero and save the day. I was an idealist.

NLP and the other ideas and technologies that I use with myself, my clients, and my trainees are all about the freedom to think and feel how you want, and to enable you to experience love more wonderfully and feel much happier with life. I know how precious and wonderful this freedom is because I know what it's like to be imprisoned in my own personal hell.

Some years ago, before I knew about NLP, I almost committed suicide. I was extremely depressed, and I told nobody. My family was wonderful, but my "friends" were treating me terribly. I was sick of life and felt hopeless. Every day when I came home I would find a space to be on my own and cry my eyes out, sick to death of the pain of feeling rejected, lost, disliked: a freak. Nobody knew. Nobody guessed. Therefore, nobody helped.

Now, I love every minute of my life. I spend it doing what I love—teaching people how to become happier, communicate better, and become more successful and free.

I travel throughout the world, from Mexico to India, sharing my knowledge and skills with people of many different cultures and backgrounds. I have the best friends in the world, get on wonderfully with my amazing family, and live in Dublin very happy, fulfilled, and delighted with life.

When I was at school, there were those who bullied me—not physically, mostly, but mentally. I was insulted by most people I knew, girls and guys. The girls were the worst, placing on me an added sense of humiliation. I had a pretty hard time all through school. There was one boy who put a shoelace around my throat and started choking me; another time he put a knife to my throat and swore he was going to cut my lungs out.

Now, everything is different. A few years ago, I saw this bully. In fact, since then I've seen most of these people, and I feel so much better. It's funny, now they seem to be intimidated by me and the confidence and security I have in myself. I never went to get revenge. I just accepted that they were cruel to me then, and maybe they aren't bad people now; maybe they've become nice human beings.

Back then, everything terrified me. I stuttered and stammered when I had to speak in public. I would avoid any halfway risky activity, which didn't help my lack of popularity. Fear engulfed my life. Worry and panic followed me everywhere. I hated the unfamiliar, and life scared me.

Today, I have trekked up Mount Everest, snorkeled the Great Barrier Reef, skied in New Zealand, parachute jumped in California, backpacked through India, and taught thousands of people in workshops in different parts of the world. I have traveled all over the planet, and I love adventure. Synchronicities and chaos are always apparent, and that's the way I like it.

What caused the change? What is the difference between me back then and me now? How did I go from feeling so depressed to feeling so happy? How did I go from hating my existence to loving my life? How did I change the way other people made me feel? How did I get to go from intense fear to becoming adventurous? How did I break the chains of the free? As I answer these questions, you will learn how to make great improvements to your own life.

People are sometimes surprised when I talk of my own problems. They are surprised that I am not ashamed of them. The truth is that I am not ashamed because there is a wonderful experience of peace in accepting your own human weakness. My imperfections are okay with me. My past, stupid actions, and humiliations are okay with me. I am just a human who has made mistakes. When you take responsibility for your choices and experiences in life, the world cannot hold your past against you. Instead you get the freedom from the constraints that limit most people—the constraints of the past.

I survived the tough times by pure determination. At that important point in my life, I had a choice: life or death. I chose life. I promised myself I would never give up. I never have. Thankfully, I am reaping the rewards. My determination and openness got me started. It was then that I discovered the ideas that would enable me to transform my life. It was then that I began to claim my freedom.

My journey to freedom was not always easy sailing. I've felt my moments of disappointment, moments of sadness, moments of loneliness, moments of worry, and moments of fear. But that is all they were—moments. I also experienced terribly sad times of grief and heartbreak. Through all those experiences, however, I was in control of how they affected me. I discovered the beauty of myself. I discovered the strength of my character. I discovered the brilliance of taking life in stride.

What I have found is that my life has often been chaotic in so many ways. I'm the guy who has had all his luggage stolen, missed his fair share of flights, lost his passport, wallet, multiple phones, and over $2,000 in cash. I've been arrested for putting my feet on a seat, have collapsed from altitude sickness, broken my ankle, and gotten third-degree burns—all on separate trips. My good friend Mark once described me excellently in one sentence: "Nothing is ever conventional with you, Fitzpatrick." Despite everything, though, my life is the only way I would have it, and when you can deal with your own life, chaotic or not, in stride, then you'll find yourself understanding how you can turn around any personal hell, brilliantly.

CHAPTER 11

The Liberation of Your Mind

I ONCE WORKED with a man who was hugely phobic of getting caught in traffic. He would get panic attacks when he got stuck behind a group of cars, so he avoided the main roads and stuck to backstreets. His fear limited him drastically. I asked him how he thought about it. He explained how he imagined himself stuck in traffic and unable to get out. He imagined himself stuck in the car panicking furiously and imagined the inside of the car getting smaller and smaller. He was telling himself nervously how awful it would be if there was traffic, and he worried about panicking.

He felt the feeling of panic first in his stomach, and then it moved up to his chest and back down to his stomach. I asked him, when he thought about the image of himself stuck, to move forward. What did he see happen next? He continued to see the same image until, after I repeated this question several times, he eventually saw the traffic moving and everything becoming okay again. I explained that his problem was not panic but impatience. Often people who panic simply have to become aware of the images they make inside of their head, and change them, and they'll get remarkable results.

The main way that we trap ourselves is through the way we use our brains. As we take information in from the world, we make images, talk to ourselves, feel feelings, and have internal tastes and smells through which we make sense of the world. So just like we have five senses to input information, we use five internal ways of representing the information. It is the way that we represent the world internally that determines how we feel and what we do. This reflects your automatic, habitual, unconscious thought processes.

The way we think and interpret the world affects how we feel and our mental state at any given moment. To think and act more effectively and feel more resourceful, we must learn to alter our natural habitual thought programs. That way, we will interpret the world in the most intelligent way, think in the smartest way, and have the wisest mental state—all of which will enable us to act in the cleverest way.

You live in different homes during different times in your life. You work in different jobs. The inside of your mind is where you get to live all your life. There is no rest or break from it—it is your permanent home. So you can either make it a heaven to live in or a hell to endure. It's your choice. True personal freedom is about learning how to make the inside of your mind a wonderful place to live.

Therefore, we need to become aware that the way we think is made up of five ways of representing the world to ourselves. Whenever we think, we do so by making particular images, sounds, feelings, smells, and tastes in our minds. Right now, if you think about what you did yesterday, you'll most likely see yourself in an image of wherever you were, and you'll talk to yourself about it. The art is for you to learn how you are thinking and to change that, so you can make your mind a better place to be.

All our thoughts are made up of images, sounds, and feelings. Once we become aware of how we formulate our thoughts, we gain the ability to change them. Since our feelings and behaviors are determined largely by how we think, once we discover how to think differently, we can achieve more effective results.

For example, people usually have problems because when they think about things that make them sad or angry or scared or lonely or over-whelmed, they make big movies and see big images of these negative thoughts in their minds. They usually talk to themselves incessantly and in degrading tones. They will often feel the feeling impressing itself in different parts of their body. Some people, however, are not affected much by their problems because they do not make big images or talk to themselves negatively. Hence, they do not create the same kinds of bad feelings.

The trick is to begin to be aware of how you make images when you are feeling bad and to change how you represent the images. Begin to become aware of how you talk to yourself and change it. Begin to become aware of how you experience feelings and change the way in which you experience these feelings.

We make images and place them in particular locations in front of us— it is as if we can see them in front of our eyes. Often when you are deep in thought, you do not see what is in the outside world because you are busy seeing what is in your thoughts. The images you make are located somewhere in front of you. They are either in color or black and white, bright or dim, focused or unfocused, life-size or bigger or smaller, close to you or farther away, and either a movie or a still image. People play movies to themselves in their mind that impact their feelings. We often refer to this as "running experiences."

The sounds you hear internally and the voice you use to talk to yourself have their own qualities, including a particular loudness or softness, tone, resonance, and rhythm. The feelings you have are located in certain parts of your body and move in a particular way. One way to change how you feel is to notice what direction in your body the feeling is moving and play around with it.

If you can imagine the feelings going faster and faster in the same direction that can intensify them for many people. If you can imagine spinning them backwards that can diminish feelings for many people. This powerful technique of spinning feelings is used a lot by Richard to help those he works with change how they feel.

It is through these qualities of your internal pictures, sounds, and feelings that you will be able you to transform the way your mind works and eliminate the bad feelings you have felt in the past.

The specific qualities of each sensory system, or modality, are known as submodalities. Like a television has brightness, color, and volume controls, so, too, our brains have their own controls. These controls determine what we feel and how intensely we feel them.

Submodalities are the building blocks of our internal world, the currency of the mind. We all make images, talk to ourselves; we can all hear internal sounds, get internal feelings, tastes, and smells. NLP explores how our thoughts are constructed through these sensory modalities.

Consider what it would be like to know how to control your own brain. What would be possible when you discovered how to control the way you experience the world? How does this enable us to build more powerful states within ourselves and others? By simply changing the submodalities of a thought or sequence of thoughts, you can dramatically enhance or detract from how powerful that thought feels.

For example, imagine seeing yourself at a time you felt really good. See a small, still, black-and-white image, like a photograph. Notice the feeling you have. Now imagine the image becoming bigger, as big as a cinema screen. Make it really bright and colorful and animate it like a movie. Step inside the image and imagine seeing through your eyes, hearing through your ears, and feeling the feelings as you experience this time more vividly. Notice how strong the feeling feels.

What you will find is that the latter experience felt much more intense than the previous experience. That's because you are telling your brain to think differently about these situations. You are teaching it to give you a burst of the similar feelings you felt back then.

Many animals work by association. They learn by the feelings that they attach to certain things. For example, dogs learn to get the attention of their master because, when they do so, they usually get food or drink or affection. They associate these positive feelings with the actions they engage in, and thus they are more likely to engage in such actions.

On the other hand, we, as humans, have the ability to think in more complex ways and forsake positive gains in the immediate future for a long-term goal. We can think abstractly, and we have a "theory of mind" and can imagine what it is like to be another person. Hence, we can predict the possible thoughts and behaviors of others and plan our own actions with respect to this. The liberation of your mind is a very simple step to take. The reason many don't take it is because it must be taken over and over again many times for it to become a habit. It is simple to explain and simple to do, but it must be replicated time and time again.

Our brain chemistry is affected by how we interpret events and how we think. Our mental state describes how our brain chemistry is acting at any one given moment in time. The liberation of your mind comes from the following principle: reality always depends on how you perceive it. Learn to perceive it more usefully and your world will transform.

This principle is something that I still have to remind myself of, but when I do, it brings me back to understanding more about the nature of reality.

This principle reflects what top scientists have been saying for decades, mystics have been saying for centuries, and philosophers have been arguing for millennia. In all this time, precious few have actually used it to experience the world.

Use the principle and your world will transform. It is what will make the difference in your life. It is the foundation of everything else within this book. If all you got was this simple principle alone, your life would improve remarkably.

What we experience in our lives is filtered by what we believe to be true. Our beliefs determine how we experience the universe. Thus, we never experience the world as "it is." We only experience the world as "we are." This principle comes down to understanding that the world changes every day, and our way of thinking about the world changes every day. Our brain chemistry affects how we take things in, how we reach conclusions about what actually happens, and how we decide to act in the face of these events.

Often, we have the same number of problems when we are in a good, resourceful, and productive state as we do when we are in a poor, unresourceful, and unproductive state. The difference is that in the first kind of state, we act more effectively, and we deal with things more effectively. The key is to begin to do three main things:

1. We must understand that our experience only represents how things "seem" to us and is not how things are in reality.
2. We must take the necessary steps to generate effective ways of thinking productively and positive chemical states in our brains as a habit.
3. We must examine the world in the most useful ways through smart belief systems and a remarkable attitude.

The client that I helped with his panic about being in traffic experienced things differently than do most of us in that situation. Some of us become annoyed; for others it's simply part and parcel of life. The difference between the way he made the chemical feeling of panic and how we make the chemical feeling of "okay-ness" is in how we think about the experience. The beliefs and attitudes that we hold about ourselves result in our being able to think and feel differently than he does. When he learned how he did what he did unconsciously, and then learned to do something different, he was able to turn the panic around.

Zana, a dear friend of mine in London and fantastic NLP trainer, taught me how there is always more than one side to a story. During some of the courses I took, I heard the participants and assistants talk about the presenters as if they were gods whom they worshipped. Zana would always point out the imperfections in everyone, while complimenting their good points, too, to open up the frame of how we perceived them. When she did this, others were often very uncomfortable. No one was left flawless. I call her the "killer of sacred cows." It's so important to realize that things aren't always what they look, sound, or feel like. If you take responsibility for yourself, things can become so much better than if you spent your time blaming the apparent causes.

That first night back in Richard's kitchen, we did little more recording. We discussed many of these different topics and decided I would design my questions and present them the next time we met. We had a solid grounding on which to base our journey to help others on their quest for freedom. I was about to uncover many secrets about life from Richard. In my next conversations with him, I would ask him about how to begin to gain control over one's own life and begin to manifest wonderful changes in it.

Mental Freedom Exercises

1. When you have a problem, answer the following questions.

   What images come to mind?

   Where are they located?

   How big are they?

   Are they in color or black and white?

   Are they bright or dim?

   Are they still images or movies?

   Are they focused or unfocused?

   Are you in them or looking at yourself in them?

   What sounds are there?

   What do you say to yourself inside your head?

   What tone of voice do you use?

   What kind of feeling do you get?

   Where is the feeling located in your body?

   What direction is the feeling moving in?

2. Play around with the qualities of these images, sounds, and feelings.

   Make the images smaller, darker, black and white, unfocused, and distant.

   Change the tone of your internal voice.

Reverse the direction that the negative feelings go in your body. To do this simply notice which part of your body feels the negative feeling first. Then, where do you notice it next? Pay attention to the direction it feels like it moves in, and then imagine the feeling going backward, in the opposite direction. This is called spinning feelings backward.

3. Write down what you regard as being the "chains" that have held you back till now. Describe what has stopped you from achieving your goals and what would happen if you made your life as wonderful as it can be.

4. Write a paragraph about some beliefs that you have about anything. Then go over the beliefs and replace the word "is" and any other incidences of the verb "to be" with "it seems like to me." For example, if you wrote in the paragraph, "America is the land of the free," you would rewrite it: "America seems like the land of the free to me."

5. Practice thinking of positive, useful thoughts, what you want to happen in your life, and make the images vivid and vibrant, colorful and bright, close and real. Speak to yourself in more encouraging and motivating ways. Imagine spinning the nicest feelings through your body over and over again.

CHAPTER 12

Random Ramblings 2:
Playing Games with Minds

It was early July and I was twenty years old. My friend and I walked into an Irish bar somewhere on 14th Street in New York City where we were spending the summer. There was a poolroom upstairs with couches and chairs around it, all facing the single table in the center. We got drinks, and I went in and placed my money on the table for a game. At the time, a brash American called Rex seemed to be on a roll. He had apparently beaten four or five Irish lads in a row and was letting everyone know about it. Girls and guys around the table rooted for anyone he faced, but he showed off—consistently beating each person, one after the other.

Soon it was my turn. I quietly walked up to the table and put my money into the slot. As the balls rumbled to the back, Rex asked me, "Do you know the rules, Irish boy?" I replied that I wasn't sure, and he filled me in while he described how quickly he was going to beat me. I asked him please not to beat me too quickly, and I smiled. Rex broke. He sunk nothing. I came to the table. I sunk all my balls and left the black over the pocket. Everyone started cheering. Rex sunk one and missed the next. I sunk the black, and I got the cheer of the night. I moved over to Rex and smiled while casually saying, "Sorry mate. I'm sure you'll embarrass me once you actually get a chance." Poor old Rex kept coming back to the table putting his money down to play me. He started making bets and began increasing his bets, and he kept losing. It was a wonderful night.

Hustling time—the art of pool.

This was one of the few times that I went pool hustling in New York. Hustling really taught me many things about how people think. There were so many mind games involved with playing people like Rex. The key always is to make sure that you are in control. It's usually the person who is in control who wins. For three months, I probably made more money playing pool than I did in the little part-time jobs I got there. I also probably learned more about people from playing pool than doing anything else.

I have always been fascinated by our ability to influence our fellow humans. I have also been a big fan of magic. Sometimes I use my NLP skills to read what a person is thinking. Although this baffles people, it is not a psychic experience or a magic "trick" but simply accomplished by using notions in NLP, such as sensory calibration, submodality eye accessing cues (which I learned from Eric Robbie), and certain language patterns.

The reason I do this is not to try to show off or to purely entertain. Most of the time, I am demonstrating what you can do when you stay outside of your head and stop thinking too much. The reason we talk about using the mantra to shut up the thoughts inside your head is to enable you to actually see and hear what is there in the real world. The biggest problem most people have is they have too much time to think. The key is to make sure that you learn to come outside into the world and see and hear things you never paid attention to before.

> *"People ask me, 'Do you ever work with the blind and the deaf?'*
> *My answer is, 'Every day . . . every day.'"*
>
> —RICHARD BANDLER

Most people will tell you everything you need to know about them without you having to ask—if you just pay close enough attention to the way they use their body and voice and the literal language they use. An example of people who are great at reading others is that of good poker players. They use the same skills as those practicing NLP. They notice subtle gestures that their opponents display that indicate if they have good hands or not. These are known as "tells." There are "tells" that give you clues about what is going on inside a person's head.

Often what's going on inside a person's head is extremely stupid. When you think about human beings and the kinds of accomplishments we have managed over the millennia we've inhabited the planet, it's hilarious that sometimes we can think in such ludicrous ways.

Apparently, at some point, there was this bang, and then there was water and trees and then big bears and huge monsters and then us—human beings. We are supposed to be the smartest of all the animals. We came along and we eventually brought "civilization." We understand the world, unlike the rest of the animals. We work while our dogs sit at home lazing about. The birds exist without depression, and bats get to sleep most of the year.

So here we are: the intelligent species. Brilliant, absolutely brilliant! We are different from the cleverest animals because of our "brain" advantage. We have brains that enable us to think and plan abstractly. We have the ability to think about thinking.

Have you ever heard of an ant that gets depressed? Have you ever heard of a dog with a stress problem? Have you ever heard of a cat with low self-esteem? Really, have you? Okay, besides on *Jerry Springer*, I'm assuming the answer is no. Now, following from my assumption, let's ask the question why. I think I know. There are three main reasons animals don't suffer from psychological problems like we do:

1. Most animals never take psychological tests and don't know about psychological problems.
2. Most animals don't think about themselves or problems continuously, they just get on with life.
3. Most animals learn from their mistakes, eventually, and do something else.

Hey, it's just a theory, but I've got a feeling that it has some truth in it. Now, I know I'm putting myself out to hang by the avid believers in the existence of dog psychology. Remember, though, until we label problems as problems, they are not problems. As soon as they interfere with our lives, we call them problems. When we talk about going with our gut feeling, we are talking about an intelligence inside of us that we share with the animals. The difference is that through our human ability to second-guess ourselves, often we learn to ignore this gut feeling that would otherwise lead us to being more successful.

Some of my favorite moments with Richard and Paula were sitting down watching reality television and one of us repeating whatever the different characters on the shows had said. Often, like with so many of my clients, what people actually say is as funny as what they do. I often thought if aliens came to this planet they would either die laughing at the stupidity of humans or would be appalled at our inability to get along with each other over the most ridiculous things.

As humans, we also are so quick to limit ourselves or limit our possibilities.

When you realize all that has been accomplished by human beings, you can begin to understand that so much more is possible. We are very quick to limit our experience or use our skepticism to reduce our perception of what is available to us in our lives. Some people will always hide in their cynicism because that makes them feel smarter. Some people will take themselves too seriously and will let other people get to them, just like Rex did. It's all about trying to feel better than others. I believe that there is something a lot nicer than feeling better than another person—making them feel good.

> *"People say they have low self-esteem.*
> *I ask, 'Do you deserve it? How many people did you*
> *make feel good today?' You don't have to change the world.*
> *Just say something nice."*
>
> —RICHARD BANDLER

Before leaving the bar with my earnings, I bought Rex a drink and chatted with him for a while. Although he wasn't the kind of person I could see myself being close friends with, he wasn't as bad as he seemed initially. Most people aren't!

Wherever I go, I remember two firm beliefs that I have. There are lots of people who are really lovely. There are lots are people who can act like assholes. I do my best to get those acting like assholes to feel good so that they start acting more nicely. I will always make an effort to get a smile out of everyone I meet. That is one of the most important goals I have for each day. It's funny, but the more people I make smile, the more I smile myself.

PART III

The Keys to Changing Your Life

CHAPTER 13

Train to Change

IT WAS PACKED, absolutely packed. The underground is usually busiest in the morning and around this time, five o'clock in the afternoon. I was in London. I was standing nudged up against the wall, as I had given up my seat for one of the old dears who arrived on the train a few stops ago. Since then, as we passed through the central stations, the train got busier and busier. It was uncomfortable, but I cared little because my mind was elsewhere. I was really excited about the next conversation with Richard.

I planned to talk to him about the nature of and keys to change. I have been extremely successful in getting people to make lasting, permanent changes in their lives. Very few people realize the importance of attitude and beliefs in any kind of change. They think the technique is what is important. Everybody can learn about what would improve their lives, but few actually make those changes and make them permanently.

I heard Richard speak about thresholds, moments of epiphany, and well-formed directions. I wanted to ask him about these ideas. I was looking for the solutions to all problems. I was looking for the "how" to altering your life. I looked around at all the stony faces and pressed suits on the train, most hiding their feelings and others reflecting their feelings. I could see in some of them that they had been institutionalized by modern culture. They accepted and settled in the rat race against the best instincts of their childhood desire for liberation. They worked nine to five, and they went home—they existed.

I began to wonder. How many people on the train were depressed? How many were stressed out? How many were scared and fearful and anxious? How many were lonely? How many hated themselves? How many were heartbroken? How many had habits they longed to change? How many felt overwhelmed with life?

My guess was that the majority of them were trapped in at least one of these limiting experiences: imprisoned in the chains of the free. To escape from chains and prison, you need to have a key. The keys to change must be understood to be able to use them. I would explore the fundamental essentials of change with the man who knew more about them than anyone I had ever met or had even heard of. The train came to my stop. I stepped off and walked through the prisoners toward that man's place. As I made my way up the escalators to the exit, I recalled a client of mine, Eamon, and one of the most memorable phone calls I have ever received.

CHAPTER 14

Understanding Change

I WAS WALKING DOWN Washington Street in Cork when the phone call came. I had expected it about that time. It was about 7:30 in the evening, which was roughly 2:30 PM in New York. Eamon, a client, had agreed to contact me after his plane landed. It was a Wednesday, and I thought back to the conversations I had had with him.

Eamon was depressed and suffered from severe panic attacks whenever he traveled abroad. He had been hospitalized at home and was on the verge of suicide. He had been seen by many people, but none of them seemed to help. He had met his girlfriend in America and now couldn't see her because he had panic attacks whenever he tried to get on a plane. This devastated him. I remembered what it was like to be away from the love of my life for a while, and my heart went out to him. When he was released from the hospital after a couple of weeks, he seemed pretty bad. He had heard about me, and for some reason, he believed I could help when nobody else could. I believed I could help him, too, and I saw him a few times.

As we talked in the various sessions, he explained how awful he felt about himself and his life and how his heart was breaking because he couldn't see his girlfriend, whom he loved so much. He believed there was no way out of his situation, and yet he was sitting there in front of me, which meant he was hopeful. I explained to him how change was not as complicated or drawn out as he expected. It did not have to take forever, and he did not have to go through lots of pain. He needed to have one trait: perseverance.

Over the sessions, I began to work with him to make changes in his unconscious. Often people's conscious minds get in their way. I had learned from Richard that unconscious work always needs to be done in some form or another—that it's usually necessary to help a person make changes that they may not be aware of consciously. When people think too much about something, they sometimes sabotage it.

Often with problems like panic, it feels to the person as if the attacks just come over them. The attacks work unconsciously, so I would deal with them in the unconscious. Eamon booked a flight, but with only a couple of days to go before he left, he was still apprehensive about going. I gave him instructions. It was okay to panic, but I wanted him to do it only when he got to his destination, and then to call me. I explained that he was going to get a surprise when he got on the flight. I smiled knowingly and looked at him knowing he was going to be okay.

I have often found that working with clients is like a battle of certainty. If I'm more certain than they are, then I win, and they can change; if they are more certain than me, it's much harder. However, in my experience, I have always been more certain. I believe in hope, always and everywhere, for everyone I ever meet.

How is it possible to change your life? How is it possible to change the automatic habitual patterns of thinking, feeling, behaving, and communicating that have been developed since birth? How is it possible to permanently create more useful habits in our lives? The answers lie in the keys to change.

The keys to changing anything in your life are to learn to change your beliefs about change, to change your beliefs and perspectives on a problem and the feelings attached to certain behaviors, and to engage in new acts or behaviors. For your life to change, you must begin by changing yourself by taking control of your habits and habitual ways of thinking and deliberately engaging in the acts that will alter the way you do things.

From thinking about Eamon, my mind traveled back to my meeting with Richard, and I stared at the large green door ahead of me. I had arrived at his London place. Inside, we sat talking in his living room in the heart of the city. I had seen him give a workshop earlier that day, and he was in top form. From the experience on the train, I was eager to explore the next topic on "the process of change." What were his thoughts on the keys to change? I took out the recorder and began the interview.

OF: So, Richard, what are the main things that you can do to help people change?

RB: I think the main thing is that you have to do something that changes their beliefs about whether change is going to happen or not. Sometimes it's some kind of a shock that is needed. Sometimes it's just a look in my eye that gets them. They will be telling me the same story they've told five other therapists, and I'll just stare at them, and sometimes they will just stop in the middle because they know I'm not buying their bullshit.

When they start talking rubbish, they need to learn to tell themselves to shut up and stop talking like that. This is why people in mental hospitals should not be left in rooms by themselves watching television and sucking back pills for years. I don't think we should give up on them. If you don't figure out what to do with them, they should be sent on to some of my students to let them try to figure something out.

I knew that Richard was talking about using a shock mechanism by grabbing a person's attention to get them out of repeating the same behaviors they had been doing for years. Often people will treat themselves terribly, and sometimes it's necessary to shock them out of this phase to break the pattern. Often this is a key to change.

RB: We shouldn't give up on anyone. It shouldn't be against the law to be crazy. They are taking people who have nutty behavior and putting them in prison for it. It's one thing if someone is crazy and they hurt somebody. There was a guy in Ireland who killed his relatives with an axe. They didn't send him to court. They sent him to a mental hospital straight away.

The guy was obviously nuts. He chopped up his relatives into little pieces. I don't think we needed to send him to a psychiatrist. In the United States, they would have sent him to a psychiatrist to see if he was mentally in his right mind. They would want to know if he knew the difference between right and wrong. He didn't know the difference between good and bad. He's never going to either. I don't think anybody will be able to teach him that in the future.

OF: Is there anything we can do to prevent people becoming like this?

RB: Well, we need to look at the way we are teaching our young children. I think we need some new TV programs. There's way too much violence on TV. I don't think we should censor it. I think we should beat it with something better. Some of these program makers have to come up with things that are more fun to watch than people getting shot. TV producers have found formulas that work, so they will keep making the same things until people come up with better things that teach people how to get smarter.

When it came to ending racism, with all the rallies, the fights, and the struggles, I still think the sitcom *All in the Family* did more to end racism than almost anything else. It made it unfashionable to be racist, and I think it was a clever thing to do. It changed attitudes in the United States more than anything else. Not that there isn't still racism, nor will there ever be an end to racism, but at least there's more freedom about what people can do.

You can't make people ride at the back of the bus. They went to all the trouble of putting black people at the back of the bus instead of the front. Only fear could be the basis of that. They made it sound like hate, but it was fear. It's stupid, the idea of splitting people up based on the color of their skin.

I remember there used to be a sign outside of a junk store in the countryside near where I lived in the United States. It said, "No dogs, No niggers, No Irish"—and the guy was serious. There was a big legal battle, and he fought for his right to admit who he wanted to his shop. He didn't want any dogs, black people, or Irish. He was probably ninety years old, and I think he died before it came to court. It was a statement about his ignorance. I think every Irish person, every black person, and everybody who had a dog should have gone over and hung out with him for a couple of weeks, to show him there was nothing to be afraid of. The courts are not the place to solve something like that. Courts don't solve things. Human communication does.

I began to think. Understanding change is realizing that it is people's beliefs that will both enable them to change and prevent them from changing. Our beliefs and our ignorance are two of the traps and chains that hold us captive. To become free to change, you need to develop new, more useful, and more resourceful beliefs. You also need to learn more about the world so that you can reach a different perspective about things. Sometimes for people to change, they have to have a motivation outside of themselves.

I remember helping a client who cut herself. She showed me the cuts on her arms. I vowed to her that if she did it again before the next session I would do it to myself, too. The next session she came in and she admitted to having done it again. With that I took a compass from the table and scraped my arm. It hurt, and I showed her it hurt. She looked at me in disgust as the blood dripped from my arm. But after that session, she stopped what she was doing. Thank God.

You see, people don't think of themselves as being as important as others. They filter their world through the blindness of their own selves. They fail to understand that they deserve as much respect from themselves as others do. People often get more motivated by doing something for others than for themselves.

During the Second World War, when prisoners of war were dying, their fellow prisoners used to keep them alive by talking to them about all the other people in their lives who were counting on them to survive. The power of love is clearly apparent when we see how people are so powerfully motivated by the thought of helping others.

When people become aware of how awful they treat themselves, it can be quite shocking. There is a fundamental truth that you are going to be with only one person your entire life. Like it or not, that person is going to be with you 24–7 in every single moment you exist. That person is going to determine how successful or effective you become. The relationship you create with that person is extremely important. That person is yourself.

Think about what it would be like to have a constant companion who did nothing but insult you, made you feel bad for making mistakes, and filled you with worries about the future and regrets about the past. The problem is that many people have such a companion. This companion can make people feel bad, or it can motivate them to make their lives better. Whether you motivate yourself by pleasure or pain, take ownership of the responsibility to motivate yourself and get yourself to take action. When you do, you'll find yourself turning things around much more easily than you could have imagined.

The most important understanding about change comes from the notion of "anchoring." Anchoring is a process in NLP whereby you associate particular feelings to create triggers, and by applying a trigger you can re-create the feeling. People can learn to take the best feelings they have and access them instantly.

Anchoring enables you to create a tap for your good feelings and to turn on that tap at will. You'll find yourself able to take the things that made you feel bad and simply cancel that bad feeling by instantly firing off the positive feeling in its place.

For example, imagine a square in front of you and yourself standing in it. Imagine a version of yourself at your most confident. See how you look; notice how you breathe. Now, close your eyes and imagine yourself getting into the square. Physically step into it. When you are in the square, imagine a time when you felt powerfully confident and strong and see what you saw, hear what you heard, and feel how good you felt. When you do this, you will create a powerful positive feeling inside yourself. When you feel this feeling strongly enough, feel the feeling coming up from the square below. Next, step out of the square and shake yourself off. Practice this again. From now on, when you step into this imaginary square, you'll find it easy to reexperience the positive feelings you have created.

Whenever you think about a time in the future, when you feel you might not be as confident as you would like, imagine the square and step into it and, inside the square, imagine going through the future scenario. You'll find yourself feeling confident and strong in the experience in the future. This is a technique we use called "brilliance squared."

You can also use these anchors with others. When people are experiencing a positive state, you can touch them on the shoulder in a particular way, and they'll associate that positive state with that particular touch. People associate feelings with what they see, hear, feel on their skin, smell, and taste. When they associate certain internal feelings with specific triggers in any of these senses, you can use that trigger to make people feel that state again.

Understand anchoring and you'll understand how you can gain control over your own "buttons" and the buttons you push with other people, and you'll learn how to make more people feel happier more of the time. You can create and use anchors to make yourself feel wonderful. You can "collapse" negative anchors or associations that already exist, such as replacing fear with confidence, sadness with cheerfulness, stress with relaxation. For example, if you feel angry at a person, you can build a feeling of laughter and trigger it when you think about the person, and you'll find that you'll no longer feel angry.

As Richard talked about change and how it came about with racism, I was beginning to understand change in a different way. You can't just tell people to change; they have to learn to change their attitudes toward things. Often people think that the only way to change people is to censor things, tell them to change, or give them drugs. Richard was talking about a different approach. It was an approach I had learned to use with great success, but I'd yet to understand exactly how it worked.

My thoughts briefly drifted back to my client Eamon. The flight he got on was to be the first of many. He called me, crying on the phone. They were tears of happiness. He couldn't believe it. "It was like getting on the 15B bus in Dublin," he said. It was so easy. He made great progress and began to discover that things aren't nearly as bad as they seem and can become even better than he could have imagined. Eamon contacted me some time after that. He was happily married and residing in America with a new job, as happy as he has ever been in his life.

This is what change is about: believe it is possible, develop a new feeling and perspective about something, and understand how to motivate yourself more effectively.

READER/CUSTOMER CARE SURVEY

HEFG

We care about your opinions! Please take a moment to fill out our online Reader Survey at **http://survey.hcibooks.com**.
As a **"THANK YOU"** you will receive a **VALUABLE INSTANT COUPON** towards future book purchases
as well as a **SPECIAL GIFT** available only online! Or, you may mail this card back to us.

First Name _____ MI. _____ Last Name _____

Address _____

State _____ Zip _____ Email _____ City _____

1. Gender
- ☐ Female ☐ Male

2. Age
- ☐ 8 or younger
- ☐ 9-12 ☐ 13-16
- ☐ 17-20 ☐ 21-30
- ☐ 31+

3. Did you receive this book as a gift?
- ☐ Yes ☐ No

4. Annual Household Income
- ☐ under $25,000
- ☐ $25,000 - $34,999
- ☐ $35,000 - $49,999
- ☐ $50,000 - $74,999
- ☐ over $75,000

5. What are the ages of the children living in your house?
- ☐ 0 - 14 ☐ 15+

6. Marital Status
- ☐ Single
- ☐ Married
- ☐ Divorced
- ☐ Widowed

7. How did you find out about the book?
(please choose one)
- ☐ Recommendation
- ☐ Store Display
- ☐ Online
- ☐ Catalog/Mailing
- ☐ Interview/Review

8. Where do you usually buy books?
(please choose one)
- ☐ Bookstore
- ☐ Online
- ☐ Book Club/Mail Order
- ☐ Price Club (Sam's Club, Costco's, etc.)
- ☐ Retail Store (Target, Wal-Mart, etc.)

9. What subject do you enjoy reading about the most?
(please choose one)
- ☐ Parenting/Family
- ☐ Relationships
- ☐ Recovery/Addictions
- ☐ Health/Nutrition
- ☐ Christianity
- ☐ Spirituality/Inspiration
- ☐ Business Self-help
- ☐ Women's Issues
- ☐ Sports

10. What attracts you most to a book?
(please choose one)
- ☐ Title
- ☐ Cover Design
- ☐ Author
- ☐ Content

FOLD HERE

Comments

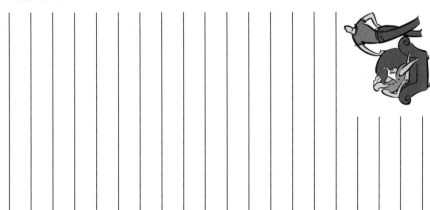

Power to Change Exercises

These exercises can be done as often as necessary to assist you in developing more resourceful beliefs about change and developing your ability to access and trigger any state in an instant.

1. What are your beliefs about how change happens and can happen for you?

2. What are more useful beliefs to have about change and how it can happen for you?

3. Brilliance squared exercise:

    a. Think of a situation where you would like to feel and act brilliantly.

    b. Choose three different states (e.g., confident, relaxed, playful) you'd like to be feeling in that situation.

    c. Imagine yourself standing in a square in front of you filled with your favorite color in a state of confidence.

    d. Close your eyes and step into your imaginary self in the square.

    e. See what you would see, hear what you would hear, feel what you would feel, and intensify the state.

    f. Feel the feeling of confidence increase and multiply itself by itself as the color of the square gets stronger.

    g. Step out of the square and think of something else.

    h. Repeat steps c through g with the states of relaxation and playfulness.

    i. Imagine yourself in the situation from step a. Imagine yourself going through that once-challenging experience and step into your square.

    j. Notice how much better you feel and go through the same experience with your new feelings of brilliance.

CHAPTER 15

Moving in Better Directions:
Well-Formed Goals

"The Best Thing about the Past is that it's over.
The Best Thing about the Present is that it's a gift.
The Best Thing about the Future is that it's yet to come."

—RICHARD BANDLER

HE SMIRKED. I wanted to win so badly. He scoffed at me and explained how he would become victorious in two sets. It was a bitter fight. We shared a set each and he was winning 14 games to 13 in the final set. It was his serve, and I faced match point. He hammered the tennis ball from side to side, and I scurried after it, each step so important. I barely made it each time, keeping the ball in play—just. The rally must have lasted almost a hundred shots. I was finding energy from somewhere.

My legs were exhausted. In fact, my entire body was exhausted. It was pouring rain, and I was soaked from head to toe. It was the final, however, and I would not give up. I felt cramps beginning to emerge throughout my body, but I just couldn't give in. I fought back from losing the first set and trailing 5–1 in the second. I was diving all over the court, scooping each ball back when all looked lost.

Tennis is not normally a game where you have to be very fit to be okay at it. When I train with my soccer team, the training is much more intense—yet during this particular match I had worked harder than ever.

I fought and I fought for every single point. It went down to the wire. I wanted it so badly.

To succeed and be happy in life, it's important that we set ourselves goals to strive for. For us to become free, we need to know what freedom is. For us to fill our lives with more love, we need to know what that would feel like. Once we know where we want to go and where we are now, it's simply a case of knowing how to get from where we are to where we want to be and taking the necessary steps.

It's not just important for us to set goals, it's also essential that we set goals in particular ways because of the way our brains operate. These have been known as "well-formed outcomes." We also want you to think of them in terms of "well-formed directions." The reason for this is that, when you achieve an outcome, it's finished; whereas when you go in a direction, you continue to do better, get better, feel better. In continuing my conversation with Richard about change, I talked with him about setting goals and the idea of well-formed outcomes.

OF: Richard, one of the things that you almost always do is help a person figure out where they want to go before working on the change with them. The notion of what we call "well-formed outcomes" in setting goals is extremely important. Could you talk a bit about well-formed outcomes or well-formed directions?

RB: Well-formed outcomes isn't about a client coming in and saying, "Well, I want to get over my fear of birds." I want the client to decide that the reason they're there is so they can achieve something, and not just get rid of a problem. When people say, "I don't want to be afraid of birds." I say, "Well, okay, I have a large axe; I'll chop your head off, and then you'll never be afraid of birds. Will that make you happy?" They normally reply, "Of course not." So I say, "Well, don't ask for that." I then ask the person what they would want to be able to do when there is a bird around, because they have to have some state that they want to achieve. They can't have "not things." I want them to ask for what they do want.

I want them to be able to say, "When I see birds, I'll say, 'Pretty bird' or 'Get out of my way.'" I don't care what it is, as long as they decide what they're going to do as opposed to not do, because the *not do* leads to the fear. They have to have curiosity. They can't have the fear.

Also when a person wants to learn a skill, it's not just about learning one strategy to become good. For example, if you are going to learn to play the guitar, you need to have a strategy to learn how to play. You need to have a strategy that makes you practice and enjoy it. There's also a difference between reading music and writing music. So you have to decide which strategies are necessary to achieve the outcome of producing a musician. If you're designing a learning program, the outcome is to produce somebody with the ability to write music and read music. To me, it must set a direction not just a result.

The clients' well-formed outcomes are different from my outcomes for them. I have to use the outcomes that they've decided they want to set as a direction, so that it not only gets rid of their fear of one thing—it gets rid of the rest of their fears, too. It has to put them on the road to a happier, richer life so that, for example, they treat their children better, and they become more interested in their work. It has to ensure they find more interesting things to do and more interesting hobbies and open up all the rest of the flower of life, so they can enjoy as much of life as possible. In that case, they'll fill their life with good things instead of building more crap.

So the art of setting well-formed directions is being mindful of what your various outcomes are and then setting things up so that you will go in a fantastic and useful direction as you achieve each of your outcomes. This is real-life design. Often, unfortunately, people fail to do what they can because they are seduced by the pleasure of the addictions of the present rather than the happiness of their lives. What do you want in the long term? Are your actions leading you into the life you want to live?

Well-formed directions must be what you *do* want and not what you *don't* want. They must be specific and sensory based. You must be able to tell when you are going in the right direction. You must know what you will be able to see, hear, and feel when you achieve your outcomes and when you are going in the right direction.

The direction must be something that is in your control and something you have the power to do. Finally, the well-formed direction is something that is ecological. In other words, it is something that is well thought out and is worth achieving. It must be good for you and have a positive impact in the different areas of your life, both immediately and in the long term.

There are certain questions that will prompt you to become clear about your well-formed outcomes or directions. Below are some examples.

Positive

What do you want?

What direction do you want to go in?

Specific

What exactly do you want?

What specific direction do you want to go in?

Sensory Based

How will you know when you are going in that direction?

What will you be seeing, hearing, and feeling?

In Control

How much of going in this direction is under your control?

Ecological

How will going in this direction affect you in the short and long
term?

Is it worth it to go in this direction?

When you filter your goals through these areas and questions, you gain
a clear focus on where exactly you want to go. For you to get there, you
must begin to make good decisions. I asked Richard for his advice on making good decisions.

OF: In helping people to make changes and go in these well-
formed directions, what suggestions do you have to help people make
more good decisions?

RB: Making good decisions is always going to depend upon the
decision, because some decisions you can make quickly, and some you
have to really think through. Everybody knows the heroin addict who
decides to take more heroin, after he has spent six months in rehab,
is making a bad decision. The heroin addict thinks of a still image of
himself, feeling the feeling he'll get after injecting, and knows that
he'll feel good and just does it. What he has to do is turn it into a
movie and get more detail and see how things work out after that. He
needs to run it on so that he sees all the horrible things that will follow when the euphoria wears off.

There are some people who play movies inside their minds with
too much detail. You ask them, "Would you like to go to the store
tomorrow?" and they spend three hours thinking it over because they
run through every gamut of every possibility and what everybody in
the world will think about it and what might happen and what might
not happen. In effect, they do the opposite of the heroin addict.

The trick is to be able to adjust the amount of information that is
considered to relate to what the decision is, so you don't get too much
information, and you don't get too little. You get just enough so that

you make the right choices and learn to trust your unconscious process. We all sort out good decisions from bad decisions subjectively by putting them in a different place in our minds, and they have a very different feeling that most people haven't gotten very good at trusting. Most people know what the right thing to do is, but they just don't do it.

In essence, making a good decision is about learning to think about things by imagining the resulting effect or consequence in some detail, but not overdoing it. It is about paying attention to how you think about good decisions and bad decisions in terms of where the images are located and what the feelings are like and then paying attention to how you think about the decision to be made—checking where the picture is and which feelings you get that most resemble your good decisions. I also discussed values with Richard. I understood from my experience with clients that problems often seem to come as a result of people not clarifying their values and beliefs about what is important. To make good decisions, I feel it is necessary for people to know what their values are. Richard briefly explained his ideas on values to me.

OF: So what about the importance of values?

RB: The problem is some people's values don't have a hierarchy, and they just change. I think people like that are dangerous and unhappy, and I try to make it so that people base decisions on what they really think is important.

Thus, setting up a hierarchy of values is important in ensuring that people make good decisions in their lives. There are two kinds of values: means values and ends values. Our means values reflect the things in our lives that are most important to us. They include our family, friends, career, car, house, and so on. Our ends values reflect the feelings and states that we regard as most important for us to experience in our lives. In other words, they are the states that we get from having the means values. For example, a house might give us security, and our family might provide us with love. When you think about the things that are most important to you and what feelings or states they give you, you'll have a list of ends values. When you figure out which ones are the most important to you, it can make decisions easier to make. This hierarchy also makes it easier to figure out what you want from life.

To me, during that tennis match, the most important thing was to win. Winning is not always the most important thing, but what is accurate is that, as the famous saying goes: "If you have a big enough why you can find any how." By which I mean that when the motivation is strong enough, you can find a way to do almost anything.

I fought for every point, and I eventually won the match 16–14. After the final exhaustive rally, I fell to the ground, completely stiff. I stretched on the soaking tarmac as the rain poured down. I felt the elation, the pride, the delight of fighting for something and winning it. That was what I was always good at: fighting back from the brink of despair, never giving up. It's been that way ever since I was a kid playing tennis. As we go through life, different things become important for us. Whatever we want to achieve, whether it be the victory in a sport or a new car or overcoming stress or beating depression, it all comes down to being determined to do it. Determination is aided by focusing on what you want to achieve and imagining it as vividly as possible so that it draws you to it. The decisions you make must be made intelligently with the future in mind.

Once we know where to go and what decisions to make, we often need an experience that shifts things in our heads. We need to change our beliefs. Often this requires us to go through a point of threshold where we reach the point of "enough is enough" and we are sick of being the way we are. Then we immediately develop a completely different way of thinking in a given context. Sometimes, it is through an epiphany, when something throws us into a state in which we get to see the world in an entirely different way.

Future Design Exercises

1. Set five well-formed goals. Ask yourself the following questions as you pick a goal you have in life:

    What do you want?

    In what direction will achieving that take you?

    What exactly do you want?

    In what specific direction will achieving that take you?

    How will you know when you have achieved that goal?

    How will you know that you are going in that direction?

    What will you be seeing, hearing, and feeling?

    How much of achieving this goal is under your control?

    How will achieving this goal affect the rest of your life in the short term and in the long term?

    How will going in this direction affect the rest of your life in the short term and in the long term?

2. Set these goals for one year, three years, five years, and ten years.

3. Revise them once a month.

Life Value Exercise

1. What are the ten most important things to you in your life?

    Put them in order of importance.

    Whenever you have to make an important decision, check to see how it fits in with your values.

CHAPTER 16

Moments of Epiphany

THE WAVES CRASHED AROUND US. We were swept at least thirty feet in the air before we crashed down. Spray covered my duffle bag. I was soaked and hanging on for dear life. I couldn't swim, at all, and I knew I was in a very dangerous situation.

It was supposed to be a routine boat trip. I was being taken by two Fijians on a small, fifteen-foot boat to meet the bigger ship that would take me the rest of the way on my journey. I was coming from Bounty Island, a gorgeous island with beautiful people and going to Nadi, on Vita Levu, the main island of Fiji. What began as a routine trip took an unexpected turn.

The small boat we were in was not at all equipped to deal with the stormy conditions on the other side of the island. That was the purpose of meeting the bigger boat. But due to a mix-up about times, we waited for the bigger boat, which passed us on the other side and was halfway to the Nadi before we could catch up. It was the last boat of the day, and I couldn't afford to miss it. It was Saturday, and I needed to get to Los Angeles, London, and eventually back to Dublin for work. It was the end of my world tour.

The guys knew this and they were determined to catch up with the boat. We left with important warnings about the terrible conditions, but they were willing to take the risk. Without thinking, so was I. We set out on the tiny boat as fast as we could. At first it seemed we were going to be okay. I was told the journey would take twenty minutes. Initially it was a little bumpy. Then, without warning, the waves got bigger and bigger until the boat was rocking all over the place.

We shot along, as if we were being harpooned through the sea. Then they slowed and stopped the engine and we endured a number of moments, each of which felt like hours, where our boat was swept up and plummeted down over and over again. My grip against the side of the boat was so strong, my hands were sore. I looked at both of my friends as they controlled the boat. Outside, they smiled, reassuring me. Inside, I could see they were concerned.

It was like I was caught in a powerful downpour. Water began to fill the boat, and I helped the lads with the buckets, pouring it out as another wave hit us powerfully. The boat was tipping from side to side. As we began to move slowly through the huge hills of waves that carried us, we were inches from tipping over. It was the kind of sea that looked like it would swallow you whole, so powerful and magnificent. I had never seen anything like it.

The lads shouted to me to move from the right side to the left to balance the boat as they predicted each wave: left . . . right . . . left . . . stay left . . . right. I moved when they told me as splash after splash invaded our tiny boat. My heart beat faster than it had the time I jumped out of a perfectly good airplane with a parachute four years previously. I was absolutely terrified, obeying the commands like my life depended on it, which I believe it did.

It's at moments like this, I've been told, that your life flashes before your eyes. The only thing that began to flash before my eyes was what I would do if I fell over. I had seen other people swim. I knew the principles. Could I stay up long enough for one of the other guys to save me? Would they jump in, or were they doomed as well?

Stupid thoughts and questions filled my mind as I realized the situation I was in. I began to think about my girlfriend back home, my family, my friends, and how they would miss me. I saw the news filtering from person to person, the sadness, the tears, and the heartbreak. Normally, this would provide me with a lovely sense of self-appreciation, knowing how much people care, but this was far too real.

Instead, at this moment as I jumped from side to side grabbing on to the boat tightly, I recalled my life—not all of it, just who I was and what I was and what I wanted in my future, and I felt a sense of tragic loss. I made a promise, which could only be made at one of those moments, that, if I survived, I would remember this experience and use it as impetus to make my life count much more than before. It was going to be another epiphany for me, where I gained essential realizations that would transform my perspective on life.

Why do we need such near-death experiences to affect us so profoundly? Why do we need to see death to appreciate life? Why does the reality of death wake us to the reality of life? Maybe it's because of the paradox of life—life needs death to exist, and death needs life to exist. We take things in our lives for granted. Living is the biggest thing we take for granted. When we reach a moment, even a second, when we no longer take it for granted, we can discover a sense of enlightenment as we understand how lucky we are to live.

I came to, from the trance that led me into such thoughts, and looked back at Richard. He was used to me trancing out when he finished his answers. I had spent many hours over the last ten years learning from him, and I had become used to having enlightening moments while speaking with him.

The whole concept of an "epiphany experience" that has such a dramatic effect on people interested me greatly. I asked Richard about such epiphany moments.

OF: Can you tell me about epiphany experiences and their importance in helping people change?

RB: Epiphany experiences come in a million forms. Sometimes we have to create them. I mean, I've created them with schizophrenics by building giant laser holograms of the devil and having them come through the window. The thing is that, whatever reality you experience, you have to take it and amplify it to the point where enough is enough, and you're not just going to take it anymore. You are not going to tolerate feeling bad. You have to get yourself to the point where the only steps that you will take are toward getting your own life back and toward freedom.

I mean, there are people who get on little tiny boats and float across the ocean and risk their lives and sometimes die just for a chance for a little freedom. Most human beings are not that courageous, but if put in the right situation, with the right mental attitude, they become courageous. I really believe in the ability of human beings to cope when they coalesce their resources.

OF: I would think with the recent events happening in the world, with 9/11 and terrorism and the "war on terror," that we should have experienced at least one moment of epiphany as human beings. What can we do to make it count?

RB: I think it's our job to get our clients and students mentally prepared so that every fiber of their souls is headed in the right direction. The chains of the free are all the fears and the doubts and the worries people have. I look at what's going on in the United States now, and I see the government trying to scare everybody.

The security measures are putting the chains back on instead of reassuring everybody. I think they're scaring the hell out of everybody. The last time I flew, they didn't make me feel safer—they made me feel like I was in Russia in 1952. Everybody was treated as a suspect. It wasn't just the measures they took, such as looking through my suitcase; it was the way that they did it. They did it as if I was a potential enemy, instead of saying, "Look, if we look through everybody's, we'll find the bad stuff." They should have looked in my suitcase and said, "This is interesting; this is interesting; this is nice. Have a nice vacation. Go on your way." But instead, they said, "Stand behind this line or you'll be shot." Excuse me, but that's not supposed to happen in a free society.

I'm looking for countries that . . . I mean, I like Mexico. Mexico is starting to blossom as a country. I think Ireland puts more value on freedom because its revolution wasn't that long ago—1916 isn't that long ago, so people haven't forgotten what people were fighting for, and the government hasn't got so many weapons that they feel confident about running everybody's ass. But you start going into some places, and it's unbelievable the lack of freedom people have, which then starts them building it inside their heads. They start to be afraid. "Every plane I get on is going to be blown up." After 9/11 was probably the safest time to fly that could have been imagined. For once, they were being careful what people took on planes.

After 9/11, I never got on a plane and heard anybody say, "Look, we've checked all the luggage; we've done *everything*—this flight is safe." And you know that may not seem like a lot, but it's a big deal. This is what I'm doing a lot with clients. "I've checked through your mind. We got rid of the bad thoughts. Everything is gonna be okay." It's not enough to get rid of all the crap inside a person's head; you have to fill it with good stuff—otherwise they'll fill it with more bad stuff.

So, in a way, I guess it's about having an internal security system that is in charge of only letting the good and useful thoughts in. Epiphany experiences must be used positively by people and not used as a reason to be scared. Moments of epiphany are the moments that we must create more of and let ourselves be affected by more. There are times when a problem you have had is suddenly solved by one of these moments. There are times where suddenly you've got an entirely different perspective and way of thinking about your situation and the experience of life. These are the times when you awaken from the trance of limited, trapped thinking.

Our lives go on. We want you to begin to stop and appreciate life now. Appreciate the moments you have with your loved ones. One day, they are not going to be around; you are not going to be around. You bought this book for a reason. There is something you want to improve in your life. Will you enable it to be an epiphany experience? If you do, it will take you through a threshold, and life will be different.

Life-Appreciation Exercises

1. Ask yourself the following question:

    What physical capabilities do you have?

    Forget any limitations or how disabled you have felt—what are your abilities? What can you do ALIVE that you can't do DEAD? (Okay, I know the answer to this is everything—what can a person quantifiably do when dead except decompose? But you know what I mean!) Really, make a list of them. Begin to realize deep down all the things you are and can do that you have accepted blindly by faith.

2. If you were taken away from this life tomorrow, what are the things you would miss most in the world?

3. If you died today, what would you most regret not having done or finished?

CHAPTER 17

Threshold Points: The Secret of Life-Changing Inspiration

In my work with thousands of clients throughout the world with all sorts of problems, I have always found that I knew they would change once they reached a particular threshold point. It was a kind of epiphany where they immediately and instantly saw things from a different perspective, and their attitude transformed powerfully. I talked to Richard about such threshold points.

OF: People need to be led to epiphany moments, so they can reach a threshold. But what creates a threshold for somebody? In other words, what needs to happen for people to be sufficiently inspired to change their lives?

He replied with a smile.

RB: Well, that's an infinite question. For some people, it's death. For some people, it's divorce. Some people just hit the point where they can't stand the pain anymore, even though the pain is self-inflicted. With some people, you have to push them over the point and get them to realize that things have to change.

Basically, there's a mechanism that's inside human beings. It's a very important mechanism that gets people to associate with certain things and disassociate from others. It gets them to say, "That's not me," or "That is me," and that mechanism is there to ensure that we can get over painful things, like the death of someone close.

It's there to help us fall in love and out of love. It plays movies of experiences over and over again to the point when you get to a threshold. The problem is that it needs to run X number of experiences within a short period of time—otherwise people can suffer for years.

Bringing people to this threshold is not just done by therapists but by any agent of change—even if you're the manager of somebody who's always slacking off. What you have to do is pull enough of the memories of how this employee has lost jobs repeatedly into his or her mind quickly enough that the person gets fed up suddenly and changes. People always talk about the straw that broke the camel's back. And sometimes you have to get the camel into the same place as the straw. Otherwise people will drag this crap out for their whole life.

One of the most important human experiences is when you get to the point where enough is enough. "Never Again." What this does is change the way that you mentally conceive things. Once you learn the mechanical nature of this tool, it helps you to direct your activity better, but most people are half-doing one thing and half-doing another, and they're uncertain. They go back and forth, but they never stack it all in one place to the point where they say, "Enough of this crap. I'm just going to do it 100 percent and find out what happens."

Great musicians, great artists, all of these people know how to commit to the moment. They may not paint every hour of every day. Neither do great writers like Robert Anton Wilson. He told me he sits down and writes for two to three hours a day, even if he writes terribly; he has made himself disciplined. Whether or not he was a disciplined person to start with, it doesn't matter.

There's a point where all of us can decide we're going to be different. If we run through in our minds often enough and fast enough and spin the feelings well enough it can work. We need to remind ourselves of how all of the lack of discipline hasn't enabled us to manifest the life we want, then suddenly it builds up to the point where it takes us through a threshold. I think, like epiphany experiences, they are sometimes created and they sometimes just happen.

Sometimes terrible things happen to people, and sometimes people have to hit bottom and end up in the gutter before they reach the threshold. Even then, there are people walking around with a shopping cart, mumbling, on whom the need for change still doesn't dawn. Most people know what the right direction for their life is, but they can't get themselves to do it 100 percent. But if they concentrate intensely on the bad stuff and build bad feelings, and then concentrate intensely on the good stuff and build really good feelings, their minds will snap into the position where they will know what to do. I think that people need to be their own taskmasters, and they need to be able to act in a positive way.

Getting yourself to reach a threshold means associating a massive amount of pain with engaging in the limiting behaviors you wish to end, or with not engaging in whatever behaviors you wish to begin. It means making the images of the worst things that you've lost from hesitating or from not telling someone something you wanted to. It means letting all your regrets stack up and be the final straw that moves you toward changing things. It means using the pain as a powerful motivator, while at the same time tenaciously moving toward the delight in making the change, taking the steps, engaging in the discipline. After motivating yourself by moving through your threshold, you can inspire yourself further by building up wonderful feelings about achieving good results. In considering the two sides to motivation, pain and pleasure, I was also curious about what Richard had to say about motivation and how he motivates people.

OF: What about motivation? How do you motivate people effectively?

RB: Well, it depends upon what it is. Some you can scare into it. Fear in itself is not a bad thing. With a lot of people, I scare them by switching their point of view in time. I take them into the future to examine their own lives down the road, and I have them look back at all the stuff they didn't do, people they didn't meet, the things they never tried, and I ask them how stupid or wasteful that is. Then I ask them if they are ready to die.

Sometimes it's enough. I do it in great detail. I do it in deeper ways to the point where, when they come back and look at their problems, things that looked like big mountains become molehills. The trick is to get people to understand there is much worse, and they create it. It's not that down the road it's not going to matter at all; it's just that the older you get, the more you're going to realize what a stupid idiot you have been and how much time you wasted.

There are people who never drive or go outside and meet anyone and people who do the same thing every day. For them, it may be fine; but, for me, it's not enough—there's always something more. I went out the other day with somebody. We went around to all these bookstores, probably six or seven, and I bought tons of books on tons of different subjects. The person I was with bought one book. I actually bought it for him. That's because the book jumped off the shelf at him. The book was calling out to him. It wasn't that he couldn't afford it, either; it was that he didn't appreciate how much of a difference it could make.

For me, there are people who are willing to make their lives less than they could be and just settle for it in lieu of having to push the buttons inside themselves to get their juices going. Most people don't create strong enough feelings to get themselves to do anything, and it requires practice. You have to make good feelings and make them strong and make motivated feelings and make them strong. You have got to have big, giant pictures, not little, tiny, stupid, blurry pictures.

That is no foundation on which to have a driven life, and from a good foundation you can live a strong life.

It doesn't mean that living a life where you do a lot means you're never going to get hurt or that bad things won't ever happen. Your life can be a lot safer if you live at home by yourself doing nothing. Some people are looking for safety. Some of us want to make sure that we have some nice experiences with the time we have on this planet. Some people fantasize about things and watch a few television programs.

Some of us want to live life to the fullest because we know that we don't get that many minutes that are that important, so we have to fight for them and make them as important as possible. Then, as your life comes to a close, you'll look back and realize that you didn't miss that much. I think the worst thing of all would be to have your life come to a close and to regret the good stuff you could have had.

It doesn't mean people have to climb Mount Everest. That could be the dumbest thing you could do, or jump out of an airplane to do something exciting. Maybe it's just to look over and smile at your wife and say something nice. For some people that is the hardest thing to do. It's amazingly difficult.

Richard hit on something important. I had done so many things I was proud of. The accomplishments meant so much to me, and yet I realized that there was something much more important. It is about making the moments of your everyday life count. Often we have so much that we can do, but we fail to do it; we neglect it because we don't feel it makes a difference. Unfortunately, these incidences of neglect do all add up and result in how we create our own futures. Success comes from engaging in a few simple, small disciplines consistently.

Motivating ourselves involves looking at our lives differently before exploring what we need to do and how we can build up an intense desire to do it. If you can realize how you think about something that you are motivated to do, then you can learn how to motivate yourself about other things. How do we talk to ourselves when we are motivated? Can we practice talking to ourselves like that when we want to become more motivated?

I once walked out of a huge bookshop in Portland, Oregon, where I'd been shopping with my cousin, carrying twenty-six books I bought there. My motivation came from the fact that I am intensely curious about things that interest me. When you can begin to formulate well-formed goals and directions, you can reach the stage where you can either achieve them by disciplined effort or let them slip by through laziness. This choice will be based upon how soon you reach the threshold. Sometimes it will take disgust with your present circumstances before you move, and sometimes you will simply feel an urge to do particular actions. Either way, it's about using your brain in such a way that you powerfully motivate yourself.

Motivation Power Exercise

1. Consider some of the goals or changes you want in your life and apply these questions to them:

> How will accomplishing these goals or changes affect your life?
>
> How will accomplishing these goals or changes affect other people's lives?
>
> What is the worst that can happen if you don't make this change or achieve this goal? How will you feel?
>
> What is the best that will happen once you have made this change and achieved this goal? How will you feel?
>
> Imagine yourself in thirty years, having failed to achieve your goal and having failed to make the changes. Really imagine how awful you will feel. Picture it vividly.
>
> Imagine yourself out there in your own future, having successfully changed and achieved your goal. Really imagine how amazing and inspired you will feel. Picture it vividly.

CHAPTER 18

The Last of the Human Freedoms:
A Remarkable Attitude

*"Nowhere does a man retire with more quiet
or freedom than into his own soul."*

—MARCUS AURELIUS

BOOK FOR THE MEDITATIONS, BOOK 4 (AD 167)

THE LITTLE BOY HELD his father's hand as they walked toward the dormitory of the concentration camp. The boy looked at everything around him with concern. His father smiled at him and gently reassured him that it was all a game, a contest that was all about fun. The father transformed the child's experience from horror to a game that was made up of certain rules. If they won, the father explained, they would win a real, live tank.

The film *Life Is Beautiful* is a fantastic example of the power of having a remarkable attitude. It is based on how a father helped his son gain a different perspective on the experiences of being held prisoner in a concentration camp during the Second World War. A real-life story similar to it is that of Viktor Frankl who, during the Second World War, went through the most horrible experience known to the world and yet still kept a strong, determined, and hopeful attitude. He was tortured and subjected to extensive abuse, and yet still he refused to develop a sense of hopelessness.

My friend Barry once described a great attitude he uses. No matter what happens in his life, he thinks, "Could be the best thing that ever happened."

He stands by this, and it keeps him focusing on the positive in every experience. Your attitude is the single most important aspect of the way you think.

With the wrong attitude, you can transform everything into a problem. With the wrong attitude, you can turn molehills into mountains. With the wrong attitude, you can turn any experience into the hardest time.

With the right attitude, you can transform problems into solutions. With the right attitude, you can turn mountains into molehills. With the right attitude, you can turn the hardest times into the most rewarding of experiences.

Your attitude is how you choose to think about things. It involves how you choose to think about yourself, how you choose to think about other people, and how you choose to think about your world. Your attitude comprises a set of beliefs and feelings that are based on the way you have processed your interpretation of your experiences. NLP is always described mainly as an attitude. I asked Richard about it.

OF: What do you believe the keys to an effective attitude are?

RB: Well, attitude is the reflection of a person's belief system. When you believe things are possible, it doesn't mean you'll do anything about it, but if you have the right attitude, then often you will. We like to call it a "Jersey" attitude, since John LaValle and I are from New Jersey, and lots of other NLPers started in New Jersey.

This attitude is called the New Jersey state because people there just get things done. It's the nature of things. People who grew up there have the attitude that if you're going to do something, then do it. If you're not, forget about it, and don't even think about it. Most people choose to just wait around and procrastinate. If you're going to clean something up, then it takes as much time to think about it as it does to clean it up. The same thing is true about most things.

When I started to look at ways to deal with phobics, all I heard was people coming up with elaborate theories of why you couldn't. In fact, they told me the purpose of psychiatry wasn't to get people to solve their problems, but instead to accept themselves the way they were. That self-acceptance was what therapy was all about. So I decided then and there that I wasn't going to be a therapist because it didn't suit my attitude.

I think that when people want to get over a problem, to get to the other side of fear or to get out of depression or to get out of whatever psychosis they are in, whatever it takes must be done. The theorists don't always tell you, but if you move on and push the fun gear to the red line and power on through, you'll find a way of doing things.

Most of the successful people I have met in my life have done this, whether they were successful physicists or businesspeople or people like Virginia Satir, who decided she was going to get something done come hell or high water, and through perseverance, and the fact that she enjoyed fighting through the difficulty, made it so she got it done.

I think that's an important attitude, and the world needs a lot more people who are willing to do this for a lot more things. It's ridiculous that the way therapy is defined is by the hour. It's not about how many minutes people sit in front of you; it's the amount you can get done. Some things are better done in five minutes; others in five hours.

Most of these restricting structures are created. It's like the way schools are structured is really about employment and nothing else. It's about having the teacher arrive at a certain time and leave at a certain time, and the same is true of the idea of grade levels. All this nonsense has nothing to do with getting people in a situation where they learn as quickly as they can and have as much fun as they can and maximizing the speed. It's about everybody getting the same stuff at the same time, so they can package it and sell it, so everyone can safely do the same thing without having to run the risk of being innovative and creative.

I considered what Richard was saying. He was making sense. I thought about the concept of an attitude. I believe that the keys to attitude involve your ability to change your attitude in the most useful ways to powerfully improve the way you deal with your experiences in life. It is essential, first, to learn certain basic fundamentally resourceful beliefs upon which to build a more useful attitude for yourself. Second, you can discover how to build on this new attitude by developing powerful internal states and feelings. Finally, you can understand how to develop multiple points of view through understanding the importance of flexibility of attitude.

CHAPTER 19

The Beliefs and States of Success

OUR ATTITUDES ARE a reflection of our beliefs. Our beliefs about the world determine how we think about and experience it. To improve our ability to think and experience the world, it is vital that we learn to develop beliefs that serve us. The main beliefs that underlie the basis of NLP are known as the presuppositions. They are very useful beliefs to hold. They include success beliefs and success states.

Success Beliefs

The Map Is Not the Territory

The way you see the world is not how the world is but simply a representation of it. Like any map, our maps of the world are only descriptions and not completely accurate or true. It's just a useful, or not useful, way of thinking about it. Change the way you think about something to make it more useful. In other words, change your map of the world.

The Way in Which We Experience the World Can Be Usefully Represented and Understood Through the Five Senses

Since we use five senses to take the world in, we can also usefully understand the way we think in terms of these same five senses. Hence, we make internal images, hear internal sounds, talk to ourselves, get feelings, and have internal tastes and smells. This is how we represent the world.

The Meaning of Your Communication Is the Response You Get

When you take responsibility for your own communication and it produces effective results with others, you will have a much better chance of succeeding than if you blame any misunderstanding on those you are communicating with. It's more useful to take the responsibility to ensure that you are getting through to your audience, as this is what ensures you perform at your best. If you are happy to blame your audience because they are not listening or understanding, you are not communicating the best you can.

People Have All the Resources They Need to Effect Change

It is because you have a brain and a sense of humor that you have everything you need to change. The key is to learn how to use them to make such changes permanent. You have the ability to alter your thoughts, feelings, and behaviors.

People Are Not Broken; Their Behavior Is Useful or Not Useful

There is a difference between who we are and what we do. The fact that we feel depressed, engage in bad habits, or communicate ineffectively says nothing about us or our worth. We simply need to learn how to think differently, feel differently, behave differently, and communicate differently.

There Is a Positive Intention Guiding Every Behavior and There Is a Context in Which the Behavior Has Value

Our behaviors and feelings are trying to help us in some way. For example, fear is there to try to protect us. A fear of spiders is useful in African jungles but not so useful in an Irish living room. If we can find out how to satisfy the intention with a more useful behavior, we can find change happens much more easily.

There Is No Such Thing as Failure, Only Feedback

Failure only exists when you place a time limit on something. It is not that we fail. It is simply that we get things wrong from time to time. When you can learn from each mistake, you can see mistakes as feedback, which can be used to improve the way we perform.

Success Beliefs Exercise

1. Take the seven success beliefs listed above and think of some ways in which you can use them to overcome problems in your life.

Success States

Underlying these presuppositions I have found valuable and essential states that are the important keys of having the best attitude. There are two main categories of these states. The first contains the states that are required for people to take in information most usefully from the world. They are known as *input states*. The second category contains the states that are required for people to act successfully in the world. They are known as *output states*.

Input States: Awareness, Openness, Curiosity
Output States: Flexibility, Determination, Pragmatism, Responsibility, Creativity

When you can master getting into these states and living in them, you will find yourself with the most useful attitude toward life. This is a shortcut to attempting to "live" the presuppositions. It enables you to experience the world through a more useful filter, thereby enabling you to act, think, and communicate in the most useful and resourceful way.

Input States

AWARENESS

Awareness involves paying attention to what is happening in the world and inside your own head—developing sensory acuity and self-insight. Sensory acuity refers to your ability to pay attention to what you see, hear, and feel in the world and to notice the distinctive features. Self-insight is improved by paying attention to how you are thinking and feeling in your life.

OPENNESS

Openness is when you are open to the idea of being wrong. It is about being open to new ideas, new experiences, new learning. Develop it by practicing looking at things from multiple perspectives and understanding that there are more than two sides to every story.

CURIOSITY

Curiosity is your ability to ask questions and wonder about things. The more curious you are, the more information you look for, and the smarter you become. Curiosity is developed by appreciating the miracles that exist in the world and the brilliance of knowledge and what it can do for you.

Output States

FLEXIBILITY

Flexibility is the state in which you are able to do different things and respond differently to the world. The more flexible you are, the more choices you have, and thus the more control you have over any given situation. Flexibility is improved by doing new things and practicing new behaviors that are different from your habits.

DETERMINATION

Determination is the state of never giving up. It is the commitment by you to continue to go for something despite failures, rejection, or disappointments. It enables you to succeed more, as success becomes simply a matter of time. Determination is improved by taking each defeat as a "learning" opportunity and refusing to give up at any stage.

PRAGMATISM

Pragmatism is the attitude of doing something usefully. It is focused on doing whatever is the most useful and smartest thing to do in any given context. Pragmatism is improved by continuously asking yourself the question: "What is the most useful thing to do right now?"

RESPONSIBILITY

Responsibility comes when you decide to be accountable for the experiences that have happened in your life. It is your commitment to take control over the way you interact and experience the world. It helps you make your life more wonderful. Responsibility is improved by focusing on what you can do about a situation and not why things happen this way.

CREATIVITY

Creativity is the state in which you can use your imagination to invent ideas that do not exist. It enables us to contribute and positively affect the world. You can use it to make things easier and better in your life. Creativity is improved by practicing combining different ideas with others and seeing what comes out from such combinations.

If you can start thinking deliberately about the world through these states and beliefs, then you will gain the ability to change how you take things in and how you respond to the world.

Success State Exercises

These tasks need to be performed on an ongoing, consistent basis.

1. Awareness

Spend five minutes every day paying attention to what you see, hear, and feel in the world and noticing the differences that exist. Notice the differences between what you can see, hear, and feel on the outside and be aware of how you are thinking and feeling on the inside.

2. Openness

Spend five minutes every day taking a belief you have about something in the world and practice looking at it from the opposite point of view. Construct as many arguments as possible, thinking about it from a different perspective.

3. Curiosity

Begin to ask more questions of everything. Buy more books. Find the people who do things you really admire and ask them about how they do it. Realize you can learn from everything. When you meet people from a different background than your own, find out about their culture. Ask enough questions to gain a good understanding of it.

4. Flexibility

Every day practice doing new things. Try new meals in restaurants; try new routes to and from work. Take up something you have never tried before and give it a go. At least once a week do something or go somewhere that you have not done or gone to before.

5. Determination

Every time you don't get what you want, simply focus on what you want, change your approach, and start again. Keep going and only focus on how good it will feel once you've done it. Avoid the possibility that it might not be achieved.

6. Pragmatism

Practice repeating the question: "What is the most useful thing to do now?" Each time you come face-to-face with a problem, repeat this question.

7. Responsibility

Whenever a problem crops up, always ask the question: "What can I do now?" Make this a habit, too.

8. Creativity

Once a week, spend twenty minutes and take three ideas that have nothing to do with each other and invent some new product or philosophy by combining them. No matter how ridiculous it seems at first, practice engaging in this exercise.

CHAPTER 20

The Illusion of Reality: The Freedom of a Different Perspective

ONE DAY, A WOMAN was sitting down in the airport after having bought some cookies and a coke in the shop. As she sat down, thinking about everything she had to do, she began to eat the cookies. She soon noticed a well-dressed man in a suit on the other side of the table, helping himself to the cookies. Although annoyed and angry at this, she said nothing, and as she continued to eat, so did he. This continued until the final cookie, which he took, broke in half, and gave her the other half. Minutes later, as she lined up for the flight, she was intensely irritated by this. How dare he? It was at that point, as she looked in her bag for her passport, that she noticed her unopened package of cookies. The cookies she had shared with the man had been his.

One of the most important freedoms we have is our freedom to see one situation from multiple points of view. When an event happens in our world, the way we think about and experience that event will determine how we act and what decisions we make about it.

The way in which we experience the world is not how the world is. It is simply our representation of the world. Our representation of the world will depend on our beliefs, values, past experiences, and mood at any one given moment in time.

It is essential to realize that reality is an illusion, and whatever reality we believe in is only true for us. Being able to look at the same experience from more than one perspective enables us to understand others' way of thinking more, as well as providing us with a more useful way of thinking about the situation. Once again, I discussed this with Richard.

OF: Richard, I've found in my own experience that what you say about the ability to look at a situation from multiple perspectives being of paramount importance seems very accurate. What do you think about the role of multiple perspectives in living a life with more freedom?

RB: Well, certainly, when you think about something . . . you're there, and your girlfriend leaves you, and it seems like your life is over, and everything is the end of the universe, but if you could float twenty-five years down the line, some people won't even be able to remember the name of the girl.

So there's time. Sometimes I tell people to just float up off the planet and look down and see whether or not this is one of the significant events. From this perspective, it doesn't seem so significant. People need to get distance from unpleasant experiences. Even in their minds, if the pictures are big and bright and loud and they seem like they're happening as opposed to having happened, they can change this view and feel different instantly.

I mean things like rape are terrible experiences, but what's even worse is that people relive it every day, like it's actually happening. People need to push this stuff away and put it in the past and make it so that it feels like it's happening to someone else so that they can get on with their lives. It's bad enough that somebody has something terrible happen to them without having it happen to them every day, over and over again. I mean, the rapist only raped them once, but mentally they rape themselves a thousand times.

They can blame it on the fact that they were raped in the first place, but it doesn't change. The most important thing is to realize that it's the job of someone like me to give people like that freedom from those chains, by being able to break those chains. Whether it's changing their perspective, whether it's hypnotizing them and giving them amnesia, whether it's welling up so much anger inside them that it just literally explodes into the point where they say, "I'm never thinking about this again. I'm not giving any power to this human being as long as I live."

I worked with a woman who had been stalked for about fifteen years, and I mean this guy was clever. He was smart. He outwitted the police. He made this woman's life a living hell. Every time she opened a drawer, there was a note from him. She would go on vacation, having not told anybody where she was going, and when she checked into her new hotel room, there would be a negligee and pictures of her naked. She had no idea how the guy was doing this. She lived in abject terror. With me, I kept running the terror by keeping her feeling that feeling. The events always happened slightly apart, and I switched all the events as if they had happened in one hour, and instead of being terrified, she exploded in vehement anger. She finally decided no matter what this guy did and no matter how much he stalked her, she was going to find ways of driving him nuts, and so she started staging events that she knew would absolutely drive him crazy.

She did things like hiring an actor who was ninety-seven. She was in her thirties, and she hired this old guy to start dating her. She also hired another person to see if they could catch the stalker. Even though the police couldn't catch him, this other guy did. Whether he turned him over to the police or not, I don't know, but the stalker disappeared after that.

She couldn't have done anything to fight back when she was afraid. It wasn't until she got that thing of "enough is enough," that instead of trying to hide with her windows closed, she started necking with a ninety-seven-year-old with the windows open. She used any kind of thing she could possibly think of to get to the stalker. She left notes for him. Assuming that her phones were bugged, she talked about this "poor, little, pathetic so and so," and that she felt sorry for him because "he probably couldn't masturbate with both hands," instead of picking up the phone and wondering whether or not he was terrorizing her.

What Richard was saying made perfect sense. When you get the freedom of a different perspective, it enables you to have a larger range of choices of what you can do to respond to the world. You gain more information about what is going on, so you can make more effective decisions.

OF: So how do you help people see things from a different point of view?

RB: Well, I always start with humor because I think that, until people laugh, they can't be flexible in their point of view. Some people find it a lot harder than others. I have met some really stuck people who are stuck in their view of the world and, as small as their lives and situations may be, they are not willing to change it. God gave us endomorphins for a reason: to stop doing the things that aren't working.

I have worked with couples who treated each other so badly that there was no way in the world they would ever find out what it would be like to be really in love—until they could start laughing at those stupid behaviors. A lot of times, it means I had to make fun of things that were hard to make fun of with people, like religious beliefs.

I had people who started to quote the Bible. So I got better than them at quoting the Bible, and as I went through the quotes, I would also bring up other things that were in there. I mean in Genesis 1 it says, "At first, God created the animals and then man." In Genesis 2, it is "man and then the animals." So there's a lot of confusion in the book. You can use it to justify stupidity.

When I tell Bible stories, it isn't to undermine the Bible but to get people to realize that what they should take seriously about religious texts are the things that make life better, and the rest of it is just an excuse to feel bad. Whether you use religious texts or politics or schizophrenia or identifiable diseases to feel bad and to justify making other people feel bad, all of it's the same. It's still just cruelty. The most important thing is to get people to change their worldview, whether they're cruel to themselves or cruel to other people, and I think that starts with a little bit of humor.

A different perspective was obviously one of the main keys to change. It's like I always say to my own clients: if you frown at your problems, they will seem bigger; smile at your problems and they will get smaller. I was curious about Richard's perspective on the true power of humor.

CHAPTER 21

The Power of Humor

MY FRIENDS EDDIE AND Dave have always helped me look at myself and my life a lot less seriously. It is because of them that I laugh so much at life. Through their hilariousness and spirit of fun, I have learned to find humor in everything. For the fifteen years I have known them, we've all developed a similar sense of humor. It was with them that I first began to understand the true power of humor.

Eddie and Dave have forced me to loosen up about life. By teasing me in the most hilarious of ways, they have made me realize just how stupid it is to feel bad about life. You see, the words of others used to be such a big deal to me. Now, I find most things funny. There are other friends I spend time with, whom I make laugh. I spend much of my time getting clients to see the funny side of their problems. I learn from the best.

Perhaps one of the best demonstrations I ever did was with a woman from one of our practitioner courses. I was to demonstrate the fast phobia cure, an NLP technique for curing a phobia in a few minutes. However, in working with her, I got sidetracked and ended up using a different mechanism.

Georgina had a fear of mice and would have a severe panic episode if she heard there was a mouse in the house. I first asked her a few questions. The dialogue went something like this.

OF: So, Georgina, do you hate all mice?
Georgina: Yeah. The thought of them turns my stomach.

OF: What about Stuart Little or Jerry from *Tom and Jerry?* Do you hate them, too?
Georgina: Well, no.

She laughed.

Georgina: Of course not. They are really cute.
OF: Okay, so what you are saying is that you are okay with Jerry and Stuart, but you don't like Frank, Mark, Barry, and the rest of the boys. That's called mice racism.

She laughed and giggled away with the thought of these mice having names and being hurt that she didn't like them. As she laughed, I casually rested my hand on her shoulder and anchored the laughter. I continued by getting down on all fours on the ground, crawling around and doing impersonations of the mice.

OF: "Hey, Frank, you find any cheese anywhere?" "No, man, sorry." "Hey, you hear that lady hates us? What did we ever do to her?" "Stewie and Jerry never get treated like this. It's so unfair, just 'cause we ain't famous mice." "I know, Frank. We are the prejudiced few."

Georgina kept laughing as did most of the audience. I got up, and again I rested my hand casually on her shoulder. I continued.

OF: So, Georgina, tell me. When you think of mice in the house, what image or images come to mind?
Georgina: Well, I imagine the cupboard closed and the mouse inside there, and I open the cupboard, and the mouse jumps out on top of me.

OF: Okay, let me get this straight. . . .

I paused for a moment. Earlier in the training I had talked about the movie *Rambo*. I described a scene where Rambo was being left on his own by his friend who is taking off in a helicopter. We get a camera shot of Rambo looking over his shoulder about 500 yards away, and we see about three tanks, four helicopters with missile launchers, and 400 men with heavy machinery obviously looking for him.

Then the shot goes back to Rambo, bloody and loaded with weapons. His friend asks him, "Rambo, Rambo, what are you gonna do? What are you gonna do?" We see Rambo looking at all the enemies approaching, cocking his gun as he speaks the immortal words, "Fuck 'em," and runs at them shooting and firing away. I used this example to describe the kind of attitude you need when faced with problems—of never giving up and of fighting your heart out.

OF: Let me get this straight. I'm a mouse, and I'm minding my own business hunting around for cheese in the cupboard.

I jumped down to the floor again and crawled around sniffing at everybody's feet. The audience and Georgina were laughing away.

OF: And then, the cupboard door opens, and I see a human that's twenty times the height of me, many times my weight, could crush me with one hand. And I do what? I jump out at her? I jump? At her? Who is this? Rambo the mouse?"

I impersonated the mouse as I jumped toward her from the ground shouting in a squeaky accent, "Fuck 'em." Georgina collapsed into laughter as she thought about the mouse with his little bandana on and all those machine guns. I simply got up and had her think about mice and placed my hand on her shoulder (retriggering the laughter). Her fear had gone. Almost a year later, Georgina came back and did another course with us. She recounted an incident she had with a mouse after the first seminar.

Her daughter informed her of a mouse running about downstairs in her house. Whereas before she would have scampered from the house, instead she spent hours searching for the mouse and couldn't wait to find out what it looked like. It's almost like she half-expected to see that bandana.

In this case, I created a powerful state of laughter with Georgina and anchored it (or associated it) to mice. That way, when she thought about mice, she felt a need to laugh.

Richard had been explaining the importance of being able to laugh at situations. I questioned him further about the power of humor.

OF: How do you use laughter to help people change their perspective?

RB: I can be more of a lunatic than they can. When a client starts quoting the Bible and about how this justifies him beating his wife and children, I say, "That's right, we should beat everyone." I'll take them out and say, "Let's beat everyone in sight. In fact, we shouldn't beat them up, we should string them up on crosses and make them die like Jesus, and then they'd know they were wrong. Let's go to the lumberyard." Then the client will say, "Wait a minute, you're going overboard," whereas the truth is that they were going overboard from the start.

I find that if I get more serious about it than they are willing to be, then there is a tendency that they have to change their worldview. Sometimes, if you put people in a hypnotic trance, you can also get them to step into someone else's shoes. Sometimes that's a lot easier.

It depends on how stuck someone is, because there are a lot of ways to be stuck, and of course, some people have been on drugs for a long time. Many of these drugs, like Thorazine and halaphine have a six-month half-life, so it takes half a year for them to just leave your system. I mean, if they are given drugs, and they still have the same damned delusion, then the drug didn't get rid of the delusion, it just got rid of the noisy behavior. That's why they are called maintenance drugs.

I want people off the drugs and bouncing off the walls, and some psychiatrists have told me I'm going to push people over the edge. Well, the truth is I'm not going to push them; I'm going to grab hold of them and jump down with them. A lot of the success I've had with these cases, others haven't. A lot of the things I did when I was younger, I don't think I would probably do now. I haven't got that kind of energy.

It's for my students to do, but I think you and I have to give up a lot of that stuff. You don't have to pretend to nail someone who says he is Jesus to the cross.

OF: But it's fun.

RB: Yeah, I suppose, its kind of fun. Everybody should do it once.

I laughed. Richard smiled back.

Richard with his grandson, Jayson.

RB: It's a lot better than "I heard you used to be a carpenter." It has a lot more of an impact on them. Things have to impact people. I know a lot more now about putting people into powerful altered states and impacting them.

I knew a lot more about tying people to crosses and lighting fires under them when I was younger, but the attitude is still the same. Whatever it takes to create a powerful emotional state where I can get people back to the important things in life, which is having a real life, that is what I will do. Most "normal" people's lives, others might not look at them and think of them as being important, but I do. I think people having families is important.

Humor is the best chemical of all, and everybody knows it without an exception. There isn't anyone who doesn't know that humor is the best chemical that humans can produce. Outright good laughter is the best therapy. Everybody says so. Everybody knows it, but they don't all practice it. Everybody knows that they learn best when they are really laughing and having fun; that's when they do things.

You go in some classrooms, and they won't even let kids laugh. They've rules against it, yet everybody knows when you're laughing you learn more effectively. That's why in my seminars, when I teach people, they are always laughing and having a good time, and people memorize everything, and they learn more effectively, and they learn to do more. Can you imagine a bunch of kids playing and no laughter whatsoever? Just serious little four year olds pushing trucks back and forth methodically without laughter—they wouldn't learn anything.

OF: Keeping that in mind, how can we improve our own ability to look at things and help others look at things from a humorous perspective?

RB: Read Frank Farrelly's book *Provocative Therapy*. That will always help. Regarding comedians, the problem is that most comedians really aren't that funny, and I mean the trick is you have to kiss a ton of frogs to find a prince, and that's true in everything. You're going to hear a hundred comedians to find one that's truly funny, and they're not going to be funny all the time—to expect them to be funny all the time is too much, so you have to be able to tell the difference between what's funny and what's not funny instead of what should be funny and what's not funny.

Most people don't find their sense of humor because they don't lighten up. They don't look at things from the point of view of how silly things are. They're asking themselves, "Do people like me?" not "What's funny about this?" A guy from India came up to me in a seminar and said, "Dr. Bandler, I have studied Gregory Bateson, and I'm always asking myself, am I in the complementary or a metacomplementary position, and you don't seem to care about that." I said, "No, I don't. Right now, are you in a metacomplementary position?" To which he replied, "Well, no, I am not." I said, "That's right, but if you ask a question, then you get the answer to that question."

"I'm only asking if we're having fun yet," I said. "So tomorrow, don't ask whether you're in a metacomplementary position or not; ask, 'Am I having fun yet?'" The next day he was laughing and having fun all day long, while the day before he had sat seriously and felt inferior while everybody else had fun. Your choice is whether to lighten the hell up or not.

From my time with Richard, I recognized he had a tremendous ability to use humor successfully in his seminars. I began to realize that there was a fantastic skill in this. If someone could manage to study how he was able to make light of seemingly any situation, then they could learn to do just that themselves. I began to study the best comedians I could find. I studied people like Ricky Gervais, Billy Connelly, Eddie Izzard, and Bill Hicks. What I found was that they all had an incredible ability to take what's happening and find the humor in it. I started asking the question, "How did they do this?" My findings became known as what I call the "laughter filter."

> *"Sometimes people say, 'One day you are going to look back at this and laugh.' My question is: 'Why wait?'"*
>
> —RICHARD BANDLER

The laughter filter involves practicing looking at all situations that trouble you from the eyes of a comedian. It involves you imagining that you have to present a comedy sketch or dialogue on a particular problem in your life. It might involve dramatically exaggerating the experience, imagining it from the point of view of an animal, mimicking yourself, or simply restating what you are thinking out loud to hear how funny it actually sounds when taking yourself literally.

The power of humor can help you deal effectively with all kinds of problems. It makes life in general easier and more fun. Humor has a built-in function of promoting flexibility in your perspective. Jokes are funny because one word can mean two things. There are ambiguities in humor. For example, consider the joke: "A man walks into a bar. He hurts himself." This joke uses the word "bar," which initially we take as meaning a pub where the man is going, probably to drink. Then a second meaning for bar is revealed in the punch line, which is where the humor lies.

By the same token, humor can enable you to take more than one meaning from difficult situations. Far too many people I know take life seriously. It's so important to learn to laugh through most of your life. When it comes down to it, there is little reason for seriousness, not to mention that we learn and perform better when we are laughing and enjoying ourselves. The power of humor is indeed an essential tool for the acquisition of personal freedom.

Richard had helped me understand valuable insights about the keys to change. After this conversation, I left his place and got back on the underground train. There were fewer people on it this time. I sat down and began to think about the answers I had gotten. Change really is possible for anyone. The true keys are the beliefs and attitudes of the person and an understanding of how goals, motivation, thresholds, and moments of epiphany work. The keys are about learning to perceive the world differently and discovering the wonderful power of humor in living a remarkable life.

On my next visit with Richard, whenever and wherever it would be, I would focus on everyday problems and how to apply what I already knew to real life. The problems people have can be changed, but the best way to help people change and become free is not always obvious. These secrets would be explored the next time. I looked around and smiled at those who sat with the same stony faces. Soon, I hoped, there would be a book that helped them to smile more and enjoy what life could really be like. Soon, they could have freedom.

Laughter Filter Exercise

1. Take an everyday problem that you have, write it down, and apply the laughter filter by exploring the following:

    Examine the way it's written literally to see if any fun can be poked at it.

    How would a stand-up comedian describe that problem in a sketch?

    How might a comedian exaggerate it or elements of it?

    How might a comedian look at it from a completely different point of view (e.g., through the eyes of an animal or alien)?

    How would comedians mimic themselves or people dealing with this problem?

    Prepare a stand-up sketch on the problem, having answered these questions, and revise it over and over again to get better at changing how you feel.

CHAPTER 22

Random Ramblings 3:
The Trance to Change Your Life

I REMEMBER SITTING down in Mexico to read the book *Deep Transformation* by my good friend Gabe Guerrero. It was written in Spanish, so I understood little of it, but I became absorbed in the book as I tried to make out what it actually said. The little bits of Spanish that were like English gave me a disjointed understanding of the first few pages. I went into a kind of deep trance. It's amazing to realize that the words you read mean something you don't understand, until you learn how to understand them, and then everything becomes clear. When I came to, Gabe was smiling at me, laughing at the look in my eyes.

Gabe and I are always practicing skills such as hypnosis on each other and helping each other go into profound altered states. We are forever giving each other suggestions and laughing as we "trance out" each other in conversations. He sometimes drops Spanish words in to conversations to do this, and I retaliate by dropping in Irish words. Both of us have been influenced for so long by Richard that we have naturally adopted many of the advanced language patterns he teaches. We have both been trained in hypnosis by the person often described as the "best hypnotist in the world." I also found Gabe's lovely wife, Barbara, to be very skilled at this. In working to improve my Spanish, I noticed myself drifting in and out of trance states quite regularly while talking with her.

Mexico is truly the land of trance. The beautiful colors of the clothing and artwork are hypnotic. I remember being in Richard's kitchen in Ireland and seeing some of the ornaments and paintings he and Paula had brought back from Mexico. When I eventually made it over there myself, I could see why they loved the country so much. The shamans of Mexico had experimented extensively with altered states. I wondered if there was a commonality between my country of Ireland and Mexico as I experienced the culture firsthand. The Mexicans were very laid back, just like the Irish. Their culture was very spiritual and intriguing, just like the Irish.

One thing that wasn't the same, though, was the weather. I thought about my training partner, Brian, back home in Ireland, where it was probably raining. I went out for one of my jogs, listening to music as I ran along the beautiful beach in Puerto Vallarta. My mind drifted over all sorts of topics. I began to think about the fact that no matter where I went in the world, from Europe to India, America, and now Mexico, the problems people faced seemed to be the same. The people I worked with had generally the same problems regardless of their location or culture.

In Ireland, Brian and I teach a weekend workshop called the Life Enhancement seminar, at which everyone writes down what they want to resolve, and we cover their problems during the two days. To ensure we make appropriate adjustments to participants' unconscious, we often do a "double induction." That means we often have a relaxation session where we both speak at the same time, in complete synchronicity. People are often amazed at how we manage to talk in unison, seamlessly, without interrupting each other. One reason we are able to do it is the same as the reason we are able to work so well at the same time on stage with each other: we are very close friends. We have a very good connection with each other and know each other so well that we can finish each other's sentences. This enables us to work very well in a humorous double act, and at the same time to perform an effective hypnotic function. Another reason we are able to do this is because we see it as similar to performing musically.

Songs bring people into altered states. I once saw my friend Karl jamming with another friend, Ben. Ben played the drums, and Karl played the saxophone. I watched as both of them played off each other. There is something about music being played creatively and in synch that creates an altered state. I remember, too, meeting Lionel, a musician friend of Gabe's in Mexico. I recall listening to his CD *Eyes Closed* and remember that, without words, each song seemed to easily bring about a state of trance. Since the time I first learned hypnosis from the tapes of the tremendously skilled hypnotist Paul McKenna, and in eventually meeting and working with Paul, I have found that rhythm and a relaxing tone of voice is so important in assisting people to relax deeply. I remember practicing hypnotic induction after induction with my friend Thomas, until we developed real proficiency in all areas of the hypnotic process. We experimented to see just how far we could push the skills, just how deep we could go.

I want to include a trance here that is a good example of something that helps explain the process of change more profoundly. Also, even though these are only words on a page, your unconscious absorbs them the same way you need to—remember they are just trance-scriptions.

You see, one of the biggest problems people have is that they don't spend enough time making themselves feel really good and spinning or intensifying good feelings through their body. The things people usually experience while they relax into trance include feeling relaxed and breathing deeply and effortlessly. Also, their bodies feel comfortable and they find it easier and easier to imagine different things. Most people are fully aware of what's going on around them, but it's just easy to relax and listen to every word. It's kind of like the state of mind you go into before you fall asleep, when you are drifting and daydreaming about different fantasies and ideas.

It's good to read the trance slowly, at a quarter of your normal reading pace, because trance comes when you slow down and enjoy the moment.

You've been sitting there . . . paying attention to what we have been saying . . . and as each word reaches you . . . you can begin to realize . . . that you've started learning about many things . . . that have already begun . . . to help you to trance form. Your unconscious . . . knows that there are many changes . . . that you've been looking for. Here and now . . . you can notice that . . . as you begin to think of . . . what you want . . . you'll find yourself seeing it positively . . . specifically . . . you'll imagine what you will be able to see . . . hear and feel . . . when you've achieved it. . . . While you'll imagine what will happen . . . as a result . . . and what part of it . . . is under your control.

As you relax even deeper . . . you'll enjoy the wonderful feeling . . . that comes with letting go . . . you'll become fascinated with the different perceptions . . . you experience that move . . . change and evolve . . . because you can find yourself letting every part of your body and mind . . . relax . . . as you allow yourself to make certain changes . . . and changes in certainty . . . while you can let go of the beliefs about change . . . that you had and understand change . . . is simply about learning that . . . you can feel this comfortable . . . wonderful state of inner peace . . . and from here you can allow yourself to experience gorgeous feelings, which seep inside your skin . . . helping you feel really good . . . and finding yourself . . . easily and completely . . . to change the way you felt . . . to all those things that did produce bad feelings.

Now, in their place . . . you can find yourself feeling only good feelings . . . feelings that inspire you . . . feelings that motivate you . . . into realizing how you can see things in an entirely new way . . . you can find yourself learning to see the same experience from multiple points of view and develop . . . inside your mind . . . a humorous way of thinking about everything . . . so that in the future . . . as you deal with the problems that no longer bother you . . . you'll find yourself seeing them in many different ways . . . from many different perspectives . . . with a wonderful sense of humor . . . that helps you laugh at everything, effortlessly.

You'll enjoy the wonderful moment . . . that allows you to understand things differently . . . and inspires you to take the action . . . that is necessary to turn your life around because you've learned many things . . . that you will find you can . . . use dramatically . . . to enhance your life . . . and as you use all these skills . . . you'll become delightfully surprised . . . with how quick and easy permanent . . . positive change is for you.

You can then come back again slowly and feel refreshed and invigorated, feeling really good.

The more I think about it, the more I understand that change must be made unconsciously and kept guard of consciously. That is why Brian and I often find that our seminars produce such effective changes so quickly. Both of us presenting and linking off each other produces a powerful hypnotic effect that induces trance in people.

The title of Gabe's book, *Deep Transformation*, was good. I knew even misunderstanding most of the text that his stories and tales were all designed to do just that—change people profoundly. I smiled at him, and he smiled back as if to say without even hearing my thoughts, "Yep, spot on and very sneaky." And then I remembered the best hypnotic change workers I had ever met and worked with, including Richard, Paul McKenna, John LaValle, Gabe, and Brian, were all sneaky as hell and as good as gold.

PART IV

Breaking the Chains of the Self

The Cocktail of Your Self

A FEW MONTHS AFTER our talk in London, I caught up with Richard again in Edinburgh. I met him in the back of a conference room at the end of a daylong workshop entitled Adventures in Neuro-Hypnotic Repatterning. Richard made some time for me after everyone else had gone. We sat down at a table near the back.

Since the end of our last discussion, I had done a lot of different things. I found that results with my clients were even better than before, and I made some brilliant changes in my own life. I decided that this time I wanted to ask Richard questions about helping people achieve freedom from the chains of the self. To me, that involved every problem people had with themselves and their circumstances. This included questions on low self-esteem, depression, stress, fear, perfectionism, eating disorders, money problems, and health problems. Although I already had good answers for these questions, I knew I would always learn more and understand more from Richard's unique perspective.

Richard had been teaching that morning about how to change your feelings about anything by paying attention to how you experience the feeling in your body and moving it the opposite direction. It was so simple and yet so effective. I was excited now about his answers to my questions, and I wanted to let our conversation take its own course.

I remembered that the concept of the "self" was a psychological concept and that many of the problems that existed came from a psychological way of understanding the self. When you look at problems simply, it comes down to feeling bad and feeling good. I wanted to explore such a notion with Richard because I understood more and more that it was all about "chemistry."

Your thoughts affect your feelings, and your feelings affect the chemistry of your brain and body. Consequently, your thoughts affect the chemistry of your brain and body. The loop begins so that your brain chemistry affects how you think and feel. Since your actions come out of the decisions you make based upon how you think and feel, it's essential that you take control over your thoughts and feelings. The good news is that, once you do, you will be able to affect the chemistry of your brain.

Your brain is composed of millions of neurons (brain cells). Every time you think or act, you make connections between neurons. This affects the release of chemicals inside your brain, which creates your feelings. These chemicals are known as neuropeptides or neurotransmitters. They affect how these connections between neurons work. So, literally, your thoughts, feelings, and brain chemistry are all interconnected with one another. So once your brain chemistry is working well, you will find it easier to think and feel more productively. This enables you overcome many of the problems in your life.

I placed the tape recorder down on the table and got out my notebook. I was ready to begin the next conversation.

The Lies of Psychology

"What you don't believe in is as important as what you do."

—RICHARD BANDLER

PSYCHOLOGY HAS ITS USES. As a psychologist, I have learned many things that are valuable from the field. I have also seen and experienced many things that have disappointed me about the field. The concept of the self has been one of the most important topics dealt with since psychology came on the scene in the nineteenth century. Unfortunately, the methods that have been used in examining this fascinating subject have often created more problems than solutions.

You see, for the most part, psychology is about studying the mind and human behavior. Its aim is to understand the "why" behind what we think, how we think, and why we do what we do. Some brilliant psychologists have enriched the quality of our lives through their invaluable research. Unfortunately, in my opinion, this is much rarer than it should be.

In my experience with clients, I have seen them change dramatically and quickly through using the skills I have taught them. I have witnessed them changing their entire attitude after just one session. I have seen people overcome phobias and immediately test them within a few minutes of my having worked with them. I have kept in touch and followed up and discovered that the changes last.

The lies of psychology are the lies that attempt to categorize people into being different kinds of "neurotics." They are the lies that attempt to suggest that any examples of quick, transformational change will only last for a while and have no long-term value. They are the lies that suggest that only those techniques or processes that have been backed up by clinical research should be used.

They are lies because what you discover in the field of psychology is that you can prove or disprove any technique, idea, or theory as being valuable or not depending on what perspective you wish to prove. There is even a study I read that suggests that being on a waiting list can help you get better more quickly than an actual therapist!

I have found the best psychologists are the ones who learn all that they can to help people change and improve, are open to all ideas, and are willing to test them in their own experience. Then they can help people change in the most practical ways. What I am interested in is that people learn to understand themselves in a more useful way.

We are prisoners of our "selves." We lock ourselves up inside the limits of our minds. The limits of our minds include our beliefs, our thoughts, and our feelings. To make things clear, the first understanding we want you to come to is the following: what you think is true isn't—but we bet it's a lot more fun and infinitely more useful!

Breaking the chains of your self involves learning how you imprison yourself through your thoughts, beliefs, and feelings and discovering how to change them and set yourself free. It's about learning how you engage in depressing thoughts, self-pity, and fear. It's about finding out how you set yourself up for disappointment by wanting everything to be perfect and how you create feelings of insecurity, worthlessness, and low self-esteem.

People can often see themselves in very unhealthy ways and have distorted self-images that can lead to many things, including anorexia, bulimia, or low self-confidence. We can be affected by panic, fear, and anxiety. We can become stressed, overwhelmed, and frustrated with life.

Breaking the chains of the self also includes knowing the secrets of manifesting wealth, becoming healthy, and making more time for yourself to do what you need to do.

We are free from these chains when we have a healthy image of ourselves and when we feel good about ourselves. We are free from these chains when we are healthy, making more money, and enjoying more time to do what we want to do. We are free from these chains when we feel delighted with ourselves, when we are happy with the fact that we are improving every day. We are free from these chains when we are secure in who we are and when we engage in only positive, useful, and productive thoughts in our minds and when our beliefs all serve us in the most effective ways.

Now, as we have explained, our thoughts and beliefs all comprise the following elements. We represent beliefs and thoughts to ourselves in the form of images, sounds, and feelings. For example, when we believe something, we will make an image of whatever it is, we will usually say something to ourselves in a certain tone of voice, and we will get a strong feeling of certainty in our body somewhere.

When I had my moment of epiphany on the boat, as the waves crashed around me, I thought back on the final few days I had had in Fiji. Probably some of the happiest people I had met lived on Bounty Island. I made friends with the locals on the resort instantly. I had a kind of rapport with them. They joked and teased each other just like we do in Ireland. From the start, they teased and mocked me, and I teased and mocked them back. It was all a laugh, and they seemed ever cheerful.

In talking with them, I discovered that they had a radically different life view than I had been used to. They didn't dwell on sad events or experiences. They didn't focus on how awful things are. They didn't spend time trying to work out why they felt bad or what it meant. If they felt bad, they just accepted it, got on with life, and kept doing what they did moment by moment. They threw most of their attention into the present.

This reminded me of some of the lads on my soccer team back home. They have very healthy views on life, and I talked to two of them, Dave and Jason, about this. Their attitude toward life is very simple: although they were certainly smart, they don't think too deeply about things. During the time I spend with them, I realize that they have similar attitudes to Mosquito, Mr. Porter, and Captain, the Fijians who became my friends on Bounty Island. It was about focusing on the present and the future and not dwelling on negative events or bad feelings, because there was no point. It was about remembering the best times from the past and feeling good about them whenever they were brought up. It was that simple. Often, life is much simpler than we make it out to be, and it is when we complicate things that we create our problems.

As I tracked through my experiences in working with thousands of people over the years who felt miserable and down, fearful and anxious, lonely and desperate, I began to realize that much of this was due to psychological labels. As more labels have been created, more and more people every year seem to have emotional or psychological problems. It's almost like psychology is partly creating more problems. The more labels we create, the larger we make categorizing books, such as the *DSM-IV* (*Diagnostics and Statistics Manual*, which presents a comprehensive list of diagnostic categories of psychological problems), the more ways we have of being messed up. These are the lies of psychology, because it is in believing them and using them as a reference for studying ourselves that we can create more problems for ourselves.

Some "ex-spurts" in the fields of psychology, therapy, counseling, and psychiatry will scoff at the possibility of change being possible quickly. They believe that it must be painful, hard, and long and that it must involve understanding everything perfectly. It's time to reject these lies of how difficult change must be and accept the possibility that change can be simpler and easier and faster than we have thought before now.

I believe that the first step in understanding how to become happier with yourself and make improvements in your own life requires that you explore these "lies of psychology" and debunk them so that you can start with the freedom from labels.

I decided to start with focusing on a useful label. I started with asking Richard his definition of happiness.

OF: So, Richard, how do you define happiness?

RB: Happiness is a kinesthetic sensation. It's a spiritual state, an effortless state. It requires no effort whatsoever. It's just something where you sit back and you slide into it. You know it takes no effort to slide into a warm bath. If the bath is too hot, you jump out; if it's too cold, you're uncomfortable; but if the temperature is just right, you slide right in, and you just float, and to me that's what the state of happiness is like. It's floating in your own kinesthetic chemicals so that you vibrate in a state of . . . not necessarily exhilaration, but whether you're exhilarated or whether you're calm or no matter how your state changes, there's an overriding vibration of comfort.

With this in mind, my next question asked what the secrets were of living more happily.

OF: So how can you become happier with yourself and with others?

RB: Practice, practice, practice. People generally spend too much time during the course of too many days making themselves feel bad, and they have to stop it and start feeling good. You have to start by making the good feelings you have stronger, and you have to learn to take your good feelings and spin them around inside your body, so they don't spin off into space. You have to find out how to take the time to attach feelings to things that enable you to improve your life.

You have to look at your children and grandchildren and feel wonderful. You know that old saying about stopping and smelling the roses? You might not be interested in roses, but you have to find the things that do interest you. People get very one-dimensional. I had a neighbor who used to sit in his garage and make these tiny wooden things, and that was his hobby. He did it for thirty years, but pretty soon, his friends died, and he died a very lonely man in a garage with lots of tiny wooden things—the weird thing is, when he died, he wasn't found for two weeks, until the smell leaked out. I don't believe that was enough for him. He didn't know how to make friends and go out and meet people. If he didn't leave the garage, he didn't stand a chance.

Sometimes you just have to take chances. I'm always the one sticking the phobic in the closet and saying, "Are you afraid with the closet doors open?" and they say, "Well, I'm not fully in the closet yet." To which I say, "How big of a closet does it have to be, and if it was a big closet, are you afraid of the closet or the stuff inside the closet?" I had one claustrophobic for whom a room this size would have been too small. He had grown up in a big house with really wealthy parents, and he would have deemed a room this size a closet. Even if he closed his eyes, he still felt the fear because he knew he was in a small place. I had to get him to the point where it didn't matter what size room he was in. I asked him, "Is it really that important? You still take up the same amount of space."

What Richard was talking about was learning to change the way in which you think so that you can think in ways that make you feel good. The basics of NLP, and of Richard's other creations, show you how to do this. If you are feeling bad, become aware of the images you are making at the time and the way you are talking to yourself and the feelings you are getting. Make the images smaller and move them much farther away. Make them black and white, fuzzy, dimmer, and white them out. Change the tone of your inner voice or the voice inside that made you feel bad. Make it squeak like Mickey Mouse or make it seductive and sexy. Take the feeling and notice in what direction it is moving in your body, and move it in the exact opposite direction. When you engage in these processes, you'll often find that you won't feel bad anymore. This works quickly and powerfully. Sometimes you'll find that your internal voice will continue to go after you and attempt to make you feel bad. When this happens, it is simply a case of repeating a special mantra over and over again. On my travels through India and Nepal, the various holy men I met taught me different mantras. However, I found that the most effective by far, and the one I have used with thousands of my clients to startling effect, is a mantra that Richard taught me years ago. He told me that whenever I'm talking to myself in a nasty way or trying to make myself feel bad about something to repeat this mantra: "SHUT THE FUCK UP. SHUT THE FUCK UP."

Many people I have worked with have said this mantra proved the most amazing mental exercise they had ever used, and they found themselves thinking more positively in a matter of days. Now, sometimes when you repeat it, you might start talking about it, saying things like, "This will never work. It's ridiculous." It's exactly at that time that it's imperative for you to keep repeating the mantra, "SHUT THE FUCK UP. SHUT THE FUCK UP."

In playing around with this idea, I came up with other mantras that I have found work brilliantly in different problematic situations. With those who worried a lot, I came up with the idea of repeating the mantra, "SO THE FUCK WHAT? SO THE FUCK WHAT?" said in a questioning, "who cares?" tone of voice. These "metamantras" as I call them are brilliant ways of cleaning up the inside of your head.

Once the inside of your head begins to become free from this negative mental pollution, it's important to replace these old habits of thinking with new, happier, and more productive habits of thinking. Richard often asks, "When you no longer have the problem, what are you going to do with all the spare time?" New habits of thinking might involve making positive images of yourself and your life, talking to yourself in more helpful ways and in a nicer tone of voice, creating positive, powerful, effective feelings that make you vibrate more happily and perform more successfully.

It might involve simply appreciating where you are. I remember standing in a rundown bus shelter in the outskirts of Pune in India. It was nearly evening, and the smell of rubbish and rotting food was extremely pungent as I waited for the bus. It was to be the beginning of a sixteen-hour journey to Bangalore, and as I stood there with all my bags, I began to notice the people around me. The shelter was located about ten feet from a local community who were housed in tents no bigger than most kitchens I had seen at home. I was stunned as I realized that each tent was the home for two parents and at least a couple of children.

As I observed the tents and their inhabitants going about their daily business, I noticed a small boy no more than four or five. He was playing away on the ground outside his tent. He was picking up pebbles and placing them down in different places. He seemed to be having a fascinating time. He was pretty thin and wore dirty white shorts with no sandals or shirt. As I watched him play around with the stones I could honestly say I never saw anyone enjoy themselves doing anything as much as he seemed to be. I watched him for about half an hour till I got on the bus as he still played with an amazing smile etched across his face. No PlayStation, no television, no computer— just stones and dirt. It really hit me just what human beings are capable of. Through nothing but his imagination and the most simple of surroundings, this boy built his own amazing entertainment world.

The people I talk with and learn from who are generally happy with life tend to think in very simple and effective ways. I remember talking with Dave from the soccer team about his attitude toward work and when he makes a mistake. He explained, "When I make a mistake, I make a mistake. I just tell myself to do my best the next time. You can only do your best. No point in feeling bad about anything. If someone ever annoys me or does something to piss me off, I just think, 'What an asshole,' and I forget about it. No point in dwelling on things that make you pissed off. Life is too short."

I couldn't have said it better myself. So I didn't.

CHAPTER 25

The Big, Bad World:
The "Poor Me" Syndrome

SHE WALKED INTO MY OFFICE with her head down. She was in her late thirties and was very well dressed. She gave me a weak, limp handshake as she slumped listlessly into the chair. I started.

OF: So how can I help you?

She sighed. I recalled the last conversation I had with her on the phone. She had called and asked for a consultation. I knew three things about her. First, she had been to dozens of therapists, from psychiatrists and psychologists to hypnotherapists, counselors, and even some NLP practitioners. None of them had helped her, or so she said. Second, I knew she was a "polarity responder." By that I mean she was the kind of person who, if you said something, would disagree with you. No matter what it was, she would disagree with you about it. Third, she was one of the best examples I had ever witnessed of what I call the "poor me" syndrome, when all a person does is whine on about how awful his or her life is. With this in mind, I had an idea of how I wanted to play it. I never expected it to go so far, but my instincts carried me along all the way.

She responded to me in a pitiful moan.

Martina: I don't know if anything can help me. My life is awful.

I agreed.

OF: I'm not surprised.

A little stunned, she continued.

Martina: It's just that everybody hates me.

Again, I agreed.

OF: Can't blame them.

She continued even more.

Martina: No. You see, I'm worthless. I'm unattractive. Nobody will ever want me.

Again, I agreed and added helpfully.

OF: Good point.

She looked up at me in disgust but continued. After about ten minutes of this, I could hear more and more anger and upset in her voice. I had agreed with everything negative she had been saying.

Eventually she looked up at me with anger in her eyes.

Martina: You see, I can't even stand up to anyone. You're abusing me like all the others. I'm just treated like a doormat.

To this day, I wonder how I had the guts to do it, but as she said this sentence I stood up, walked around the table, and wiped my shoe on her cream trousers. She looked up at me in absolute horror. After another few minutes she began to scream abuse at me. She called me every name under the sun as she explained that she was going to prove me wrong.

OF: I'm sorry, my dear.

I said as patronizingly as possible.

OF: I'm afraid I can't help you, and no one else can because you are unhelpable. There is nothing that will make any sort of a difference for you now. You're ugly, stupid, fat, annoying, boring, lazy, and disagreeable.

I had covered everything she had said about herself in the previous twenty-five minutes, more or less.

OF: What's more, you have tried everything, and nothing has worked; therefore, your problem will stay with you forever.

She cursed me and told me how she was going to turn her life around.

Martina: You are an absolute disgrace. I'm going to show you. How dare you? You have no right. I will prove you wrong. You're an absolute disgrace.

She was going to shut my mouth, and I was going to regret what I'd said. With that, not even thirty minutes into the session, she stormed out angrily. Initially, my heartbeat raced, and then I sat back and realized what had happened.

Three months later I received a letter. It was four and a half pages, handwritten, and began "Dear Mr. Fitzpatrick." I read along and began to laugh as this lady savagely insulted me over and over again as she explained how she had turned everything around. She explained how she had met someone new, had made new friends in the new job she had, was moving to a house in a nicer area, and how everything was working out wonderfully. She finished her long abusive letter with: "So I told you. Now my life has changed, and all of those awful things you said, well, you were wrong. Everything is great now. You aren't very accurate. How does it feel to be wrong? Things are working out for me. I am making things work out for me."

As I finished the letter I realized there was only one thing to do. I responded with a letter made up of one line: "Yeah, but for how long?" This meant that, to keep proving me wrong, she would have to keep making her life wonderful. About a month later, I received another letter in the mail, along with a check for the session with her. This time it was only a page long. This time it began "Dear Owen." She went on to explain how she eventually figured out what I had been doing. She apologized for all the angry words and explained how the thing that had made her really change was the anger and determination to prove me wrong. All she kept thinking, she said, was, "I'm going to show that bastard." That determination was what got her to take action.

The boy I saw in India playing so happily with the stones and the dirt didn't feel sorry for himself. Most people I met in India, living in severe poverty, didn't feel sorry for themselves. In contrast, I have often found that it is people from the Western world who come to see me who have their own horrible self-pity, poor-me stories. They explain for hours how awful their lives are. I find it extremely difficult to get them to focus on their futures as they will continuously bring the topic back to the past. Again, this is not always their fault. They learn to do it because there is a good feeling that comes from playing the poor victim. Self-pity can be quite comforting as you give yourself some love and connect with yourself more.

The "poor me" attitude is one of the traps that limits people from overcoming their problems. I asked Richard about this phenomenon and what the best way to work with people who feel sorry for themselves is.

OF: How do you help people who feel sorry for themselves?

RB: Well, to feel sorry for yourself, you first have to "feel sorry," which is a complicated set of sensations. Then you have to know when to do it, and then you have to make a set of pictures that blame your problems on other people. It's like that blues song, "dudawndandan . . . my wife left me, dudawndandan . . . she even took the dog, dudawndandan . . . then my car broke, dudawndandan . . . so I rolled down the stream on a log."

It's just like it goes on and on and on, and yet there are people with absolutely nothing sitting in the middle of India smiling away, because you don't need certain things to be happy. People think if this happens or that happens, everything will be perfect. People think that if all these things happen, then they'll be happy. I know multi-billionaires who are absolutely miserable, and they have absolutely everything. But they are still miserable, because being happy is not connected with what happens in the outside world.

It's something you have to know how to do, and you have to practice it, and if you don't practice being happy, it doesn't matter what happens. The problem is that these people have practiced being sorry for themselves, and they have become really good at it. So you have to get them to stop practicing that and to start practicing being happy, and until they do that, it doesn't matter what happens in this universe.

They could get a billion dollars and have the world's sexiest partner, and be put on the cover on every magazine, and they'd still be miserable because they don't know how to feel happy. People always think, "If I had a billion dollars I'd be happy." If you can't be happy with a dollar, how could you be happy with a billion dollars? It's not what makes you happy; it's what makes you obsessed.

I know people who lecture for a living who have to do lectures over and over and over again all over the world because they feed off other people's admiration, which is an addiction. They can't sit around like I can. I live in the middle of nowhere; there's nothing but cows, the country, and my wife.

This was such a huge secret. Overcoming self-pity is about learning how to be happy with little and practicing feeling good. It's about focusing on two areas: first, the actions you can take to improve things—instead of asking yourself "Why me?" you ask "What can I do?"—and second, appreciating what you do have and enjoying it. If you set high standards and rules for yourself to feel good, the feeling will be a lot harder to achieve.

People often get stuck in their past and get into the habit of dwelling on their past circumstances. I once worked with a guy who did this. I said to him, "Change your past." He said he didn't understand. I repeated again, "Change your past." Again, he looked at me confused. Finally I shouted at him, "Change your past," and he screamed back, "I can't." To this I said, "Well, what the hell are you living there for, then?" He got the point.

Being happy and generating powerful positive states essentially comes down to four things:

- It's about making more positive images, creating better feelings, and talking to yourself more usefully.
- It's about appreciating the wonderfulness of life and the present moment and enjoying every activity you engage in as fully as possible.
- It's about appreciating how lucky you are for all that exists in your life.
- It's about feeling really good about yourself and who you are.

If you can do this, you'll move from blaming everything to becoming much happier with your self.

Blame to Aim Exercise

1. Write down what you find is a problem in your life and immediately write out an action plan of how you will tackle it:

What *resources* will you need?

What *information* will you need?

What *contacts* will you need?

What must you *do* to sort it out?

Ask yourself the question: "Can I change the past?" If not, why live in it?

CHAPTER 26

Mirror, Mirror on the Wall: The Problems with a Distorted Self-Image

WHEN I WAS FEELING depressed all those years ago, I remember spending time with a friend of mine. When I would pick him up at his house, he would jokingly stop at the mirror as he was leaving, look in it, and exclaim to himself, "You look so sexy." This had an impact upon me. I began to realize that he was holding this belief for himself and that this belief made him feel happy. I wasn't happy with myself, but as I began to fight the depression, I began to repeat things like this as I looked in the mirror. I began to focus on being nicer to myself.

I notice that often people feel bad about themselves and who they think they are. The notions of self-concept, self-image, and self-esteem are things I come across every day as clients try to diagnose their own problems. I questioned Richard about labels like self-esteem.

OF: What are your thoughts on concepts such as self-esteem?

RB: Well, I think it's just a stupid concept because it's self-referential. Basically, people don't like feeling bad, but they create more ways to feel bad when there are enough ways to feel bad as there is. People say, "Well, I don't feel good about myself." I always ask them the question, "Is there any reason to?" And they always reply, "What?" So I say, "Is there any reason why you should feel good about yourself? You're sitting in my office moping and whining. That's nothing to feel good about. Is this what you do all day?" And they always say no, and I say, "Well then, when you do good things, do you feel good about yourself?" To me, when you are doing worthwhile things you should feel good, but they make up a bad feeling and start spinning it inside themselves till it becomes a habit.

It's just like there are people who have a habit of scratching their left ear, and once they start they can't stop, yet you can break these neurological connections because they are neural cortical pathways that are just looping. You can get people to stop looping these things if you have the right technology. That's definitely what Neuro-Linguistic Programming provides and also what Neuro-Hypnotic Repatterning is specifically designed for. It's designed to bathe people in different chemicals at the neurological level so that they can't get access to habitual negative patterns of behavior, and then you have to put something new in so that they do something worthwhile.

The trick is to create a void and fill it with something worthwhile. Most people don't have any idea how to be happy at all. I mean they really don't have enough practice. They haven't spent enough hours every day being happy and practicing it. They've spent most of their lives feeling either frightened, scared, less than others, blah blah blah, and what they really need to do is to get up in the morning and, for no reason, feel good, and get better at it so that when good things happen, they can feel ecstatic.

There are a lot of things we could learn from cultures other than our own: from "primitive cultures." There are a lot of primitive cultures that don't have the conveniences we have and don't have all these wonderful things. The one thing they place a higher value on, though, is how good they can feel, because they consider it a tribute to their deities. Whether it's a tribute to a deity or not, I think it's your birthright to feel good and that you don't need a bloody reason to do it; what you need is the skill to know how to run thoughts through your mind in a certain way so that you create good feelings.

As I listened to Richard, I realized that, often, people think about themselves in a negative state, and they feel bad about themselves. They assume that it means they have low self-esteem when, in reality, it is because their view of themselves is distorted by the bad chemistry of their negative state. When you can realize that your self-esteem means nothing about who you are or how "good" a person you are, you can discover how to focus on making yourself feel good instead of trying to find your "true" self.

Since the way you interpret the world is not how the world is, but just your representation of it at that moment of time based on the way you feel, the same is true of the way you think about yourself. When you can focus on feeling really good, you can then examine yourself from a better state, and that way you will find that you feel a lot better about yourself.

You can feel good by making images inside your mind that make you smile and making those images big and bright and vivid. You can talk to yourself in a nice tonality. You can do things that you enjoy and make other people smile more. There are so many ways of creating good feelings inside yourself and the more often you practice them, the more wonderful a difference to your self-esteem they'll make. Low self-esteem simply means people don't feel great about themselves at a particular time.

Similarly, when people feel insecure, it does not mean that they *are* insecure; it just means that they feel that way. Richard gave me a great way to help people who feel insecure.

OF: How do you help people who feel insecure?

RB: I use paradox. When the insecure person comes in and tells me, "I'm not sure about my future," I say, "Are you positive about this?" They usually say yes. The person who is racked with doubts is absolutely sure about that, and when you point that out to people they have to laugh. It's the importance of humor.

Then, they have to move on and ask new questions, because when you ask, "What can go wrong?" you'll find out. It's the same when you ask, "What if I'm not right about this?" You will always notice the tonality the question is asked in influences the feeling it produces. It's the tonality of your own internal voices and the pictures that you make with good tonality and good feelings lined up inside of you that is important. Anyone can move in good directions, and to me, that's a good start.

I liked Richard's take on highlighting the paradox in people's problems. The idea is to show people that what they think they lack in one area of life, they are actually demonstrating in a different area. For example, people who believe they need to be motivated are already motivated—to sit at home and do nothing. People who hesitate don't think about hesitating—they do it immediately.

Remember, you are not who you think or feel you are—you are everything you can become. You are you at your best. Sometimes you become fuller and show your best, and sometimes you don't. But you are still it, and it is still you. You must understand this because it means that, instead of trying to compare yourself to others, you can realize that it's only about comparing yourself to yourself and asking the question, "How much better am I today than I was yesterday?"

The reality is that when we begin to ask this question, life gets so much better. We can only feel good or bad about ourselves compared to something—either others or a perfect image of ourselves. If we can instead accept our imperfections and accept our uniqueness, we can compare ourselves to how much we are improving, and that will enable us to make continuous progress in our lives as we reach our potential.

Perhaps the most serious problems that are associated with the way we think about ourselves are the eating disorders: anorexia and bulimia. As I have had good success with clients with these disorders from using the skills I learned from Richard, I knew that Richard would have some excellent advice on them.

OF: What suggestions do you have for people dealing with eating disorders?

RB: I'm very successful when dealing with people with eating disorders. I've never had a problem with them. I worked with somebody in London who oscillated between anorexia and bulimia. She was in her midthirties. She was at one of the personal change workshops, and I'd say it took me twenty minutes. But I focused on the simple things. What makes an eating disorder?

It doesn't have to be an eating disorder; it can be any disorder. It's an ultracompulsive behavior, and what makes something compulsive is that it doesn't have an "or" gate. Perfect logic: if there was a point when there was "or"—take it or leave it— it wouldn't be a compulsion. So what I do is take the driving compulsion that a person has and make it so that the feeling spins in the body in the opposite direction, and when it spins, since it's moving differently and doing the exact opposite of how it normally does it, it creates a very altered state.

I also use a little hypnosis to help this along, and when a client is in that altered state, I simultaneously install the same sensations they have with anything they feel they can "take or leave" so that the minute it kicks in, whenever they see food, their response is, "It doesn't matter. I can take it or leave it." I do this because, if they have to look at drugs and say, "I won't take drugs. I won't take drugs. I won't take drugs," instead of "I could take them or leave them," then it's harder. They need to make good choices, because that's the trick.

You've got to get people to make good choices and only make choices that are good, because then they go into the "either/or" gates—"I can take it or leave it" —where the good choice is to leave it, and they do. That's real freedom. It's been quite a bit of time, six months now, and that client hasn't had any problem, and most of the others don't either. I mean, it's not a good choice to be vomiting out all your food. It's not the way your metabolism is supposed to work.

It's not healthy, and these people are going to become sick, but most of them feel bad all the time because they're chemically imbalanced. I'm sure doctors can give you plenty more reasons about why bulimia is bad for you.

I had noticed also when working with people with eating disorders that there were two main problems. First, the compulsive behavior and, second, the way they were so distorted in the way they saw themselves in the mirror. As Richard had already discussed the compulsive side of these disorders, I asked him about the distortion side of things.

OF: Why do these people often see themselves in distorted ways?

RB: Primarily because they are in such profound altered states based on starvation. I mean, while they're in altered states they may as well take bizarre drugs. Most of them do take a lot of drugs so that they don't get hungry. They look in the mirror, and they still look fat, but that's because they practice doing that. Even if they were never fat, that doesn't matter. They've rehearsed this so that they have this feeling that, no matter what they look like, they'll feel the same, and you can take your feelings and alter your visual perception. It is not a hard thing to do, especially when you are really hungry.

There are things that we are not compelled to do and things that we are compelled to do. When you stop and notice what sort of images, self-talk, sounds, and feelings make you feel compelled to do something and what sort of images, self-talk, sounds, and feelings are there when you can "take it or leave it," you can begin to play around with them and learn how you can be compelled to do more useful things and how you can "take or leave" nonuseful behaviors.

Furthermore, it's important to realize again the importance of chemistry and altered states and to practice getting into positive powerful altered states that make you feel significantly different when you think about yourself. When you can focus on getting yourself into positive states, you'll find it much easier to get effective results.

Looking in the mirror is not just about affirmations. If you don't look good, your brain will know that you are lying to yourself. It's about making yourself feel as good about yourself as you can. Being nice to yourself means saying nice things in nice ways and making sure that you take whatever action is appropriate to help you feel better about yourself.

Self-Image Sweetener Exercise

What kind of person do you want to be?

What kind of person do you think you are?

What do you need to do to develop the qualities of the person you want to be?

What is the most useful way of thinking about yourself now to become more of who you want to be?

How do you talk about yourself to yourself?

How would your best friend talk to you?

Start treating yourself more like your best friend would treat you.

CHAPTER 27

Destroying the Problem Machine

WE WERE OUT DRIVING on a road he hadn't been on in years. My client couldn't believe it. He looked for the panic attacks, but they were nowhere to be found. I knew the secret about panic attacks. Try to get over them and they can become worse. Try to make them worse and you'll feel much better. So I encouraged him to make the panic a lot worse. The more he tried, the more he couldn't. The panic would not work anymore.

Since I began working in the field of NLP, I have met some people who felt really bad because they were still feeling bad even though they shouldn't because they knew NLP. This whole notion of feeling bad about feeling bad causes many people massive problems. People who suffer from problems such as panic, actually panic at the thought of panicking. It is the thought of the problem that feeds the problem. In other words, the biggest problem is not the original problem; it is the problem you have with the problem.

The key is to get people to the point where they don't mind having the problem. Often I use humor. I get clients who stutter to laugh at themselves stuttering. Anything and everything I can do to help people care less about their problems, I do. I talked to Richard about this phenomenon.

OF: What I've learned, Richard, is that often it is not people's problems that are the problem; it is their problem about the problems.

I worked with a client recently who had done a couple of courses in NLP and was depressed because he was depressed, and yet he had the NLP skills to get himself out. How do you help people like this?

RB: That's just meta-stupidity. I mean, to begin with, he was lying. He didn't have the skills, because he wasn't using them. That would be my definition. They have to break it down to the truth. They're saying, "I have all these skills, but I can't use them on myself." Well then, they don't really have the skills. I mean, I've developed most of the things in the field of NLP to help myself to do something first and foremost.

Every once in a while, a client comes along, and I don't know what to do to help. Then I may go out and find something for him or her, but you know, there aren't any techniques that I use on other people that I don't use on myself. So that's kind of a goofy statement. That's like saying, "I have a shovel, but I can't dig a hole." To which I would say, "Yeah, you have a shovel, and you're not digging a hole, and what stops you digging the hole? Stuff that's inside your head. You don't motivate yourself to want to do this and to get it done."

This is the difference between voluntary acts and self-indulgence, and I don't put up with self-indulgence. I don't put up with it in myself, and I don't put up with it in my clients. I hear a lot of the same kind of crap when people come in the door. They've been in therapy for twelve years, and they whine and moan, but I don't listen to it. I just tell them to shut up, and I go back to the most important thing, which is always, "What do you want? What are you doing?" If you stop what you are doing and start doing something that will work, you'll get there. Period. And all the rest of it and all the reasons and all the excuses are not going to buy anybody anything.

It used to be believed that if you understood your problem, it would change. We've discovered pretty thoroughly that that's just nonsense. Lots of people understand themselves till they are blue in the face, but they're no better off. What you really need to do is understand what you're not doing, and if you're feeling lethargic, and you're not motivated, then whatever you're doing in your brain is producing that chemical reaction in your body. So the first thing you need to do is the opposite. You need to spin your feelings in the opposite direction. You need to make the opposite kind of pictures, in which case you will feel different. If you think differently and you talk to yourself differently, you're going to feel different.

The marvelous thing about human beings is they're so malleable. In thirty-five years, every person they've sent me who was supposed to be impossible has been easy, because I've had that basic principle. I just look for what they're not doing, and whatever it is that they're doing, I get them to stop doing and start doing something that will work. We're not dealing with a humungous number of variables. We're dealing with the fact that people make pictures, and they talk to themselves. The pictures they make are in a certain place, at a certain distance, and the voice is moving in a certain direction; it has a certain tonality and a certain speed.

Insomniacs can't sleep because they talk to themselves. They say, "I'll never go to sleep, blah blah blah blah blah." You get them to talk more slowly and lower and put in some yawns, and the next thing you know they're sound asleep. It's good to add to that some "hypnotic" skills because the other thing that makes human beings go into repetitive behaviors is that they go into the same state of consciousness. The same class of whining produces the same class of altered state—the "I can't do it," bad-feelings state. Whereas, when you put people into profoundly different altered states, whether they're states of excitement or states of deep relaxation, the fact that it's a different state enables you to install different behaviors.

Richard in a different world.

It is much more useful to realize that, if you are not using a skill, you don't have it. You only have skills when you use them because, if you are not using them, they are not there. Years ago, when I began to allow myself to be okay with feeling bad and focused on applying the skills I had to feel better, I found myself getting out of the problem states I was in.

Sometimes, I felt that these skills were just sorting things out at the surface level, and I needed to deal with the problems more deeply. So I began to write out everything I could about a problem and what I needed to do. Once I engaged in this exercise I found myself feeling comfortable with being able to use all the skills and mantras because I had dealt with it as fully as possible.

Sometimes, clients or training participants will try a particular exercise and begin to panic when they can't do it. They begin to run the age-old questions inside their heads, "What if I get this wrong? What if I can't do this in the real world?" Those questions have positive intentions in that they are attempting to prevent disappointment in case the techniques don't work. What most people don't realize is that these techniques do work for everyone, and with practice, anyone can do them successfully. It's crucial for them to understand that they must let go of the need for them to work and instead enjoy feeling good for no reason. That way, the skill will come more easily.

CHAPTER 28

Being Perfect Ain't Okay

I HAVE FOUND THAT, as a society, we have become too spoiled by choice and too focused on perfection, and this gets in our way of being happy. As the modern world brings with it an improved ability to control things, many people get caught up trying to control everything and comparing themselves to a perfect image of themselves. This was the next topic I introduced for Richard's input.

OF: How do you deal with people who compare themselves to perfect images of themselves?

RB: Well, to begin with, I would disagree with the idea that those are perfect images. Their perfect images have no slack. A perfect image would cut you enough slack, and the perfect image would be an image of somebody who doesn't make images they have to live up to. You don't have to live up to an image to be happy; you can just do it anyway.

With people who make a perfect image of themselves, I would change the picture. It's as simple as that. If they won't change the picture, I smack them once or twice, and I tell them to change the picture. Typically they do—or I make it worse. I've had people come in who have told me they were going to kill themselves because they didn't get this job, or they didn't get that girl, or their life didn't fit their plan. I'd say, "You don't have to do that. I'll do it for you, and I'll do it right now." I pull out a huge knife and start across the room, and they always shout, "Wait," and I say, "Well, what am I waiting for?" Then they say, "Well, there must be something else." I reply, "Well, start visualizing it right now. Don't waste my time." But most of them don't realize there's lots of people who do things by "matching."

You can always tell people who do things by matching in seminars because they always raise their hands and ask if it is the same as some guy's concept of self. And whenever they say, "Is this the same?" The answer is no. They think sameness is good, and I think sameness is boring, and you have to teach them that if they actually got exactly what they say they want, it wouldn't work. When people are not moving toward a visual image they are trying to match, they should get rid of the image rather than going into self-criticism, low self-esteem, and years of therapy.

I found that it was often the disappointment that was experienced by clients that led to perfectionism affecting them so negatively. I had heard an expert talking about the notion of not setting up people with false hope in case they were disappointed by an unsatisfactory result. In considering this, however, I knew it was of paramount importance that people kept hope alive, yet at the same time, not set themselves up for disappointment. I asked about this.

OF: What are your thoughts on the notions of hope, false hope, and disappointment?

RB: I have another name for false hope—stupidity. False hope is just stupidity. It's "I know that some day she'll take me back." Even if she took you back, she'd go leave you again, so it doesn't really matter. That's just stupidity; that's not false hope. That's just not accepting what is and turning around and realizing that even if you go out with another girl, you're probably going to mess it up. You have to do something with yourself so that you can actually have a relationship.

There are some people who have very unrealistic expectations and therefore they're disappointed. To me, when you talk about false hope, I think a lot of people plan to be disappointed. They don't really look at the criteria of what would make them happy in the first place. Even if they got what they wanted, they'd still be unhappy in essence.

They look at the unattainable girl and wish they could go out with her, even when they don't even know what she is like. She could be a total bitch, but she looks good from thirty yards, so they imagine she's the girl of their dreams. Then, when they do finally try to go over and meet her, it turns out she is happily married to someone else, and then they're disappointed. They do this instead of going and meeting her and finding out who she is and then saying, "Well, she's not available," before finding someone who is and who would actually make them happy.

Real hope is when you realize anything is possible, but as soon as you reduce the variables down—"It has to be this girl," "It has to be this job," "It has to be this amount of money by Christmas"—you set yourself up for failure. Failure is determined when you put a rule about what the end is or what the location has to be. Whenever you get stuck, you should expand your horizons.

If you don't get that job, it really could mean that there's a much better job out there for you, and if you start expanding the range of what you could do, you could find something you enjoy doing more and make more money from and work fewer hours. But most people think that "Oooh, I didn't get this thing, therefore I'm gonna feel bad, so I'm always gonna feel bad, and then anything I want is gonna make me feel bad." They descend into a cycle. But it's really more about their internal dialogue and the pictures they make that cause them to feel bad than it is about their potential on the planet.

If you really look out there, there are tremendously stupid, inept human beings who are very wealthy and very happy and are having great relationships, so there's no excuse for people who have half a brain. The problem is that they're not using the half a brain they have. If they would just learn to get their internal dialogue aimed in the same way, with the right tone of voice, put those pictures up, and start making good decisions and really looking around and opening up the options, believe me, the sky is the limit.

Perfectionism all relates to obsessive-compulsive visualizing. They make a picture, and if their experience doesn't match that picture, they feel bad, when the easiest thing in the world to do is to change the picture.

I once worked with a lady in India who always wanted things to be perfect. What she began to realize as I talked to her was that her ideal of a perfect day would actually turn out to be a letdown because there was no element of surprise in there. The paradox of perfection is that something has to be flexible and able to improve to be perfect, and if it can improve, then it's not perfect. When you attempt to have everything exactly as you want it, you set yourself up for disappointment if you don't have something else put in place.

What you need to put in place is the idea of what you want and add the flexibility of what you will do if it isn't exactly like you want it. You need to have the outcome of how you want things to be and the freedom to be able to be happy regardless of how things work out in the real world. You need to accept the things you cannot change and be able to change the things you can and, as the proverb says, the wisdom to know the difference.

When you know ahead of time that things will not always work out exactly as you want them to, you can enjoy the parts of the experience that do work out and feel delighted about that. You can also appreciate the things that didn't work out and be happy in the knowledge that it is exactly what makes life so interesting.

When I worked with this woman, I was able to make her aware of the pictures she was making inside her head. She made images of how things "should" be, and I made her realize that she could be aware of those pictures and accept that reality would be different in some ways. I had her begin to make images of different scenarios working out and got her comparing them with the worst-case scenarios. When she got to see these new images in a new context, she began to appreciate the good parts of experiences instead of always focusing on what was wrong. In essence, she began to enjoy the uncertainty of life.

Probably what really struck me from what Richard had said was, again, a very simple point.

> If you really look out there, there are tremendously stupid, inept human beings who are very wealthy and very happy and are having great relationships, so there's no excuse for people who have half a brain. The problem is that they're not using the half a brain that they have.

This made a strong impact on me. It was a fantastic point. I began to realize that the secret to all this freedom we were talking about was not about how clever we are or how skillful; it was truly about our attitude, ways of thinking, and taking certain actions that would lead to certain effects and consequences. Success is not the possession of the smart or capable; it is the product of thinking in certain ways and acting in certain ways.

CHAPTER 29

Declaring War
on Mental Terrorism

*"Most people plan by disaster. They think of what
can go wrong and then they master it."*

—Richard Bandler

WE HAD SEPTEMBER 11. It was a day that shook the world. Thousands of people died in one of the most significant terrorist attacks of all time. All over the world, tragedies occur on bigger and smaller scales every day. Terrorism brings terror, and people die. Inside our own heads, we engage in a different world of terrorism that brings its own casualties: ourselves. Every day we set off negative feelings that act like bombs, causing injuries to our self-image and mood. Every day, we develop beliefs that trap us under the rubble of stress and anxiety. Every day, we are terrorized into feeling fear more and more.

The war on terrorism is an effort by certain countries to end terrorism in the world. Some would argue that the war itself is terrorism. Regardless, I want to talk about declaring a different kind of war: the war against mental terrorism. It is a war that aims to put an end to the negativity of your mind and the bad feelings that you feel. It is a war that aims to end the tyrannical reign of the nonuseful mind and deliver you into the freedom of the promised mind. People die in mental terrorism, too. Fear, stress, and anxiety destroy your health and peace of mind. Depression can kill you.

The battles that must be won in this war are the battles against fear, against sadness, and against stress. This requires you to hold particular attitudes toward these enemies. The first attitude is to realize that these were not always enemies. There are evolutionary reasons behind all three factors. Fear protected us from harm. Depression kept us close to home when we needed to be. Stress kept us aware of the fact that we needed to take action to keep ourselves safe. The second attitude is to remember, once again, the power of humor in dealing with these problems. When we can laugh at something, it no longer scares us, it no longer depresses us, and it no longer stresses us. The final attitude to keep in mind is that there are many different ways of thinking about fear, sadness, and stress, and we can learn to change the way we think about them.

These three battles are not separate from the rest of this section. Many people think stress, depression, and fear are far too big to be "sorted out" through a few exercises. What you will find, however, is that the exercises at the end of the following segments, if they are completed in full, will come dangerously close to completely ridding you of these problems. Please complete them with an open mind, and you will find the difference in the way you feel about yourself, your life, your problems, and your fears will be huge.

When people come in and say they "have" depression, fear, or stress, we ask them to "show it" to us. This gets them to realize that it is a *process* and not a *thing*. Once this is known, people can change the process. The exercises at the end of the following segments enable you to make powerful changes to this process and transform the way you experience your life.

Battling Fear

I looked out at the crowd. Outside, it must have been ninety degrees. It was one of the highlights of my life. It was July 5, 2003, and the workshop in Bangalore, India, was about to start. I began.

Minutes later, I asked for a demonstration subject. Richard had always taught me the best way to win an audience over was through a demon-stration. I wanted someone who had a fear of public speaking. Reluctantly, a few hands went up. I picked out somebody, and he came up. He was shaking like a leaf. I turned him with his back to the audience and taught him how to change the way he felt.

One of the greatest problems we have in this world is fear. Battling against fear requires that you learn how to change the way you experience feelings in your body. When I spoke with Richard in the conference room in Edinburgh about fear, he explained more about how to help people over-come it.

> OF: How do you help people overcome fear?
>
> RB: I start out neurologically. I take the sensations, find out where they start, how they move through the body, pull them out of the body, turn them upside down, stick them in, and spin them backward—throw in a little circus music, just so they know it's silly. As odd as it sounds, I've cured thousands of people by doing nothing else.

I had found Richard's very simple approach to be highly effective in eliminating fear. This was the technique I used with my demonstration subject. I helped him imagine he was turning the feeling around in his body and running it in the reverse direction. As he did this, he felt so much more relaxed and was able to speak. I sent him back to his seat expecting it would be the final time I saw him.

Helping people with fears and phobias has never been much of a prob-lem for me. It was always simple to get people to imagine "spinning" or "running" their experiences and feelings backward. To "run an experience backwards" means that you get a person to play a movie in their mind of something they have experienced and imagine it running backwards. This often changes the feelings about the experience. You can also notice how their feelings move through their body. Where they start, move to and fin-ish up. Then by spinning those feelings in the same direction it tends to make them stronger and by spinning them in the opposite direction it tends to change them.

Panic attacks, on the other hand, are different. Although I had an effective way of working with panic, I was curious about Richard's approach to dealing with this different kind of fear, which originated from anxiety.

OF: So what about panic attacks, then?

RB: Panic attacks are a little different. You can help people with the fast phobia cure, but panic attacks have a tendency to come back, so it requires a bit more of an altered state. You have to get people who have panic attacks into a different state of consciousness, where they're really relaxed. I use hypnosis for that and create a very powerful state of relaxation, and then, when they start their panic, I trigger the relaxation so that panic causes relaxation. It's paradoxical, but it does work, and I've had tremendous success over and over again with it.

Richard also suggested that it was important to be aware that fears often have a purpose and to ensure that purpose is well cared for.

RB: I don't like the notion of fearlessness. I think some things are worth being afraid of. I think men should be aware of sleeping with their next-door neighbor's wife. I think they should be terrified of it. I think that men should be terrified of losing intimacy with their wives and their children. These are things worth being afraid of. I think that you should be afraid of big snakes when you don't know about snakes.

There are people in India who grow up sleeping with cobras. They know everything about cobras. They don't have to be afraid of them, but if you stick me in a room full of snakes, I'm going to be terrified and get the hell out of there because I don't know anything about snakes. I grew up in the city, and the only types of snakes we had are called lawyers. They're the most time consuming. They'll kill you with tediousness.

So in getting rid of fear and panic, it's important to respect the intention behind them and ensure that those intentions are being looked after through a different means. Fear was an important mechanism for survival. It's simply useful sometimes, and other times it's not. People fear embarrassment, rejection, and failure. They fear talking to people. All of these fears are based in misguided, fuzzy logic. There is no reason to be fearful about approaching people to ask them out or speaking in front of a group of people. It's just that we learn to associate fear with these experiences, and we practice experiencing it in the same situations over and over again.

Indian smiles—my audience and me in Bangalore, India.

When you can run your feelings backward and create altered states in yourself, you'll discover how you can begin to feel confident and curious where once you felt fear. It's not about being fearless or even courageous. It's about learning to change your associations to certain things.

Later that day, when I was finishing the seminar, I saw a figure walking down the aisle toward the stage. My heart raced as I continued to talk, unsure of what was happening. The man made his way onto the stage and moved toward me. It was my demonstration subject from earlier that morning. He asked for the microphone. Taken by surprise, and not knowing what else to do, I gave it to him. He began to thank me profusely and explain to the audience that for so many years he had this phobia of public speaking and now it was gone and he could do anything. I smiled. What a testimonial. "Only in India," I thought to myself.

Beating Fear Exercises

1. Spinning Fear Backward

    Think of an undesirable feeling you have had.

    Where did you notice the feeling first? Where did it move to next? Where did it go then? Notice which direction it moved or "spun" in your body.

    Bring the feeling on, and as it moves, imagine taking it outside and turning it around, reversing it so that it moves in the opposite direction in your body.

    Keep spinning the feeling in the opposite direction quickly and notice how the feeling completely changes and is no longer negative.

2. Panic Destroyer

    When you are panicking, attempt to panic more. Try to panic as much as you can. The secret is that when you try to do it, you will find it extremely difficult.

3. Reframing Fear

    Find out what the intention is behind the fear. It is usually an effort to protect yourself, but from what? Once you know this, find out how you can fulfill that intention without the fear.

4. Fast Phobia Cure

    Imagine yourself in a cinema behind a projector booth watching yourself sitting in the cinema watching yourself on the screen. Imagine you are seeing yourself watching a movie of a time during which you were fearful.

    Imagine the movie running right through from before the experience till after you had survived the experience.

Imagine stepping into the screen at the end of the movie, and run the entire movie backward. See the sights backwards, hear the sounds backwards, feel the feelings backwards.

Run it backwards really quickly while you are in it. Do this a number of times.

You will find it difficult to feel the fear the same way.

Battling Sadness

Many people ask me about that suicide call that came at 3:30 PM on the Tuesday afternoon. Did I try the same tactic I used with the lady who engaged in self-pity? The answer is no, of course not. Every client is different. As he cried on the other end of the phone, I was not in control of much. He could have hung up at any stage. I didn't even know his name at that point. He eventually told me it was Martin. His number was unidentified. I had to keep Martin on the phone and get him focused.

I couldn't afford to try and provoke him into anger. I had to get him into a state of hope and belief in me. Once I did that, I could get him into the clinic for a session. As I talked to him, he pitifully sobbed, and I found it hard to make out what he was saying.

Martin: It's so painful, so, so painful. The pills don't help. The doctors don't help. Nobody understands me. I need out. I need out now. I'm going to take them. They said you could help, can you? Well, can you?

I had no time to even find out who "they" were. I gave him the hope he needed.

OF: Yes, I can, and I will. Listen to me. You can change things around. You can turn your life around. I swear to you. You can. It is possible. I promise you. I promise. I will help you. I can help you do it.

Every fiber of my soul attempted to convey an absolute sense of certainty because I was sure, absolutely sure, that I could help him change his life.

Martin: But I can't see how. Everything is so messed up.

OF: I know everything seems really messed up right now, Martin, but I promise you we can turn things around. I know what you're feeling like. You're feeling absolute agony, like there is no way out. Nobody has a clue what you are going through, Martin, and nobody can understand you. I can't pretend to understand what you are going through, but I know how I felt. I was suicidal, too. I almost killed myself, like you, but I managed to find a different way out. Let me show you the way, Martin.

I asked him how he would feel if he overcame this and turned it all around. I asked him what his life would be like if he sorted out the mess and a year from now he was happy and moving forward. I described it as vividly as possible. After some effort, he responded.

Martin: You really think that is possible, Owen?

OF: I know it is. It's so possible. You just need to be determined. We're going to do this together, Martin, and I need you to do what I ask.

I worked with Martin, and he was soon living happily with his life back together again. I still hear from him today.

In battling sadness, I began to think about what Richard had said about people feeling sorry for themselves and those searching for perfection. There was much wisdom and insight in applying these ideas to those suffering from depression. I had also had excellent results in the work I had done with people who came to me looking to feel happier and better about life.

I think that the best place to bring depression to is to a state of determination. If you try to make people who are depressed feel happy, often it will be a hugely challenging thing to do, and they can always go back toward being depressed. On the other hand, when you help people who are depressed become determined, they are in a position in which they can deal with any and all challenges that may come their way. Like the woman who was determined to prove me wrong, the determination provides people with an energy that they badly need. Many people who are depressed have a lack of energy and an apathetic sense of helplessness and hopelessness. If they can get energized, they can use that to begin to make some changes in their lives.

Another factor that is really important is to keep busy and have lots of things to do. There are so many great self-help books out there. Reading them and using them will make a difference. Exercising a lot ensures that your mind is distracted from the negative thoughts and that positive chemicals are being created inside the mind, which helps people feel better about life. Physiology is important because how people sit, stand, and move will make it easier or more difficult for them to feel depressed. (It's easy to feel sad when your shoulders are slumped, your posture is crouched, and you are frowning.)

You can also begin to see the distortions of your thinking. Depressed people are no more realistic than optimists. As we've made clear, we all have a different way of thinking about the world. When we feel down, we see the world in a negative way, and we believe our perception of the world is accurate and true. In the work I did with Martin, I taught him to use his brain to stop making negative pictures and to stop talking to himself negatively. It involved getting him to become aware of his limiting beliefs and how they were distorted.

I would ask him how he knew he was no good. I would ask him how he knew he was stupid and unattractive. I would ask him for evidence, and I would ask how that evidence proved anything at all. I would get him to be specific about everything and rigorously made him justify every negative thought he had. He soon became aware that what he had thought was as far from reality as you could get.

I beat my own depression through determination, by challenging my own negative thoughts, keeping busy, and by using my brain better. Anyone can do that.

Beating Sadness Exercises

1. Use meta-mantras.

Regularly use the mantra, "SHUT THE FUCK UP," when you are giving yourself a hard time.

2. Change the tone of your inner voice.

Change the tone of your inner voice to make it ridiculous so that instead of it sounding depressing, it sounds like Mickey Mouse; or make it a deep, seductive tone.

3. Use the laughter filter.

Use the laughter filter to frame every negative thought in a highly humorous way.

4. Change your internal pictures.

Pay attention to what images you make when you are sad and make them smaller, move them far away, and make them fuzzy and dim. Replace them with happier images and make the new images big, bright, colorful, and vivid.

5. Adjust your physiology.

Pay attention to your physiology. Change it until it represents how it is positioned when you are happy and feeling good. Bring your shoulders back, lift your head up, breathe deeply, and smile brightly. Do this whenever you wish to change your state.

6. Challenge your thinking.

Write out a couple of paragraphs of your internal speech when you are depressing yourself. Challenge each statement with the following questions:

How do you know that is true?

Who says that? Isn't it an opinion not a fact?

How can you conclude that "A" causes "B"?

How can you say that "A" is the same as "B"?

Is that true in every case?

What do you mean specifically by that?

Be more specific.

Answer all these questions and rewrite your paragraph accordingly. You will find that there are many loose arguments in your internal talk.

7. Get plenty of exercise.

Exercise stimulates the release of endorphins, which make us feel good. Fresh air is also good because it puts the body in a higher energy state, which is harder to be depressed in.

Battling Stress

Stress is something that has become a paramount problem in the modern world. When I visited India, I was surprised to discover that it was equally problematic in a country famous for knowing the secrets to meditation. I recall a question from one of the participants regarding road rage and my answer, which helped him gain a different perspective on it.

Seminar participant: How can you help people with road rage?

I looked up. I could understand the question, but I couldn't see who it came from. Indian names are much different from the ones I am used to. In my first few days there, I nicknamed three of the friends who took care of me Jan, Van, and Dan. I remembered Sajani, the name of the woman who looked after me, primarily because it was only three syllables. I could only handle three syllables. Eventually, I saw who was asking the question. I smiled. I couldn't pronounce his name either.

OF: First of all, you guys don't have road rage over here. You know how I know? Because I've been in Pune. You only get road rage if you get caught in traffic. In Pune, they don't stop—at all. It's crazy. Cars beeping all over the place with no apparent logic or system at all. Unbelievable. I got into one of those auto-rickshaws, and let me tell you right now: does the film *Star Wars* mean anything to you? We were flying along through the traffic, and I don't know how the hell we didn't crash. It was mad. And the few times I saw traffic lights, it was like they weren't even there, or at least green meant go, yellow meant go faster, and red meant go really fast but beep and hope for the best.

I was trying to get out to Osho's commune. I was told I should prepare myself spiritually for it. Let me tell you something, I was really prepared. I must have said more prayers than the Pope on Sunday before I arrived at the commune, and this was just as I was getting the lift in the rickshaw. "Oh, God, please help me get there safely."

The one time I did actually see cars and rickshaws stop, though, was when a cow was in the middle of the street. Now that was cool. I loved that—cows just sauntering around through the streets. And it's almost like they know it. They fear no car. It's like they're thinking, "Come on. What's wrong? You chicken? Cluck. Cluck." They walk out, and every vehicle in sight comes to a screeching halt, and the cows, cool as they like, breeze slowly across the road.

And I got an idea. What the city of Pune needs to do is use the cows as traffic lights. They can get some bloke standing there with his own cow, and every time the light turns red, he can take the cow onto the road. What do you think?

I smiled at them. They were laughing their heads off.

OF: So let me talk to you about road rage. Before we go any further on that, are there any people who want me to also tackle a problem similar to this?

From the audience another name I couldn't pronounce shouted eagerly.

Second seminar participant: What about wife rage?

The audience laughed. I responded immediately.

OF: What do I look like to you? Not even God knows the solution to that. It's like trying to find the solution to why guys are so stupid at trying to help their wives with their problems. They don't know the secret is to listen and not help.

From road rage to spousal rage, we can give ourselves stressful feelings. Often these feelings can overwhelm us and sometimes lead to anger or anxiety. What's important is that we learn how to find the laughter in a situation and develop attitudes that enable us to relax easily. What I was doing during the training in India was getting them to think about stressful situations in traffic in a humorous way so that the next time they were caught in that situation they would be able to smile.

In the battle against stress, I began to ask Richard about the secret to helping people to stop worrying.

OF: How do you deal with worriers?

RB: I give them more to worry about first. I tell them worrying leads to death and that gives them something good to worry about. Basically, the worry machine is just something where they start to generate infinite possibilities of bad things that could happen, and if you take the same machine, they could generate infinite possibilities of things they should do now, not in a year, and if you build in them a little wanton anticipation, you can get them going in the right direction.

I found in working with clients who worried that, often, it all came down to them asking the same question over and over again: "What if?" In understanding this, I suggested that people begin to keep a "worry book" with them during the day. This book is where they write down their worries. Each time they wrote down a worry, they had to ask themselves, "Is there anything I can do about this problem now?" If there was, they were to take the appropriate action, and if there wasn't, they just kept it in the book. Eventually, at a prearranged time in the evening, they gave themselves ten minutes of "worry time," when they go through the worries they wrote down and worry for those ten minutes. They would then finish with asking the question, "What can I do about it now?" The clients who have used this system have reported back remarkable results. I continued on this path with my next question to Richard.

OF: So what about people working with stress?

He replied with a coy smile.

RB: I recommend people don't work with stress. You'll do a much better job without it.

I rephrased my question, knowing too well my inarticulate wording would not get a response. Richard always listens literally to what people say. I once asked him which personalities, living or dead, he would most like to have dinner with. He replied, "I'm sorry, but the idea of having dinner with dead people is repulsive to me!"

"Literal listening" was the reason he was able to understand more about what was going on inside people's heads. People usually tell you everything you need to know in their body language and in the words they use. With this in mind, I clarified my question.

OF: How do you help people overcome stress?
RB: The problem is that they're usually real good at it, and I will

say, "I can tell you that you're already stressing about that, madam. You're really good at that, madam. God, I can't get a headache that quickly. Look at what you're doing, madam. Look at the lines on your face. Jesus, you know you could win a fecking award for that!"

It's because until they learn to laugh, they're not going to do anything other than stress, so I would say that you can put them in a state of absolute paradox so that they can learn to laugh at themselves and at the very things that cause them stress.

I always get them into the state where they can't stop laughing and anchor it, and every time they start to talk about serious shit, I fire off the anchor, and so they just laugh. Then I tell them, "Now go ahead try to be serious," and they start laughing. I put them in a loop, and that loop itself burns up the stress. I don't think the trick is to teach people to get out of stress, but to avoid it in the beginning so that they don't go into it; they just go do what needs to be done and do it without all the thinking.

There is too much thinking going on all the time. People are thinking of all the things that could make them feel bad. If you don't have a list of all the things that make you feel bad, then you won't get what you don't want. You know, if the list of things to make you feel good is you can be relaxed, you can be happy, you can be busy, as opposed to you can be stressed, you can be terrified, you can be this or that, then you are setting yourself up to feel good.

OF: So what suggestions do you have for people to relax more?

RB: I think meditation is good. I think trance is good and creating good states. The more time you spend feeling good, the more you won't want to give it up, and the more you realize that it's more of a natural inclination for humans to be relaxed. The problem is that we live in these rat races where we can't get taxis, and we have to keep time schedules, and we get idiots at the airport. It's tough to stay relaxed when you're surrounded by a bunch of bogus things that are environmentally inconvenient. If you just give yourself a little extra time, you don't have to worry as much.

You see, many stress management courses promote the ideas of basic visualization and relaxation rituals. Unfortunately, most people never find the time to engage in these activities. They walk away from the course with tools to deal with stress, but they become too stressed to use them—and sometimes they become stressed about using them in the "right" way. The key is to learn how to develop attitudes that enable you to relax in difficult situations.

It's about learning to think of yourself as a relaxed person who takes things in stride. It's about learning to laugh at situations by using the laughter filter to make everything that is stressful as comical as possible. It's about seeing things from different points of view, so you understand that things aren't as important as they seem. When you can begin to do all this, you'll find it easier to think less and do more; you'll find yourself organizing your time more effectively and learning to stay in the present moment more.

Furthermore, you'll discover that the trick is to make the states of relaxation, humor, and focus the states you go into consistently and to use those states as a background. You'll find yourself dealing with everything more comfortably relaxed, and with a wonderful sense of contentment and peace of being able to live in the moment.

Beating Stress Exercises

1. Use meta-mantras.

   Regularly use the mantras "SHUT THE FUCK UP" when you are giving yourself a hard time or "SO THE FUCK WHAT?" when you are worried. Repeat these mantras over and over, especially when you hear yourself say "What if?"

2. Stay in the present.

Take some time each day just to notice where you are and to relax, letting the sights, sounds, and feelings you experience simply be there. Do this for about five or ten minutes.

3. Reframe stress.

Find out what the intention is behind the stress. It is usually an effort to protect yourself, but from what? Once you know this, find out how you can fulfill that intention without the stress.

4. Practice relaxation/meditation.

Set yourself five to fifteen minutes every day to find a quiet place to relax. Take this time to close your eyes, daydream your favorite fantasies, imagine your body completely relaxing, and imagine how you would feel if you knew you couldn't fail. Make the images as vivid as possible and enjoy the relaxation with complete abandonment for a few minutes. You can also offer yourself some positive suggestions or affirmations while you are relaxing. The secret is not to try too hard to get it right. Focus only on how much you are relaxing, not whether you are or not.

5. Finish things.

Remember to write down all the things you have to do the following day in your work before you leave. Write things down and use a diary so you can afford to put things in the "back of your mind."

6. Close off things.

At the end of the day, finish your time at work by turning on and off the computer once, opening and closing every door and drawer and cabinet. By doing all of these actions once, it provides your brain with an indication that everything has been closed off and finished for the day. Write a list of what you are to do the following day, in what order, and note anything you have to finish the next day.

7. Keep a worry book

Get a worry book and take it around with you. Every time you notice yourself worrying, think about what you can do about the worry at that moment. If you can do something about it, then do it. If not, simply put it in your worry book and take ten minutes every night to look over your worries—just worry solidly for that ten minutes.

8. Change your inner pictures.

Pay attention to what images you make when you are stressed and make them smaller, move them far away, and make them fuzzy and dim. Replace them with more relaxing images and make the new images big, bright, colorful, and vivid.

9. Change the tone of your inner voice.

Change the tone of your inner voice and make it ridiculous so that instead of it sounding stressed, it sounds like Mickey Mouse, or make it a deep, seductive tone.

10. Use the laughter filter.

Use the laughter filter to frame every stressful situation in a humorous way.

CHAPTER 30

Freeing Up Time

I LOVE KIDS. They are so much more fun than adults. Often I get the feeling that I have much more in common with them. A few years ago, I was at a NLP workshop in Orlando. One of the mornings, I babysat Irene, the two-year-old daughter of my friends Dave and Holly. Reenee, as I call her, and I played lots of different games. She was just learning to talk. While we played, time stood still, and I realized something amazing about children. Children at such a young age have no real concept of time. They just live in the moment. There is such a freedom in this, I thought—not simply being devoid of all responsibility but truly living in the moment, free from the past and future. Children can teach us some wonderful lessons.

Einstein, one of the greatest geniuses of all time, argued that "time is relative." Yet, despite this, we rarely use it in a way that helps us. The more we develop technologies that enable us to do things more quickly to save time, the more we take on, and we end up losing time. With computers, laptops, mobile phones, planes, and fax machines, we are continuously looking for ways to do things more quickly. While we do this, however, our world seems to move faster, and we seem to have less time than ever in which to do so much more.

In *Time for a Change*, Richard's fantastic book, I read about how he taught people to change their perception of time by going into a state of time distortion. They were able to make enjoyable events feel like they took a lot longer and not-so-enjoyable events go by in what felt like a flash. Time distortion is achieved by going into a state in which you perceive time slowing down or speeding up in the past and retriggering it when you need it.

As I employed this technique in my own life, it made things so much easier, but I still found myself busily doing many things at once and running out of time. I talked with Richard about this.

OF: Have you any suggestions about time management?

RB: I think most people waste most of their time. In terms of managing time, I think the most important thing is to spend less time worrying and less time feeling bad and to understand how your mind works, so you make decisions quickly and you do things quickly. You learn to motivate yourself, get things done, and get it over with effectively. The amount of time people spend hemming and hawing while doing things is absolutely crazy.

Most of the clients that I work with spend anywhere up to 70 percent of their waking time nagging themselves and making horrible pictures and 15 percent of their time planning things that they never do, and another 14 percent of their time complaining about what they didn't do, and maybe 1 percent of their time, if they're lucky, actually doing something. To me, the most important thing is to change that ratio around to the opposite. The mind is a marvelous thing; it can plan and plan and plan, but we have to learn to plan things and then do them.

Human beings are happier when they are manifesting. My next-door neighbor said to me one time when he looked over at some horses that had been kept in a field behind my house for a couple of years, "Those are very unhappy horses." I asked him what he meant, and he said, "Horses aren't happy unless they are doing something. If they were in a herd, they'd be romping around looking for food.

When I worked them on my farm, they couldn't wait to get hooked up to things and go out and do what horses do." He continued, "Ever since we got tractors, the horses are just standing out there. The horses are lonely. The horses are bored, and then they start doing things like gnawing on trees and chewing on themselves."

Humans are a lot the same way. If they are not doing something that they enjoy, they start gnawing on themselves. They do it with internal dialogue and bad pictures, and then they start gnawing on the people around them; they start picking on their children. When I look at the generation that's grown up after me, one of the things that amazes me is that we've scared these children worse than what was done to us.

When I grew up, we thought a bomb was going to blow us up, and a lot of us thought, "Who cares? Let's try anything because it doesn't matter." But the situation now is even more insidious. It's the idea that the world is a dangerous place. The police are spying on you. The terrorists are spying on you. All you see is millions of cop shows with everybody getting shot—this is how teenagers grow up. In many ghetto neighborhoods, people who are successful move out so that the only role models left are prostitutes and drug dealers.

We have to learn to intermix things; we need to put successful people and poor people in the same environment together. We need to take people from different religions and let them have lunch together for Christ's sake. I mean, the more Muslim people I meet, the more I really like them, and if I had let the government determine this, I would have been afraid of them all. I would have avoided them all. I'd have thought they were all lunatics and nuts, but the truth is when you get to know people you realize what they are really like. The more we travel and meet others, the more we do things to break down not just the fears between people but the fears that we have inside of ourselves, the better we will be. Fear is an indication that you are being stupid and should be taken that way and should be dealt with that way.

The keys to time management are really about learning to arrange your life so that you are performing at your best more of the time. It's about ensuring that the moments you spend with your family are all about your family. It's about never letting work invade your personal time and making sure that the time you spend with your loved ones is not unnecessarily affected by problems from your job. It's about organizing your time and priorities in the best way possible for you. It's about setting time aside every day to write down all the things you are doing and have to do and checking that list every morning.

Another great idea on managing time effectively is to study how much time you spend on different tasks. Take a watch with you for a couple of days and time and record everything. This will give you a fantastic insight into where all the time "went."

Freeing up time is about realizing that we can't make more time; we can only make better use of the time we have. Prioritizing your tasks into different categories will enable you to take action on what is urgent and important and to stay ahead of things. It will involve delegating things and sometimes refusing things to do what you need done. But as you focus on ensuring that you are in the best state possible and doing all you can, you'll find yourself getting more done than ever. It's also about disciplining yourself to keep to a schedule while still remaining flexible. That way, we can best learn the enjoyment and satisfaction that comes with the freedom of living in the present, just like children.

Time-Changing Exercises

1. Organize.

>   Set aside a day to get everything organized.

>   Design your diary/appointments/schedule around the information you've just read. The amount of time that you'll save over the next year will be well worth it. Make this a regular habit: once a week, once a month, every three months, every six months, once a year.

2. Catch up.

>   Give yourself an extra couple of hours to catch up and finish up things each week.

3. Prioritize.

>   Some things are more important or urgent than others. Make sure you know your priorities. You'll never get everything done all the time.

4. Get a notebook.

>   Get a notebook and take it everywhere. Write down anything you think of that you have to do.

5. Time yourself.

>   Take a watch around with you and record in your notebook how much time you spend doing each activity during the day. Do this for a few days, and you'll understand exactly where your time "goes"!

CHAPTER 31

The Art of
Financial Freedom

MONEY IS REGARDED all over the world as being one of the most important things that exists. Even in places like India and Tibet, where spirituality is so important, there are many people asking for money on the side of the street. Worldwide, money enables us to do more things, go more places, meet more people. Money provides us with freedom to enjoy the pleasures in life or simply to survive. The idea of financial freedom is really the idea of having enough money to enable you to do what you want and live how you want. Since we are all different, the amount will differ from person to person.

In studying the wealthiest people I know and examining the literature available on wealth, I learned the fundamentals of increasing wealth. I also wanted to gain Richard's perspective on wealth, as he is someone who has successfully acquired financial abundance over the years.

OF: How can you increase wealth and gain more financial freedom?

RB: To increase wealth, you have to aim your mind at answering the question: "How can I be selling my time?" There's a point at which you can increase how much your time costs, but there has to be a point at which you productize somehow or else recapitulate. You either have to train other people to do what you do so that you are using their time, or you have to be able to do things differently.

The reason I write books is because it's a way for me to be there when I'm not actually there. I make audiotapes and CDs and DVDs and all these products because it's a way of manufacturing my skill and putting it out to a larger number of people without it taking a long time. You have to have a thing inside your mind that says, "How can I spend half the time making four times the money?" At first, it always seems an impossible question; however, people have been doing it for centuries. It doesn't have to be with the same skills that I have. I happen to have the skills I do, so that's what I sell.

Some people right now are working on a house. Somebody's paying them $15 an hour to build the side of a house. They have to answer the same question, "How can I spend half the time making four times the money?" A lot of people think that you can do it easily with the stock market. I find the stock market very dangerous. You can do well for a while, but you can do really badly very quickly, too. Unless you really understand the stock market and keep reunderstanding it, you are going to do badly. However, by the same token, the guy building the house could turn around and say to himself, "Well if I saved up enough money and built one extra house and sold it, then I could build two houses, or I could buy one trailer and sell it and buy two trailers." People have been doing this since the beginning of time, finding things and finding niches in the market.

When my grandfather got to the United States, he was penniless because he'd lost everything to the Germans, and he was driving around New York state in an old car that broke down. He went into a gas station, and they said it would take a week to get the parts because they couldn't close down the gas station and drive to the city to get them. So he said to the guy, "Well I'll tell you what. I'll drive your truck to New York and get the parts." Then he said, "By the way, do you need parts for any other cars?" So he drove in to New York, and he added 10 percent on the parts prices, and he came back and made money getting his car fixed. In five years he was a multimillionaire. He had people driving all over the city to all the gas stations in trucks with parts in them. He started with nothing and made millions of dollars.

These kinds of stories happen all over the planet all the time. There was a guy in the northeastern United States who was making crates to put baby carriages in. He looked in a truck, and he thought to himself, "You know, if we just put runners in these trucks, we wouldn't have to build these expensive crates. I could put myself out of a job." So he bought an old truck for $50, put the runners in it, and told the carriage maker he could take it to every store in New York, and he wouldn't need a crate, so he'd save all that money. This guy ended up owning a trucking company in New England. Fifteen years later, he was a multimillionaire.

Stories like this go on and on, where people take one idea that makes sense and they do something with it. The most important thing for people to realize is that, whether or not they become ultra-wealthy with money, there are lots of really rich people who are really unhappy. Real wealth is being happy with what you have and being intelligent enough to make more.

Financial freedom is, therefore, about making your time worth more to you. It is also about figuring out ways of making your money work for you while you do something else. Prosperity consciousness is when you develop the beliefs and attitudes that support you being wealthy. Often we can learn negative beliefs about money in childhood that we carry with us into our adulthood. We learn that loving money is bad and that the "poor person will enter the gates of heaven."

While such beliefs and stories are designed to ensure that people do not value money as the most important thing in the world, taking them as the absolute truth is not useful. Instead, you can realize that "loving money" can be bad, but acquiring it is not. The more money you have, the more of a difference to the world you can make. The most successful people who have made the most difference to the world have done so either by their own wealth or their ability to access those with wealth.

Another idea on financial freedom is the art of being the "bigger tip" person. Whenever you have a choice between giving a small and a large amount, it's essential that you give the larger amount, as the way you behave will affect how you see yourself. As Jim Rohn says, it's about being the "bigger tip" person. If we give the small amount, we'll see ourselves as misers. If we give the bigger amount, we see ourselves as richer. Finally, it's important to set financial goals to get your brain focused and tuned into an abundant way of thinking. When you come to these realizations, you can do all you can to achieve as much wealth as possible.

Wealth Mentality Exercises

1. From your earnings, invest 10 percent, save 10 percent, and give away 10 percent. This enables you to begin to practice managing your money successfully.

2. Write out your beliefs about money and what beliefs are more useful to have instead.

3. When you have a choice between paying two similar amounts, always pay the larger amount. It gets you thinking from a prosperity consciousness rather than a poverty consciousness.

4. Define your well-formed goals around money.

    What do you want to be able to afford?

    How much do you want to earn per year?

    Set a yearly schedule for the next fifteen years of how much you want to earn and what you want to be able to afford.

    How much money would it take for you to be financially free?

CHAPTER 32

Looking After Yourself

TO CREATE A HEALTHY environment inside your head, it is crucial to create a healthy environment inside your body, too. This does not mean rigorously following what people describe as the "perfect diet" or exercising religiously every single day. It simply means being good to your body by using some old-fashioned common sense.

We know that if we drink too much or take drugs, it will affect our bodies in negative ways. Most people know what it's like to wake up with a hangover and experience the negative mental state that comes with it. We know that if we eat too much or too little or the wrong kind of foods that our emotions will be affected negatively. We know that if we don't exercise regularly, we will not be in a positive mental state. We know this through experience, not just through the many statistics and studies that prove it scientifically.

The key is to begin to follow some very simple guidelines about the way to treat your body. Eat healthy (fresh if possible) foods. Drink healthy drinks. Avoid alcohol and other drugs as much as possible. Sleep well and exercise regularly. I asked Richard for his ideas on this.

OF: What suggestions do you have in helping people with their health?

RB: That depends upon the person. Oddly enough, most of the people I know who are pretty healthy are also pretty happy. Unfortunately, though, there is no way of predicting things. I caught diseases even though I was profoundly happy, but I lived through them, and that was not the prediction that doctors had. This thing about health has not been figured out. In the end, we're going to figure out that it's highly determined by genetic code and chemicals. I think that it's very important when you're feeling bad to change as much as you can, and I think it's a good idea to rotate whatever regime you have.

I take vitamins for a while, and then I stop, and then I'll start again. I think if you just take the same vitamins all the time, your body habituates to them and just gets rid of them. It's a good idea to introduce new things. The more you keep introducing new things, the more vibrant I think your body will stay. If you take vitamins, you should change your regime of vitamins. If you exercise, you should change your regime of exercise. The more you keep things the same, the more the body habituates to it, and it does very little good. In fact, I think at a certain point, it becomes counterproductive. It's best to keep trying things, and when you try things and they make you feel bad, just stop it.

What Richard was pointing out was that varying our disciplines and habits is a good idea because when the body gets used to certain things, those things do not always have as positive an effect as when they were first introduced. By combining different approaches, it is possible to continuously impact the body positively. So with food, the idea would be to eat foods that are nutritious—but be sure to eat lots of different kinds of food. The idea is to exercise in different ways. It's good to get into a routine with food and exercise, but inside of these routines variation is the key.

The bottom line is that you know some foods are more likely to help you put on weight, so if you want to lose weight, the key is to avoid those kinds of food. A few other tips on eating would be to make sure that you eat slowly. Research suggests that chewing improves digestion, which improves your overall health. My granny always taught me this, and yet it was only when I actually started to do it more often that I noticed the difference. Drink plenty of water because keeping the body hydrated is essential to staying healthy.

I began to talk with Richard about sleep. I had heard many conflicting reports on how much sleep people need to function effectively. I asked Richard about this.

OF: Regarding sleep, how much sleep do people need to function effectively?

RB: It depends on who you are. Some people need more sleep; some people need less. I think most people sleep too much. I think it's like a drug, and people should wean themselves off it to find out what maximum performance is. Most people have very low energy because they sleep too much, and it produces a chemical inside them.

This crap doctors tell you about how you need eight hours—I mean, excuse me, I think somebody just picked a day and divided it by three and came up with this number. They don't say, "Some people need eight hours and ten minutes, and some people need seven hours and five minutes." They say, "Everybody needs eight hours." That's just nonsense. Most of my life I've slept three to five hours a night, and I've always felt fine. If I sleep more than that, I feel groggy. People need to find what's perfect for them. However, every once in a while, you're going to sleep for fifteen hours and then sometimes not sleep at all. You know people should learn to only eat when they're hungry, not when they feel hungry. They should learn the difference between real hunger and just wanting to stuff something into their mouths. When you listen to your body, it will let you know how much sleep or food you need.

Richard's beliefs seemed to fly in the face of some conventional medical theories about people requiring a certain number of hours sleep. The crux of what he was explaining was that it was up to the individuals themselves to study their own patterns of sleep and to find out, by trying different things, what works best for them. His warning about the danger of getting too much sleep was enlightening to me. I had never really thought about this, but as I remembered some times when I stayed in bed, and I noticed it was days like that when I felt constantly tired.

People who find it hard to get to sleep are often trying too hard to do it. When you can get to the stage where you don't "need" much sleep, you'll find it easy to drift off. I remember a little trick I learned when I was in Europe traveling with Gillian, a friend of mine. We arrived in Krakow, Poland, after our adventures in Frankfurt and Prague. The morning we arrived, it was a special holiday in the town. I was sick and had gotten little sleep on the uncomfortable train. We managed to get a place to stay. Over the next few nights I got little sleep. I was exhausted. On the final day in Krakow, we met Veronica, a lovely woman from Norway, and her nine-year-old son, Patrick, as they booked a bus trip that we were on. As we traveled with them, Gillian got on great with Veronica, and I got on great with Patrick. Although he spoke little English, I managed to make him smile as I clowned around.

We got to know them, and they traveled with us to Budapest, our next stop on the train. I noticed Patrick had absolutely no trouble sleeping, regardless of how uncomfortable the train was, while I still struggled and felt the exhaustion as bad as ever. I asked Patrick how he managed to sleep. He pointed to the Walkman I had seen him put on from time to time. He placed the earphones on my head, and I heard slow Spanish music. I felt myself slipping off for the first time in days. "Yes, but I've seen you sleep without the headphones, Patrick," I said curiously. "I hear the music in my head," he replied. I smiled. A nine-year-old boy had been my therapist. I could sleep.

Another thing that fascinates me is the amazing feelings that I have had at different times when sleeping. I have often woken in the middle of a dream that felt like pure bliss. Inside the dreams we enter can be a feeling of absolute security, love, and inner peace. I was interested in Richard's opinion on the notion of dream interpretation.

OF: What is your perspective on the whole notion of dream interpretation?

RB: I think it's neurology's way of making neural cortical connections and that it has absolutely nothing to do with content. The most meaningful dream I ever had was when I got a job working a staple machine. I worked for eight hours stapling things, and that night I went home, fell asleep, and I stapled for another eight hours. I did that for five nights in a row, and after that I never dreamt about stapling again, but I've never had any problems running the staple machine either.

I've had some of the weirdest dreams that you could possibly imagine, but I don't believe that they're connected with content. I think this whole concept of interpretation of dreams is absolute malarkey, and I think that both Fritz Perls and Sigmund Freud, or as I like to call him Sick Man Fraud, don't have it right. It's a nice idea, but it is bull. I believe that people have psychic dreams when they are in psychic states, and if they could pay attention to those and learn to do things, then that's a different phenomenon. It's a different kind of a dream. Most of the dreams that people have are just really nothing more than neurology readjusting itself just before you wake up and as you go to sleep.

This again opened up another topic for me.

OF: What are your thoughts about psychic phenomenon?
RB: I think it's fun.

He smiled.

RB: I think that everybody does it and that everybody ignores it and that it's more the rule than the exception and that it's evolutionarily: just what's on the way. My favorite thing that I've heard a physicist say at a conference was that "all psychic phenomenon is just nonsense." I said, "I had a prediction that precognition is going to be proved to be false," and he didn't laugh, but another 1,500 other people did.

To me, that's what it all boils down to—having a sense of humor and realizing that anything is possible and therefore will happen eventually. Some of it will happen slowly. I think that most people don't really look at the fact that we're not very evolved as an organism and that we're in the process of evolving and the more that we cognitively evolve, the faster we'll evolve physically.

OF: So how could we improve our own psychic abilities or at least our own intuition about things?

RB: By sorting out the good ones from the bad ones. When you have intuitions—notice them. If they turn out to be wrong, notice the difference between that feeling and an intuition you had that was right. If people take the time to do that, they will start using a lot more right intuitions than wrong ones.

One day I was talking to my friends Gemma and Joe about the fact that there were a few people I had not seen in years that I would have liked to keep in touch with. I had no way to contact them. I named three people in particular. Following that conversation, I was e-mailed by one for the first time in three years. A week later, I met the second in some bar I randomly ended up in. Two weeks after that I met the third friend, again randomly, as I had hooked up with other friends. Coincidences, I believe, are synchronicities. There is some sort of universal intelligence out there.

Things always happen for some reason. That reason might help you or hamper you. What most people don't realize, though, is that the reason something happens depends on how you deal with it. Everything happens for a reason that helps us if we choose to take it that way. Remember all perceptions are just perceptions. How we see the world is just how we see it. The key is to let your intuition guide your decisions, and the universe can conspire to help you. Whether it does so in the form of "god," "angels," "luck," or the "power of the mind," the same result is possible. That's my take on it.

I thanked Richard for his words of wisdom. It was time to head back to my hotel room. I walked with my tape recorder in my hand through the streets of Edinburgh as his words resonated through my head. So many things were becoming clear for me. Many of the answers I learned from him, I had experienced on my own already, but he had a phenomenal ability to articulate them brilliantly.

Better Life Exercises

1. Decide on particular kinds of exercise you can do and spend at least thirty minutes to one hour engaging in them at least three times a week.
2. Make a commitment to begin to eat healthier food. Buy fresh fruit and vegetables in your weekly shopping.
3. Study your sleep patterns and pay attention to the patterns that work best for you.
4. Pay attention to coincidences and write them down.
5. Pay attention to your intuition and notice the difference between the feelings that you get that turn out to be correct and the feelings that turn out to be wrong.

CHAPTER 33

Random Ramblings 4:
Being Serious About Laughing

BELIEVE IT OR NOT, I am not perfect. Now I know what you are thinking. "Rubbish. No way. You are perfect, Owen." But, alas, I am not. Indeed, I have some flaws (albeit not that many ☺ YES). Sometimes I talk way too much, am self-absorbed, am annoying, get into a mood, get too intense, ask stupid questions, eat too fast, drink too slowly, say the wrong thing, and make an idiot of myself.

Richard is not perfect either. He is a normal human being with flaws, too. As he says himself, he has made more mistakes than most people. That is why he has learned so much. The key is not to make the same mistakes over and over again. So many people hold themselves back because they care about what others might think. They hesitate and wait and wait and wait. Their biggest problem is that they take themselves and their world too seriously. What people really need to do is to learn to lighten up and decide to feel good instead of trying to be important.

> *"Never get too serious. Too many people get serious and try to be 'right' all the time. If you are not getting where you want to go in your life and still feel being right is the most important thing, more important than being happy, this is where you waste life's energy, and then, after ten years, you'll discover that you weren't 'right', and it didn't matter."*

—Richard Bandler

To me, self-importance is what leads people to stupidity. Being able to laugh at myself is something that I have had to learn. I remember once I was out with a friend who had learned about creating rapport with others. During the evening, she accused me of "mirroring" her, using an NLP technique. What she forgot was that mirroring is a natural part of the process of getting on well and that it happens in everyday communication between friends. Now sometimes when people learn a little NLP, they get carried away with what they think is going on. What is important to remember is that so much of NLP came from studying what was already out there in the real world when communication was happening successfully.

Once a woman in a course came up to me and told me that there was a "deep, dark lurking sadness" somewhere within me. Another time, a man I just met at a conference asked me what I was talking about at the conference, and when I told him it was NLP, he proceeded to tell me it was all a load of "codswallop." These are just some examples of the kinds of things that happen in the real world. Some people will be skeptical because that is how they have learned to think. Some people will assume that you are being manipulative, perhaps because that is how they think. Some people will look for problems in you because that is what happens inside of them. So many people miss the entire point.

Trying to seriously convince them of the opposite is often the worst mistake you could make. Often, the more defensive you get, the more guilty you seem. So the key is to relax and simply let other people have their ideas. My friend believed I was "using NLP" on her; this woman believed I was "deep down hiding my inner sadness"; the man at the conference believed NLP was rubbish. They were convinced that they were right, and there was no need to convince them otherwise. Instead of feeling bad about it, I just realized it was where they were at and simply laughed.

There are also people who have done NLP courses who walk away from them thinking that they know everything and that they are experts. The truth is that it all comes down to perception. We all come up with an idea, and then we work to prove that idea is true. People develop ideas about me or Richard or you, the reader, and they prove those ideas to themselves. We love to think we have "figured out" somebody. The reality is that it is all about perception, and there is no point in taking any of what people say to heart. When you can laugh at yourself, you don't have to identify with other people's delusions or distortions, and you can simply focus on feeling really good.

Being serious about laughing is about recognizing the humor that exists in life and going into the future with a different attitude. Whenever something annoys me, I will usually go on a rant about it to a friend and do my best to describe the situation in an exaggerated and funny way. This helps me see it in a more useful perspective because I begin to laugh about it immediately.

Otherwise, it is easy to get caught up in feeling angry or pissed off with people or circumstances. If we hold ourselves as too important, we fail to recognize how silly this is. There are many people who try to become more important by getting a new title. There are many people who try to seem to be more intelligent by being critical. Of course, there will be people who will take this book and criticize it to show how intelligent they are. We can learn from the feedback, but to feel bad about it is going against the whole notion of personal freedom. Again, it is often such people who miss the point. It is not written to be "good" for them. It is written to enable people to learn about things that help them to develop more personal freedom.

What will "people" think? Well, you've got to ask the questions "Which people?" and "Who cares?" The people that matter are the ones you truly love and who love you for who you are. If you start by being able to laugh at yourself, then you have the freedom to be at your best. When people are at their best, it is because they are so immersed in the activity and not in how they are perceived. That is the trick.

One of the things that I will often do is let people think that they have figured me out or gotten to me. There are many people who love to think they have control over you or that they see the kind of person you are immediately. They live in a cloud of their own delusional perceptions. The problem is that we all do. Seeing other people without putting them above or below you is a good step toward being able to feel great about who you are.

Once you become very skilled in NLP and you get to meet the best in the field, you start to realize just how elegant and skillful you can become with language. You learn about concepts such as nesting loops, sequential phrasing, and semantic packing. You learn about understanding "meta-programs" and "modal operators," which are simply generalized patterns we use to sort and organize information inside our heads, and how to elicit them verbally and nonverbally. You learn about how you can twist and turn words to dramatically affect other people's brains through your use of placing the right words in the right sequence at the right time. You learn how to ask questions that can turn a person's life around and use verb tenses in ways that completely alter the way people perceive their past, present, and future.

All of these really cool and fascinating skills are the things that I still love working with, teaching, and learning. But none of this matters, and none will really be effective unless you recognize the importance of being able to laugh at the humor that is everywhere. We can transform our worlds if we can just learn to laugh a little more. We can laugh at those who try to make us feel bad by making themselves feel important, and we can smile at the ridiculousness of human beings sometimes. Or we can go around in this serious world with our serious heads and our serious expressions.

Somewhere in this world, there are far too many people taking far too many things seriously, especially themselves. There are times to deal with situations seriously, but there are very few times to treat yourself seriously. I am not perfect, and I have two choices: feel bad about why or laugh at how. I prefer laughing.

PART V

The Art of Loving Freedom

CHAPTER 34

Love, Actually

IT WAS ABOUT TWO O'CLOCK in the afternoon, and I was driving along the familiar road. The sun was shining for once. I had the windows open as I listened to the songs on the radio. It was a surprisingly cloudless day in December. Outside it was cold, but there was little wind. My mind continuously wandered from topic to topic, only being brought back to reality occasionally to remember which turns to take. The farther I went into the countryside, the more the fresh, clean air filled my lungs. I was becoming more and more relaxed every mile I drove. I felt I was becoming healthier, too.

I was on my way to visit Richard and Paula once more. It had been an especially chaotic few months. I had not seen them since just before my world tour. I had so much to tell them, so many questions to ask. Since the last time we had met, I had taught NLP in India, trekked up Everest, skied in New Zealand, and had a really amazing set of adventures along the way.

I was thinking about everything I had been through in the previous six months. My questions were questions for me, for my own life, but deep inside, I always knew that those questions were highly valuable for so many people in the world. The reason was that the questions would revolve around the most important concept on the planet: love. I was going to explore this topic with Richard to see how it fit with my own experience.

I had already applied all that I had learned from my past conversations with Richard with remarkable results. My focus was now turned to our relationships with others and the problems and solutions to be found in them.

As I drove, I heard some experts on the radio discuss love and the nature of romantic love and infatuation. It was yet another synchronicity that I was used to in my life. I began to think and ponder on love as a concept, and as I drove, I was aided by the intermittent songs dedicated to love or heartache of some form.

CHAPTER 35

Love Makes the World Go Around

LITTLE FIVE-YEAR-OLD JOHNNY was in the hospital with his parents visiting his eight-year-old sister, Jessica, who was very sick. The doctors explained to his parents that Jessica needed a blood transfusion to stay alive. After completing the blood tests on the family, it turned out that only Johnny had the same blood type and was the only potentially viable donor. The doctor asked Johnny if he would give his blood to his sister. He hesitated for a second and then agreed.

During the procedure, as the blood was being transfused, color started reappearing on his sister's face. He looked up at the doctor and asked with a tremble, "How long before I start dying?" He had misunderstood the doctor. He had thought his sister needed all his blood.

Love is perhaps the most important quality in life. People will do anything for those they love. When I think about my friends and family in this world, I am often overcome with emotion. The emotion I'm talking about is love. The people I have in my life, what they have done for me, and how grateful I am to know them—it all makes me understand why we are all here together. We depend on each other. We care for and help out each other. We do the act of loving each other.

Sometimes, however, we do not practice this act. We compete with each other. We become fearful and resentful toward each other. We attack each other. We hurt each other. We kill each other. We do the act of hating each other. Some people in particular seem to be more likely to do this, but we are all capable of it. The wars of the world reflect, on a mass scale, the things we often mirror in our own relationships.

We always seem to idealistically ask for world peace, and yet we fail to take any actions to create our own inner peace and our own relationship peace. We criticize the world's leaders for their ignorance when we are often guilty of the same ignorance in our own lives. Change happens one person at a time. What is vital is that we make ourselves and our own lives as good as they can be and create such a powerful example that others can learn and improve.

As humans we are presented with many difficulties around relationships. First, there is the art of getting in a good relationship. Second, there is the art of making relationships better and improving them. Finally, there is the art of dealing with relationships when they are in conflict or have ended.

There are many different kinds of relationships: with your partner or spouse, mother or father, son or daughter, family members, close friends, work colleagues, strangers. Most of life's problems come from difficulties in our relationship with ourselves or our relationship with someone from one of these categories.

As we've already looked at your relationship with yourself in the last section, it's time to examine the three arts of what I call "loving freedom": getting into relationships with others, making them happier and better, and dealing with them when they end.

We are born on a planet with over six billion other people. In our lives, we get to meet thousands of people. We build great bonds with some of these people, and some we meet only briefly and never see again. That's life. The bonds we build with people enable us to experience the most wonderful sensation known to humankind—the art of love. I call it an art because there are different kinds of love and different ways to do it.

Now some of these bonds can last our whole lives or at least most of our lives. These bonds can be tested and broken, made stronger and closer.

They can arise when you least expect them, and you'll also learn the unyielding lesson that exists about all things: what has a beginning will always have an ending. You will meet people, and no matter how close you are or how deep your connection, no matter how much you love them or they love you, at some point, your relationship will end.

Some hope for their ideal scenario of dying at the exact same time as their loved ones, so both are spared the pain of grief, but it is very rare that happens. Often relationships will end before death, and sometimes you'll be lucky enough to make it last until one of you passes away. So with this unavoidable, tragic truth looming in the back of our lives, what is there to do? How can we make the moments count more? How can we love properly and live as well as possible knowing this inevitable truth?

Loving freedom, to me, means having the freedom to love yourself deeply, others deeply, and accepting the never-ending truth of change. It means having the freedom to be happy on your own and happy with others as they come in and out of our lives. It means having the freedom to connect wonderfully with those you meet and deal successfully with those who are difficult to relate to well.

As I got closer and closer to my time with the Bandlers, I decided where I would begin. I would talk to Richard about loneliness and go from there.

CHAPTER 36

Escaping Solitary Confinement:
Breaking from the Prison of Loneliness

MY CLIENT, BRYAN, looked at me with curiosity. We were sitting in a hotel bar in the center of Dublin. We were there for therapeutic purposes. Bryan was about to make a huge leap in his progress.

OF: Right now. Do you see that girl over there by the bar, with the black top on, blonde hair?

Bryan: Yes, I do. What do you want me to do?

OF: Okay, go up to the bar and order two bottles of beer, and when you get them, on your way back, go over to her, tap her gently on the shoulder and say excuse me, give her some genuine nice compliment, and then excuse yourself again and come back to me here. No hanging around waiting for a response. Your function is to compliment and leave. Do you understand?

Bryan: Yeah, but what if she . . .

OF: No matter what she does, make excuses to return to me as soon as possible. You have to learn what it is like to compliment someone to make them feel good, not always in the hope of getting them to go out with you or get them in the sack.

Bryan: Okay, here I go!

We did the brilliance squared exercise we had practiced. He remembered to imagine himself looking slick and confident walking over toward her. He repeated silently to himself, "She's so lucky. She's going to love you." He imagined her smiling with delight in response. He quickly got up and walked to the bar. He got the drinks and went over to the blonde girl and her friend. He tapped her on the shoulder.

I have always been intrigued by people. I am a people watcher and can be fascinated by watching people walking on the street. I travel around the world, and what I love most and remember best are the people I meet. They are my highlights. I adore my friends and family and spending fun time with them. I love the process of being in love when it happens and simply being in the same space as my loved one.

I had been remembering my work with Bryan on a television program called *Ask Anna*. It was an Irish program on the channel RTÉ that took different people who needed help in a particular area of life, and the charming Anna would get them specific experts. I was chosen to help Bryan with flirting. This exercise in the bar was one of many we did to enable him to flirt more effectively.

This came to mind because I was thinking about the whole notion of loneliness. You see, I have worked with lots of people over the years, teaching them how to improve their social skills, flirt better, love themselves more, and develop friendships and relationships. What I found was that I learned more and more about how all of this worked. I was still fascinated by the area of social communication, and the opportunity to learn more about it from Richard was something I relished. Also, I remembered what it was like to feel lonely, and I was curious to find out what could improve my own way of helping people overcome this emotion.

Now very rarely, if ever, do I feel lonely. Once I learned what "loving freedom" was really about, I began to understand how to live without loneliness. I have so many friends whom I have met on almost every continent of the world and whom I love dearly. My relationships with them are different and all special in their own way. I am lucky in one sense, but in another sense it is not just luck. I have attracted the friends I have into my life.

I have fallen out with friends before. I don't always get on with everyone I meet, and I don't always manage to keep in touch with people. Generally speaking, however, I never feel lonely even when I am alone because I make an effort when it comes to the relationships and friendships in my life.

Loving freedom is about reaching out and connecting with more people and building more relationships with people. Not everyone is going to be your cup of tea, nor you, theirs. What's critical is that you begin to meet more people and master your communication and relationship skills. When you have achieved this, everyone who comes into your life will be there for a reason that helps you learn something. Some will stay for the rest of your life or for the rest of theirs.

Loneliness is rampant in today's society. Some people are lonely because they are not in a relationship, some people are lonely because they are in an unhappy relationship, and some are lonely because they have few or no friends or family in their life to talk to. I have worked with many people with such problems. It's actually a lot simpler to go out and make friends than most people think. Most people try a few things and then claim that they have tried everything.

What's essential in the process of making friends is to keep in mind that it is a process. It's not just about getting out there and going to the right places. The way you think, your beliefs and feelings about people, is important for you to make effective first impressions.

I contemplated love, relationships, and friendship as I made my way down to meet Richard. As well as working with my client Bryan, I had worked with a number of people earlier that week who had consulted me with a desire to meet someone. They felt desperately lonely, and they wanted, more than anything, to be in a relationship. I had plenty of advice for them and ideas, but the more I talked to them, the more I realized that they had to let go of the need for a relationship before they could enter into a happy, healthy relationship with somebody. Even the process of simply making friends with people would be a problem when it was too important to them.

I soon arrived and met with Richard. We sat in his kitchen once again, and I started the tape recorder. I began to discuss my thoughts with him. My first question looked at the notion of friendship.

OF: Richard, why do some people struggle to make friends, and what are the secrets to making more friends or improving your social life?

RB: Often people don't know what to do. If they knew what to do, they would actually do it, because what to do is usually so much simpler than what they say about it. They say, "Well, I'm lonely, so I should go out and meet people." But they're lonely because they are not nice to themselves. They've made a feeling called loneliness, and they feel it so strongly that it stops them from going and meeting people.

They don't know how to feel good before they meet people, and if they did, then people would want to hang around with them. When they go out feeling bad, and when they are around people still feeling bad, other people don't want to hang around with them. These people don't know how to start with the important thing, which is to make themselves feel hope.

If you take all the bad feelings you have inside of you and just spin them in the opposite direction one by one, round and round and round, eventually those part-body sensations will switch to whole-body sensations that are pleasant. I think once you feel good and start to glow more that you are attractive, and people will be attracted to you.

It was simple and I liked it: pay attention to how you feel, run your negative feelings of loneliness in reverse, and generate positive, happy, good feelings in their place. If you feel good, people will want to become friends with you. It made perfect sense, but I wanted more.

OF: So overcoming loneliness is not really that complicated then? How exactly can people start to do this?

RB: Well, I would say start with yourself. If people can't make their own internal worlds pleasant, if they can't talk to themselves nicely and make nice pictures inside their own heads, then it's going to be really hard to get along with others. If they can't really empathize with themselves, to be able to empathize with somebody else and to listen to people enough is going to be a problem, too.

If people say, "I like blue," and you don't give them blue things or buy them blue flowers or blue shirts, then they're going to think you're not listening. The truth is that if you say to yourself, "You ought to stand up for yourself," and you don't, you aren't listening to yourself. Then if you aren't listening to yourself, most likely you're not listening to other people.

Therefore, in addition to spinning feelings backwards, you have to make your internal world pleasant by making nice pictures and talking nicely to yourself. Again it made sense. Listening more to others was something simple that I agreed with. Far too often, people spend so much time thinking about themselves that they barely hear the other person. They spend time trying to tell the other person how fantastic they themselves are. As I contemplated this, Richard looked at me and continued.

RB: There's what? There are about 550 million people who feel lonely. The problem is that, whether they meet somebody or not, they're going to be lonely because they haven't learned to enjoy themselves. You can make yourself feel good for no reason, for absolutely no reason whatsoever. You could be the most pathetic person, or you could be the most successful, wealthy person. I've had them both in my office telling me the same thing.

I've had the person who is homeless with warts all over his body and who has absolutely no future, no education, and no prospects telling me the same thing as a multibillionaire. They're both there telling me how unhappy they are and how lonely they are and how miserable they are, and neither one of them is ever going to get out of that until they stop and just make it so that they feel good for absolutely no reason. Until you learn to saturate your own neurology with your own chemicals to feel good for no reason, it's very difficult to make it in life, because otherwise everything that happens in the world is going to matter too much.

Someone will say something to his or her partner, and suddenly the partner's feelings will get hurt, and this may even lead to divorce. The divorce rate is based on chemistry as far as I can tell, and it's not good chemistry. No one should be allowed to have arguments until they're on dialysis machines, because then they will realize in most arguments people say stupid things. People have to learn to stop arguments and just say, "Stop. That's it. We're not going to do this."

Richard kept drilling this point into me. The vast majority of information out there on overcoming loneliness was about having the confidence to approach people, getting out there and knowing what to say. What this missed was that the real first step is essentially the need for people to make themselves feel as good as possible because this will affect those around them. Richard had used a good example in discussing his wealthy and poor clients. It reminded me that all problems can be tracked back to bad feelings.

There is an important distinction between making yourself feel good enough to go up and talk to people and making yourself feel good because that will affect the people around you. We all know people who exist in our lives who seem to drain all the good feelings out of a room. I heard them once being called "mood hoovers." Then there are other people who walk into a room and just seem to shower everyone with wonderful feelings through their shining energy. They are like shining stars.

The state that we are in will affect other people without us needing to say or do anything. There was an experiment Richard told me about. A bunch of scientists took two cartons of yogurt, placed them a few yards apart on a table, and hooked them both up to a machine that measured the amount of electrical activity present in them.

They added milk to yogurt A. Yogurt A responded wildly on the machine as the bacteria from the milk mixed with the culture from the yogurt. At the same time that Yogurt A responded wildly, so did Yogurt B. No milk was added to Yogurt B. Now this anomaly in science was replicated several times, and as they tried to alter this seemingly invisible affect, the only thing that would eventually prevent Yogurt A from affecting Yogurt B was to place a wall of yogurt between them.

Richard's explanation for this is that "yogurt knows yogurt," which is the same as when you pluck a musical string at a particular frequency and other strings at that frequency respond by vibrating. The same is true for human beings. People know people, and when you go into a particular state, you'll vibrate good energy in your body, and this will affect the people around you. You have met the "mood hoovers," and you have also met the "shining stars." Now when you begin to generate powerful positive feelings yourself, you'll shine these feelings to those around you.

Richard made one particular comment that provided me with a wonderful moment of epiphany. It was when he said, "The divorce rate is based on chemistry as far as I can tell, and it's not good chemistry."

I kept running this idea over and over again in my head. Almost every problem, I realized, was based on chemistry. It was based on both the chemistry inside your head and the chemistry between you and another person. So when you learn how to create better chemistry in yourself and with others, you'll take a giant step toward eliminating the problems of your life.

If you can remember that whenever you feel bad with another person, it is because the chemistry isn't right, and you can either figure out how to change it or accept it for that time. Either way, it is nothing personal. It is just about how you are creating chemicals inside your head and sending energy to others.

With this in mind, I wondered why some people don't like me and some do. If it is all about chemistry, how come I had good chemistry with some people and bad chemistry with others?

> OF: Okay, so why is it that I get on well with some people and not with others? What is that all about?
>
> RB: Well, it doesn't matter what the reason is. If people don't like you, then they don't like you because you're not making them like you, and most of the time it's because you're not likeable.
>
> If you feel really good on the inside, so that you are really happy on the inside, so that you are really shining on the inside, so your internal dialogue sounds really good and your pictures are really wonderful, then people will want to be around you. If you exude joy and vibrate joy, people will want to be around you. It's the most important thing. I mean people will dress up. They'll get their hair done. They'll do everything to look good, but they'll forget to take the steps to feel good. If you feel really good when you meet people, they'll like you; it's just that simple.

Richard went to the kettle and asked if I'd like a cup of tea or coffee. I said I was okay and grabbed a bottle of water from the fridge. I began to let all he had said sink in. Richard had repeated again this concept of the need to feel good inside before anything else. Feel wonderful on the inside and others will feel great when they are with you. So that's the crux of loving freedom. By reading up to this point in this book, I'm sure you have already practiced many of the suggestions for how you can feel more wonderful more of the time. What is essential is to feel good first rather than relying on other people to lift your spirits.

We look our best when we are having fun. I remember a comedy show I went to where I was at the door with Kevin, my friend who was organizing it. I watched as the people went in, and I watched them as they left. I could have sworn that the vast majority became far more attractive by the time they left the show. Feeling great and having great fun is actually a brilliant way of looking your best.

Probably one of the most important states to get into to make friends and potential lovers is the state of playfulness. Take flirting. Flirting is not the same as seduction. It is not based around attempting to make the other person feel sexually attractive and attracted to you. It is based on laughing, joking, teasing, and messing with the other person. It is based on enjoying the company of the other person and indicating that there is possibly some interest there, but maybe not.

When we flirt, we must do it in the state of playfulness where we are not hanging on desperately to this one person to talk to. Instead, we must feel an abundance of opportunities out there. That feeling gives us a sense of independence that is attractive to others.

People sometimes ask me, "Why is it that nice guys finish last?" Well it's not because they are nice—it is because some nice guys are not a challenge. Most women seem to be attracted to someone they have to work to have. Men are generally the same. The reality is that if you give a person the idea that you are interested but that they have to "earn you," it stops them wondering whether or not you are "good enough" for them. They are too busy trying to prove that they deserve you! The playing-hard-to-get rule has some merit in it. Of course, this is not always true, but it offers a good explanation for why people often seem to go out with those who don't always treat them well. The well-known phrase "treat them mean, keep them keen," has plenty of truth in it.

I considered how many of the single people I had met had described their feelings. I remember many chats I'd had on nights out with single friends as a drunken loneliness filled the air. As a single person, if you are without a card on a day like Valentine's Day, you often can't help wondering why. You look around again and see all the happy couples doing everything together, including most of your friends.

There are lots of people who are just happy to play the field and are in singles' paradise. I have a young friend, Richie, who is great when it comes to flirting and seduction. Whenever I go out with him, he charms girls. He doesn't always succeed, but he never stops trying, and he finds the whole process easy. Some people don't find that kind of life as easy as he does. For others, it's not the kind of life that they want.

For many people, going out and playing the field is great for a time, at least. But the enjoyment doesn't last forever. Meanwhile, as you go out with many different people, there's always the danger that you'll fall for one—I say danger because it's a "complex web we weave" as Shakespeare would say, when what started as fun becomes much more important to us, or to them. If you manage to stay disconnected and just "have some fun," then you will one day have to come face to face with the fact that there will be a time when you can no longer do it.

Often, when people are single they ask, "Why me? What's wrong with me?" The bottom line, however, is that the answer is simply, "Because that's just the way it is." Everyone could find someone to go out with, if they could just go out and meet people and ask them out. You'd definitely find people to go out with, but you might not necessarily like them or get on with them. The whole point of holding out is to achieve this wonderful aliveness of meeting the "right person." The good news is that there is no single "right person." There are a few that would suit you perfectly.

I like the idea of Cupid because I think it makes more sense somehow than the "soul mate" idea—Jack and Rose on the Titanic, Romeo and Juliet. These couples seem to suggest that a person's soul mate does exist. But, realistically, the idea that there are a variety of people that you meet in your life and that you could fall for any of them if Cupid shoots his arrow is actually a more reasonable one. They are all potential soul mates because they could potentially fit you and your spirit and your soul. (Please note: I'm not saying Cupid exists or doesn't exist. I'm simply saying it's a useful metaphor for explaining the stories of love.)

The scientific explanation of falling in love is much less romantic but is similar in nature. In evolutionary terms, we become attracted to those who have an immune system that complements our own. We sense this through our sense of smell, through tiny little chemicals given off by the other person known as pheromones. This is complemented by our past experiences in which we have developed certain preferences and attraction for particular kinds of people. In a given context, we build on this attraction by engaging in thought processes that help us fall in love. These thought processes result in chemical changes in the brain as chemicals, such as phenylethylamine (PEA) and oxytocin, are released, giving us a powerfully strong high. Again, however, it is only particular people that we can feel this way for.

Now with this in mind, if you are single, fear not. Valentine's Day need not be torture anymore. Every year, I always send a card and sometimes flowers to someone I know who is single, and I do so anonymously. I do so if I think this person won't be getting any other cards. When my focus is on making someone else feel good rather than feeling bad about myself, I feel much happier. It's also a day to fall back in love with yourself (in a nonnarcissistic way, I might add!). When you think about a day of love, you must use it to express your gratitude and love for the most important person in your life—you!

This doesn't mean send yourself a million cards or get yourself flowers. It means something more important—stopping to recognize who you are, how you are improving, and how much love you have to give. It means being aware of the mistakes you've made in relationships and promising never to make them again, and focusing on all the wonderful qualities you could bring to a relationship and all the wonderful reasons someone would be exceptionally lucky to be with you. I promise you, there are lots of reasons.

I have always been a hopeless romantic. Now I feel I have become a hopeful romantic. It's not about being perfect in relationships or flirting and so on, it's about stopping and being aware of your brilliance, and your potential brilliance. It's about working on yourself to make you more of who you really are at your best. It's about using your brain to make yourself feel as amazing as possible as often as possible. Like attracts like—it's a law of the universe. So as Richard suggests, feel wonderful and you will attract wonderful people to you. The best way we can do this is to really enjoy living.

Enjoying living involves really responding to life: letting life touch you, letting ourselves fall in love, losing ourselves in music, surrendering to the emotions of a movie. We find ourselves most when we are truly lost—lost in music, lost in art, lost in sport, lost in performing, lost in conversing, lost in loving, lost in being, lost in the moment. In those times of losing ourselves, it is so easy to find ourselves. In such moments of surrender, we really live. We are also at our most attractive when we lose all self-consciousness and become absorbed in the moment. Then, hopefully, the right person will come along. Of course, luck is a part of it, but there are many ways to meet the right person, and there is more than one right person out there to meet.

In today's world, many of us are searching for the perfect partner, perfect career, perfect car, perfect life. There is no such thing. Everyone has flaws. Everything has flaws. It's about finding a partner whom you love, a job that you love, a car that you love, a life that you love. You can see a few things on a menu that you love, and you can choose one. Idealizing over the perfect meal will always lead to disappointment. Our imaginations can conceive of more good and bad that exists; that is our real power. What's essential is to look for a partner whom you connect with and can feel great with, a career that makes you feel great, a car that feels great to drive, a life that feels great to live.

When you are focused on feeling good and making other people feel good, you will get on far better with people. When the desire to make other people feel good is your intention instead of needing them to like you,

you'll make friends easily, and you'll make people more attracted to you. People love being in the presence of someone who makes them feel good about themselves.

Bryan went up to the cute blonde at the bar and delivered his compliment. She smiled in surprise, and he made his exit. She mumbled, "Thank you," and as he walked away, although he could not see, I could see how she looked at him. Her night was made, and he was all of a sudden far more attractive to her. What's more, Bryan had walked away, and he had learned the concept I had been trying to get him to master: if you want to get what you want, you need to let go of neediness.

He had walked away when his instinct was to try to "hang on" in case she showed any interest. His focus changed from giving a compliment for what it might lead to, to how it would make the other person feel, and that led him to get back to the self that he was, who needed nothing outside him to make his life worthwhile.

Bryan was a lovely guy, and I was delighted to help him. A couple of days after we finished filming the program, he got his first kiss in four years, and a couple of months later he began going out with a lovely lady he met all by himself. We still stay in touch. He describes what we went through as him being given back his life. In reality, it was only about him changing his focus in a variety of ways and, from there, the answers appeared.

You see, love is not a measure of a person's worth. It is an experience that exists in the world—probably the most powerful experience. To make it happen for you, to find the right person as a single, the key is to begin by loving yourself. Become the kind of person whom you would be pleased to introduce to any potential partner. How do you love yourself? It is simple. Start by being nice to yourself inside your head and being nice to others in the world. Then get out there and meet people. When you least expect it—whether an old flame, a new work associate, a friend of a friend, a complete stranger, or someone right in front of you—you'll find someone with whom you feel a connection.

You'll find yourself feeling really great when you are with this person, you'll spend hours talking together without getting bored, you'll feel like he or she understands you more than anyone else, you'll look forward to your time together, you'll feel like you know this person and can touch his or her soul. He or she will be one of your soul mates and hopefully your fairy tale will finish with the words "happily ever after"—and if it doesn't, then start again until you write it yourself.

I came to and realized that while I had been considering all of this inside my head, Richard was smiling at me, a cup of coffee in his hand, his eyebrows raised, and awaiting my next question.

RB: Got caught inside your head a bit, Owen, did you?

I smiled.

OF: Yeah, but I'm back now. Where was my next question?

I muttered to myself as I racked my brains to find my next question. "Eh . . . uh . . . em . . . I know it's here somewhere. Oh, yes," I smiled. "It's about good communication."

CHAPTER 37

The Art of
Good Communication

BRIAN COLBERT, my good friend and training partner, has fantastic communication skills especially in a business environment. He is one of the best negotiators I have ever seen in action. He knows how to get people to do things—quickly. On the other hand, Brian always laughs at my ability to talk people into things in everyday life. You see, I'm the kind of person who will take my chances in all sorts of situations. From talking policemen out of traffic tickets to convincing airline staff to reopen the boarding gate when it is closed, I always seem to manage to convince people to do things they ordinarily wouldn't do. Well, not always, but most of the time!

Me and my buddy and cotrainer Brian Colbert.

Many people assume I learned this from my training in hypnosis, but in reality there is one major secret to how I manage all of this: I pay attention to every interaction as if I were the other person. I always try to look at every situation in which I want to be effective from the other person's point of view. That way, I can better adapt my communication in the most effective way. Before doing this, as we have already explained, ensure that you are in a good state yourself. Then, what else is important? The way you walk, talk, and use gestures and the language you use all affect how other people perceive you.

I had jotted down in my notebook to ask Richard about basic communication skills, but I wanted to be more specific with him. I had a number of exercises that I found helped people improve in this area. A good way to practice your communication skills is to present yourself to a video camera, or even to the mirror, and talk away in imaginary contexts. As you do, you'll discover how you come across.

You will notice certain things you do well and certain things you don't do well. This will enable you to become aware of your natural habits of communication and will help you to deliberately improve how you come across to others. Practice walking in different ways, saying hello in different ways, smiling in different ways. Watch people who are brilliant socially and model them. Do what they do. Smile like they smile. Shake hands like they shake hands. This will help you become more effective socially.

I present a course called the Art of Charisma in which I teach people how to communicate more charismatically. The key is to get them to practice trying out new things and finding out how that makes them come across. It is also about being aware of how their communication affects other people. The ability to pay attention to other people and how you are making them feel is an essential quality that makes you great at doing many things, from how you perform as a comedian to how you perform in bed. It is all about the same thing—learning how to make other people feel really good and being aware of how your behavior affects them.

I considered the various elements of social communication and what I felt was one of the most important: tone of voice. I found that a person's tone of voice is one of the most critical factors that gains interest from another person, and that it is one of the most important tools out there that can be used to change a person's internal state.

OF: I found that, in communicating, your tone of voice is extremely important. Do you have any suggestions on how people can improve the use of their tone of voice?

RB: I do have a suggestion. It's a really primitive one. I would use "listening," and changing your body position, and taking some voice lessons. People have been teaching voice for years. Go get yourself a voice coach. Learn to project your voice. Learn to make higher notes, lower notes, deeper tones, and richer tones. Variation is what real learning is about. The more variation you can make in your voice tone, the more accents you can do, and the more flexibility in your voice you will have.

In my trainers' training, I always teach people to do five or ten different accents. Learn to talk like a Texan, like somebody from New York; speak with a Spanish accent or a German accent or a French accent, and make it sound silly and exaggerated so that you can improve your tone of voice, because the more variation you have, the more control you will have. This is not just true about your tone of voice but variety also helps your sexual performance.

I listened to Richard's voice. It was hypnotic. I recalled all the training sessions I'd been to, with him as teacher. He could keep an audience of 500 people captivated for a few hours without anyone moving. Tone of voice is so important because it enables you to tell your stories and capture people's imagination more dynamically. When you use your tone of voice more expansively, you enrich the quality of your communication massively. Your "tone of face," in other words, your facial expressions, will help you use different kinds of tonality to produce powerful changes in how you affect other people.

Make your own tone of voice interesting to listen to. Make your gestures and facial expressions expressive. Remember the art of good communication is your ability to express yourself well. Practice telling stories over and over again in such a way that you make them more intriguing to listen to. Pay attention to the rate at which you talk, and talk more slowly to people who talk slowly to you, and faster to people who speak quickly to you. Begin to be aware of how you are communicating in the world and how you can improve it.

As well as expressing yourself more effectively, bear in mind how people think when you communicate. Since we think in the five senses, the more you begin to use all five senses in constructing experiences for people, the more vivid and real the experiences will be. I have a saying that people don't fall in love with facts about you but they fall in love with the way you tell your stories. Remember, every time you communicate, it's not about how you can express yourself and your thoughts; it's about how you affect those around you. If you want to be successful, you have to learn how you can affect those around you powerfully and positively.

Good communication is about presenting information clearly, taking in information easily, and affecting other people with your words, gestures, and voice. I resolved to make my own communication skills even better, as my mind drifted to something else that I had momentarily forgotten.

The concepts of failure and rejection caused more hesitation and absolute fear in so many of the clients I have worked with. Both of these concepts must be dealt with before I even considered exploring more about love, friendship, and relationships.

CHAPTER 38

Rejecting Rejection and Failure

ONCE YOU HAVE DEVELOPED an irresistible tone of voice and improved how you communicate with others, the next step is to go out there and meet people. Unfortunately, fear usually holds most people back. They hesitate because of what I consider to be the two biggest fears of social freedom: the fears of failure and rejection. These are the two things that I've found hold most people back from achieving success in their lives. I talked with Richard about them.

OF: The fear of failure and fear of rejection seem to be two of the biggest things that hold people back from doing well in life. We seem to learn about failure in school, and I've found that many of the teachers I have worked with have a huge fear of failure themselves.

Richard interjected.

RB: People who fear failure are the very people who should never be teachers. I mean to me, if I was going to qualify who should be a teacher or not, it would be to find people who did not have a fear of failure.

This was an interesting point. I knew that many teachers, since they taught in the school system, had constantly been working from the principle of pass and failure. What surprised me was that it was possible for them to change their view radically in a short space of time. Many of the teachers I worked with, when they turned around their perspective on the notion of "failure," reported a dramatic improvement in how they taught their students.

OF: So with that in mind, how do you help someone who has a fear of failure?

RB: I just take the feeling and spin it backward, because if you have a fear of failure, think about how complicated it is. To have a fear of failure, first you have to know when to fail, so you have to set up a thing that says, "This is when I'm going to feel bad."

OF: In fact, the rules for how we are going to feel in response to the events of the world determine many of our fears and bad feelings. Just as you say "disappointment requires adequate planning," so does failure. When we can change the way we define failure and the rules we hold about it, we gain freedom from the fear. Is the same true for rejection?

RB: Yes, but most people can be rejected before they even talk to a person. They look at somebody, and they look away, and they think, "I'm rejected," making a picture of themselves talking to that person. I mean they take any behavior whatsoever and make it so that they can be rejected on the widest range of possibilities. Instead of interpreting all behaviors as successes, they interpret all behaviors as failures and so set up a fear of failure and make everything so that it says, "I failed." This means that they actually don't test their own theories, and if they didn't set this up in the first place, they would be free.

I work to make people free. I don't work to make people so that they live up to a bunch of pictures they don't need in the first place. I mean, I want people to be truly free. I want them, when they look at somebody, to think, "I feel like talking to that person," and so they walk over and say hello. And then, if the person is an asshole, they can walk away, and if the person is nice, they keep talking to him or her.

It's so much simpler than people make it out to be. And when people come in and say, "I have a fear of failure." I respond by saying, "Please put it in the top drawer and take out one of the other things."

They then say, "What are you talking about?" And I continue, "Excuse me, you're the one who said you had it. You know, you're talking about it as a thing, not me. Okay, how do you know when to have a fear of failure? Because you don't do it all the time. You have to plan it in advance. Do you sit in bed at night and make lists, so you can know when to feel bad?"

What a waste of time. You know how many hours a day some of these people spend planning so that they know when to feel bad? Worse than that, people who fear rejection feel bad while they're talking to people and they're not good at communicating, because they don't actually know when they failed and when they didn't. For example, when a woman looks away and twirls her hair, they would know she's enticing them not rejecting them.

These things I have to tell men because they know nothing about women. A woman comes out wearing a dress and carrying a dress and asks, "Which one do you like best?" and guys start thinking about it, like they're fashion designers. Excuse me, if someone just wants to be complimented, just compliment her and leave it at that. It's simple. You have to learn the magic words that make all relationships work, "Yes, dear."

OF: That also seems to be something we could learn about. Have you any advice on how people can learn to understand the opposite sex better?

RB: Well, I don't think they have to understand them. I think they need to appreciate them. Women are different from men and men become mad at them for not being more like men. Why do you think gay guys get on so well? Your choice is to become gay or like women for the way they are, and not for the way they are not. Women like to do different things than men do. You have got to accept it, or you won't spend much time with them. I have been married for a long time, and that's because I have always enjoyed it.

I let this sink in. What we need to do is reject the concept of rejection and fail to accept failure. This comes with understanding what these concepts really mean. To be rejected means that someone said no to you in some way to a request you had. To fail is that you didn't do something that you wanted to do or achieve something you wanted to achieve.

First, if you realize failure only exists when you put a time limit on achieving something, you can take every result you get, good or bad, as simply information that lets you know what to do next time. So this means that you will never fail again because your rules for failure are that it only exists when you accept it.

OF: So if you take the concept of rejection and realize that whenever anyone says no to your book, or a date, or your job application, all that means is that, in their opinion, you weren't right for them at that point in time. They don't know the truth. All they have is their opinion, which is based upon how they feel toward you and what they think about you with their limited knowledge and understanding and their limited experience with you.

When you can accept that this is what's actually happening, you can realize that you can reject rejection and understand that it's not about you but about what's going on inside the other person's head, and you can learn from the experience, so the next time you have a better chance of succeeding. It's important to appreciate that people will have different opinions and preferences than you have and to enjoy this quality in them. Is that it?

Richard smiled and nodded as if to say like he often did, "You got it, kid." I smiled. I was ready to move on. It was not just rejection and failure that I felt were stumbling blocks in the world of communication. I also wanted Richard's insight into how to deal better with difficult people. As usual, his wisdom explained a lot.

CHAPTER 39

Sticks and Stones and Words That Hurt

I REMEMBER BEING absolutely terrified. The shoelace was held around my throat. "I'm gonna choke you now unless you say it." I couldn't breath. I felt it tighten around my throat. "I'm gonna choke you, Fitzpatrick. Say it. Say it NOW." I tried grabbing his hands, but he was too strong for me. He was a few years older, and I was just eleven. I watched as his friends on their bikes laughed, though they looked a little concerned. "Come on, Fitzer, say the word 'fuck.' Say it now."

I never did say it, and eventually he let me go. That was not the first time, nor was it the last. The final time it was a knife to my throat. I used to be terrified of running into him.

You see, when I was younger, I didn't curse. In fact, I wouldn't curse. I got taunted for this often in school, and many kids made my life hell. It was pretty stupid, when I think of it, making such a big deal over stupid words. It was exactly like Socrates refusing to denounce his teachings and preferring to take poison (except, obviously, for the whole death thing!). I was stubborn, and I got myself in lots of trouble because of it.

They were only words, and I didn't realize it at the time. What can I say? It was stupid. I was just a kid. My mum used to say to me, "Sticks and stones may break your bones, but names will never hurt you." I only figured it out years later. She was right—names and words only have the impact we let them have.

In some of our training sessions, we will use profanity because we are expressing ourselves in a particular way. If you feel hurt or offended or uncomfortable when you hear a "bad" word, then it is your response to that word that is the problem. Words are not "bad." They never were. It is simply that we have attached and associated negative feelings to certain words.

I always explain this with a simple example. If I say the words, "I hate you," I believe that is "bad." If I say the words, "I fucking love you," I believe that is "good." Every word has a meaning in context, and once we all get smarter about this, maybe we can stop being scared of words and focus on saying nice things to ourselves and each other more often, instead of trying to censor the world. What is sad is that some people will be turned off reading this book because there are "bad" words in it. It's pitiful that people's fear of words can trap them so completely.

I met the guy who used to bully me with the knife, in a bar almost fifteen years after we had last met. Initially, I felt a negative feeling toward him, and then I just let it go as I realized he may have moved on. I was now taller and bigger than him. We said hello, made some small talk, and that was it. I had no need for revenge because I knew that he had probably moved on from where he was, and I had, too. It's essential to remember that you can deal with those who bully you or attempt to intimidate you more successfully. I asked Richard about this.

OF: How can you learn to deal with others, who say nasty things to you, more usefully?

RB: Well, you have two choices. One is a baseball bat, and the other is to realize that they're just words. If you don't think you can avoid a fight, then you should start it before the other person is ready.

I remember being in the Deep South, and people were hassling me about being a Jew and talking about how they hung Jews down there. What they didn't realize is that I was holding something under the table, and I had it ready under my jacket while they sat at the table. And I realized at that moment that I could just get angry and hurt these people, and I could hurt every one of them. I had the ability. There were only four of them.

The only thing that would make me do that is if they made me feel bad, and I stopped and thought, "These people are so ignorant. How can I possibly take anything they say and turn it into a bad feeling?" So I just started playing happy music in my head, and they were saying all the same things. It started to sound like a silly song. I just smiled; then one of them said, "You're a coward. That's right. Born and bred a coward," as I listened to the music.

One guy said, "Well I don't know if I should beat you up or not." And I said, "You really shouldn't, because I'm not good at it. If you beat me up, I'd get hurt." He stepped forward, leaned over the table, and grabbed hold of me, and as he grabbed me, I opened my coat, and all he could see was what I had sticking in his throat. I smiled and said, "I'm terribly afraid that one of us is going to get hurt." I always remember how he got up and said, "I think we should leave now." The other guys were asking, "What about that Jew?" and he said, "Well, maybe we should just go get us a beer." I said, "I'll buy you guys a beer," and I got up and bought them each a beer. It was easier to buy them a beer than it was to hurt them.

Most of the time people use bad tonality when they become angry with their kids. It's ludicrous to get angry with your kids. It doesn't make any sense. If you yell at your kids, you shouldn't feel any anger. You should yell at them because you feel it will help to accomplish something. You should always be thinking about the moment they were born and how you felt and what you want to teach them and finding good ways to teach them the things you think are important. Making bad feelings inside of them isn't going to be helpful most of the time.

I began to think about the people I had known in my life over the years whom I had felt intimidated by. I noticed that nobody intimidated me anymore since I had been learning from Richard.

OF: So how can you protect yourself from really aggressive people?

RB: People who are really aggressive? There is no easy way to deal with them when they outnumber you. They are like dogs in a pack. The best thing to do is to get the hell out of there, and if you can't get the hell out of there, then you just have to deal with it. Sometimes violence on this planet is unavoidable. If you see it coming, you should get out of the way before it starts.

Most people just stick around too long, and things get far too out of hand. It's really better just to avoid it. When I was a musician, I was stuck in bars where I didn't necessarily want to be for years, and these chumps tried everything under the sun to create problems. We were more like an army than a band. We played in all these rough places. We had all met in a dojo. If we beat someone up, we weren't going to be any better off. That's the bottom line. What you learn as you get older is that it doesn't matter how many fights you're in if everybody gets hurt.

Hearing Richard say that the best way to deal with people who try to start fights is to walk away was something I didn't really expect, but it made absolute sense. He was talking about walking away from a fight not because of fear but because of intelligence. He was talking about having the freedom to feel comfortable enough with a person to be able to guard against their attempts to manipulate you. Instead, you do what you need to do of your own accord.

OF: So does that include dealing with mental bullies?

RB: You bet it does. The fact that people feel the need to bully someone else is just a reflection of their own weakness. People try to bully me intellectually; I just smile at them, and it pisses them off, and the more it pisses them off, the more I look at them and say, "Look, you got two choices: you can back off, or we can go for it. It doesn't matter to me. If you're going to intellectually mess with me, you will discover I'm the wrong person to be screwing with."

I can make people sane, and I know how to make people totally insane, but that's not the goal in life. The goal in life is to find out how to avoid those people and find the ones who are nice—and to spend as much time with the nice people as possible. You have got to pay me to work with the others.

Everything was becoming so simple. The secret was to realize that no one really has any power over you unless you let them, and regardless of how they attempt to get to you, if you refuse to let them, you are free. If Viktor Frankl could go through what he went through in that concentration camp and still feel he had the freedom of mind to choose his own attitude in any given set of circumstances, then you, too, have that freedom. It's about having the freedom to feel in control and at the same time walk away if it's the smartest thing to do. That way, those who try to get to you, can't, and you'll be living life your own way.

I remembered an experience I had in New Zealand as I walked back from the cinema in the center of Christchurch. I was on my way back to the hostel I was staying in. I was walking over an overpass. It was deserted and dark, about eleven o'clock at night. Someone shouted from under the overpass, "Hey, you! Got any spare change?" As I was in the middle of texting someone back home, I simply shouted down, "No, sorry, mate." From below he called again, "Hey! Give me some spare change, you bastard."

Without even thinking I shouted back, "Ah, get lost." I continued to walk and noticed that there were no cars at all in sight and no other people around either. It was extremely quiet, and as I put my phone back in my pocket, I heard footsteps running on the pavement behind me, getting closer and closer. I turned and saw this young lad around twenty, a little taller than me, running directly for me. He wore a tight gray T-shirt and blue jeans. He began to shout abuse and threats as he neared. I considered my options.

I thought of fighting or running, but I was too tired to do either. I had been on a long journey that day. Then I thought of a third option. As he neared to within twenty feet I walked toward him with a smile and out-stretched hand. In shock, he stopped, and after a moment of confusion, he took my hand. I put one hand on his shoulder as I shook his hand and asked him, "What the hell are you doing running after me trying to pick a fight, my friend?" Completely shocked, he mumbled, "Eh, I wasn't." A few minutes later he had his head down, ashamed, as he listened to me. For the next ten minutes I talked to him about his life and his problems and gave him different pieces of advice. It was a fascinating conversation, and I hope that, in some way, I got through to him. When I left him, he seemed a lot more focused and knew what he had to do. I never saw him again.

It always interested me how words could have such an impact upon people. I was curious particularly about the notion of "bad" words. In some of our seminars, people have complained occasionally about our use of language. I asked Richard about this.

OF: I have found there are a few people in the world who get offended by profanity and certain words that are regarded as being offensive. Have you any thoughts on this?

RB: Well, that's a fucking shame, isn't it? The fact that some people can get so upset by a word when it's just a sound sequence is ridiculous. These words aren't even the same in different languages. What we do is take a word and decide that we are going to feel bad about it. Take the word "Mick." Sometimes it's some person's name, and sometimes it's slang about the Irish. The word "kike" is a slang word for Jews. People then decide that when they hear this they are going to feel bad.

So a bunch of people get together and say a word in bad tonality, but it's the tonality of words that make people feel bad, and if you let a whole lot of words make you feel bad, then you're doing something stupid. I can go through and get that to change in a cold second.

As Richard explained, the tonality is what makes the difference when you use words with people. Words are just words, and they rely on the meaning we give them. What is important is that we recognize that they do not have any power over us. I thought about what I had heard that caused much disorder and disagreement—the rap songs that discussed sex, drugs, death, and murder. I wondered how Richard felt about such songs.

OF: What about rappers who use these words? Some people say that they have a bad affect on the listeners.

RB: I don't really listen to rappers. If they're saying bad things on records, then it doesn't really matter to me. I believe in free speech. I think that if we don't make fun of it, then kids will take it seriously. Saying that it would lead to violence over and over again is probably going to be more destructive than what is on the tapes, because when you start to hypnotize people saying, "This makes this happen," then it probably will. The last thing this country needs is the government advertising these rap songs and saying that listening to them will turn you into a criminal.

It's kind of ironic. They're saying that, "Saying things makes bad things happen," and they're saying a bad thing; therefore, they're making it happen in a way. To me, it's paradoxical. It's just like the insecure person who is very secure in his or her opinion about that one thing. There's always a paradoxical level. People who suffer from uncertainty are absolutely sure about it, and the people who are out there listening to bad language or bad things said or watching TV programs with the idea that "violence makes bad things happen" are going to end up saying something horrible, much worse than what is being said now.

They're saying all this artificial stuff is going to become real, which is the biggest nightmare that you could possibly say, and that if they believe that saying things made it true, they wouldn't be saying this out loud. So, here's the paradox, what they really should do if they believe what they're saying is shut up, because they are doing the biggest disservice of all. So, to me, this is always the paradox. To me, the real essence of how we evolve as human beings is where we find the point of paradox, and we change the subject.

I liked this perspective. To me, the idea of censorship never really worked. In fact, it often made people more likely to try to get their hands on the music. Instead, the trick was to get people to laugh at it. What always struck me when I saw any of these rappers being interviewed was that they were just like some of the stand-up comics I have seen and listened to.

They were expressing some brutally true things about the world, with exaggeration, in a humorous way. They were not afraid of words, and they got a kick out of provoking the conservative traditionalists. If we could only learn to laugh at these songs like the rappers do and teach our children to do the same, then maybe the world wouldn't be so full of violence, because we would be changing the mentality of our culture and not simply trying to deny what exists out there. Laughter enables us to escape the negative pain and suffering that exists through taking things seriously.

CHAPTER 40

The Art of Good Friendship

I REALLY ENJOYED spending time with Richard and Paula. To me, our conversations were great because of the obvious good fortune I had in learning answers to life's most fascinating questions. Separate from this, they had become good friends. As I thought this, I asked Richard about friendship.

OF: I want to talk about friendship for a bit. What do you consider to be the qualities of a good friend?

RB: Start with honesty and loyalty. That's what a good friend is. A good friend is loyal above and beyond all things. To me, that's what makes a good friend. There are friends and good friends. John LaValle is my good friend and always will be because I know I can depend upon John anytime, anywhere, for anything on this planet, and he knows I'll do the same. If I'm capable of it, I'll do it, and I won't ask why. He doesn't have to explain it to me. He doesn't have to justify it to me. It is what we've always done for each other because that's what good friends do.

They don't expect or need an explanation. They just need to know what you need, and they provide it if they can, and if they can't, they're honest about the fact that they can't. That's why the mafia worked so much better than the government. These people were family and friends, and they were loyal above all things. That's why they would have wiped the government out if it wasn't for the government cheating—I mean by electronic surveillance and basically inventing laws so they could put people in prison. They could never beat the mafia. They had to invent income-tax evasion because they couldn't convict anybody of a crime.

I smiled. I thought of John LaValle. I knew what John was like, and Richard had described him perfectly. John and his wife, Kathleen, have always been terrific examples of loyalty and friendship. They are excellent role models whom I feel glad to consider as friends. I thought about some of my own closest friends. I realized that, despite the fact that they were all radically different and unique, they all demonstrated the qualities I valued so much: loyalty, honesty, integrity, love, generosity, and kindness. I began to feel immensely grateful for knowing these people and being so close to them. I knew that if I ever needed something, my closest friends would be there for me. Indeed, when I went through my toughest times, they were there for me when I needed them the most. They had all contributed so much in my life.

At that point, it was time for a break, and we went outside and walked around for a bit. I began to think about my own life. I thought about the people I was close to. I have the most wonderful friends. I have my best friends from home. I have my best male and female friends. I have friends I've made from the courses I've been in and ones I've taught. I have friends from the soccer team and friends from my travels. I have friends I met randomly and just connected with. I have friends from all over the world.

I have friends I can say anything to and those who just make me laugh. I have friends I go out with regularly and those I meet a few times a year. I have friends who do the same kind of things as I do and friends who have little in common with me but whose company I enjoy. I have friends I'll spend hours talking to and friends I can sit beside for hours feeling comfortable with not a word between us. I have friends who make me laugh with whom I am at my best and friends for whom I enjoy being the butt of their jokes.

My closest friends all hold loyalty as being an extremely high value in life. People like Eddie, Dave, and Brian all value this trait. No matter what, we always do our very best to come through for each other. So how did I manage to make such wonderful friends? How come I was so lucky? Then I realized it wasn't about luck. It was about making connections and keeping them. It was about being friendly toward people and building friendships with them. You have to do things for yourself to have wonderful friends. You have to demonstrate these qualities and make an effort to do nice things.

I have met people randomly in bars and met people in courses, and sometimes we've just connected and gone on to become friends. Some people think it's strange to make friends like that, but I have a different philosophy. Some people I really enjoy being around and some I don't. By making the effort to spend time in touch with people I have met and gotten to like, I get to experience the delights of having many friends. If everyone comes into your life for a reason, you may as well stay in touch with them as long as it works for you and find out what the reason is.

To me, the art of being a good friend is being a good friend in different ways to different friends. It means making your friends laugh, smile, and feel good about themselves when they are around you. It means being interested in them and listening to them and finding out how they are doing. It means respecting them on the same level as yourself. It means sharing your experiences, stories, and feelings with them. It means letting them know, whenever you can, how much they mean to you and that you love them.

It means staying in touch with them as often as possible. It means getting in touch sometimes for no other reason than just to check how they are and to let them know they are in your thoughts. It means doing nice things for them when you can and being there for them when possible when they need you.

My friend Gillian once sent me a note all the way from Australia when I was going through a tough time in my life. It was a note from a dear friend sending the nicest wishes and love for me to help me through this time. I was touched. To me, it was the best gesture of friendship I had ever experienced. It's so amazing to know that someone cares and that no matter where they are on the planet, they are there for you. I thought of all the brilliant friends in my life who care for me so much. I felt so lucky again. I realized that friendship comes from the heart and manifests itself in the way you treat those you love.

My family is so wonderful, and I have had the opportunity to express to them how I feel about them. My Mum, Dad, sister, and my extended family and cousins all know how I feel about them. By your family, I mean the closest friends you have, not just your blood relatives. It's not just about always being perfect and nice to them, but it is crucial that those closest to you understand that you love them and are inspired by them. It's important that you treat them well and are grateful to them for being in your life. That way, you can properly enjoy the wonderful merits of good friendship.

By that stage, as we chatted about the weather and cows in the field nearby, I began to recall what I was most interested in finding out from Richard. I still had the most important questions left to ask. My recent experiences had been very chaotic, and I needed Richard's advice.

CHAPTER 41

"How Come We Don't Even Talk No More?"

PEOPLE COME INTO our lives and they leave. I believe that sometimes friendships need to end. Sometimes friendships are right for a certain point in your life. You are there for the people in your life for a certain reason, and they are there for you. Whatever that reason is, it happens to help you in some way.

I'm the kind of guy who has found it hard to break away from a friend, regardless of circumstances. Being pretty nostalgic, I would always try to save a friendship at all costs. At the same time, I know many people who will stubbornly cut off all contact with others if they feel hurt or betrayed by them. Neither way is really the secret to dealing with people when your friendship is affected. I knew that Richard had had many friends over the years and that many of them had turned on him and treated him terribly.

I had had a falling out with a friend of mine a few months earlier. I felt hurt and betrayed. I knew that if anyone could help me, Richard could.

OF: Over the years, Richard, you have had friendships with many people. Many of them have stolen from you, betrayed you, cheated you, and bad-mouthed you. How do you deal with people in your life when things change and something bad goes on between you?

RB: Well, the trick is to realize that every day you meet someone, it is like you are meeting them for the first time. Therefore, even though you've known someone for three months, and he or she has been a good person, it doesn't mean that person won't be an asshole the next time you meet. People's modus operandi changes, their beliefs change, and their ideas change, and what we know about thresholds tells us that once something goes through threshold, it's never the same.

Many people go through thresholds, and once they go through a threshold, their morals change; their values change. They may have good values, but then as soon as something happens, which has nothing to do with you, everything changes—the way in which they interact with you, their willingness to steal from you, their willing-ness to criticize (whether or not they're grateful for what they've gotten from you), the way in which they treat their families, the way they treat their children, the way they treat their spouses—everything else changes so that you have to keep your eyes and ears open to be aware when somebody becomes an asshole and to stop hanging around with them.

People notice when someone has changed and is no longer a good person, but they keep expecting the person to change back. The truth is that if somebody is treating you badly, that's the time to stop it. If people don't change back immediately, they're probably not going to. People are either getting better or they're getting worse, and once they're getting worse, they are not going to stop and start getting bet-ter just because you want it to be that way.

OF: So what do we do with people who have gone through such a threshold?

RB: It's better to stay away from them, and if they come back and start apologizing and talking about, "Well I had a drug problem," or "I was off my rocker," or something, just ignore them and realize the time you spent with them wasn't a lie; it's just that they've changed. People change for the better, and people change for the worse—and to expect otherwise is to do nothing but feel like an idiot when you weren't really one.

I don't feel bad, even though there are people whose lives and fortunes are based upon what I taught them and who do nothing but criticize me and steal from me. The thing is that, the time I was working with them, they were working on becoming better people, and then their lives changed and turned them into idiots. That's not my fault; they became idiots by themselves, and if they keep being idiots, they'll pay the price themselves.

I sat back and let this sink in. I had never thought about things like this. It made so much sense. I was curious about what Richard meant when he talked about ignoring people. Did he mean forgive them? I asked him.

OF: So what do you think about forgiveness then?

RB: I don't deal with the concept of forgiveness. I don't have to forgive people for what they do because I either forget about it because they've stopped and are doing other things, or I remember it so that I don't get taken again. To say that I have to forgive somebody means that I have to do something.

If you screw up, why should I have to do something? If you screw up, you should have to do something. It's not about me forgiving you. If you do things that are better than what you were doing, then I'll forget about what you did. I am not going to go through some act of forgiveness, and I think this whole forgiveness thing comes out of Christian nonsense.

That people should be forgiven without actually changing, that you go in to the priest, and he says, "Okay, your sins are forgiven," well, God may forgive you, but he doesn't forget; you still have to go afterward and do something better, and I'm the same way. To me, if you change your behavior and start good behaviors, I'll forget any previous bad behavior.

OF: How do you do this?

RB: You don't think about it. You think about the good things people do. But if people continue with bad behaviors, I'll remember them all. But I'm still not going to feel bad about it, because I'm not going to feel bad because you made mistakes. That's one of the problems people have. People say, "Oh, he hurt my feelings; therefore, I have to forgive him." I think that's nonsense and to even think about it is nonsense.

I don't think about what people did to me in the past. People bring it up, and I'll think about it, but I don't think about it often. There's no point worrying about it. They're the ones who screwed up, not me; therefore, they're the ones who should have to do something. I think that's wrong that I have to say, "I forgive you," so that they can feel okay when they screwed me. I don't participate in it, and I don't bring up things to feel bad about unnecessarily.

If they try to make me feel bad, they make themselves feel worse every day. That's the way I think about it. I can't think of any punishment worse than to actually be someone like them. I think it's a thing that takes care of itself. I can be so much happier with so much less. I make new ideas, and I know their minds. They have to lie to themselves; I don't.

It struck me that what Richard described as "forgetting" was similar to my notion of "forgiving." You see, as I listened to him, I agreed with what he was describing, but I couldn't help but remember that, when I forgave people who had hurt me in my life, I felt much better. Then it suddenly occurred to me. My concept of "forgiving" is to make peace in my head with people and let them go. It involves being aware of what they did and what they are doing now. I won't carry around bad feelings or resentment toward them, but I won't do the act of telling them it's all right when it is not.

My notion of "forgiveness" is not "Your sins are forgiven. You now have a clean slate." Instead, I simply realize that everyone has a different perception of reality and that, sometimes, people do the wrong thing because they just act stupidly, and sometimes they do the wrong thing because they change their values after reaching that threshold Richard talked about. When they do, it's often necessary to cut them loose and become free from them.

As Richard explained, it doesn't mean your time with them was bad or a lie—it just means that it's over now, and it's time to move on. Then with freedom from thoughts of them, you can move on, and if they start doing good things again in the future, then maybe you will have a connection with them once again, and maybe not.

I don't believe in bitterness. One of the gurus I met in India told me, "Everyone is on a journey. Most people don't mean any harm, really. They are just lost souls." We are all just going around doing the best we can, and one day we will die. Therefore, what is the point of holding a grudge? What is the point of holding awkwardness and hurt between you? There is none. You can learn from the behavior of people you love. And you can move on when a friendship is over. I believe in letting bygones be bygones because, as Richard says, "The best thing about the past is that it's over." We are all human and will make mistakes.

Similarly, sometimes we will make mistakes, and it is us who will do wrong. We will all hurt people without meaning to and will all take out our own hurts on others occasionally. It's wrong, but we're not perfect, and it's more important to focus on doing good things instead of feeling bad about what you did. Guilt serves a function. It is there to let you know that you did something that you feel was wrong, so that you can decide to do better things in the future. You only need the signal, not the emotion taking over your life. Once you accept this, you can get on with doing good things and being happy in life.

I thought about my friend. If there was a way to save the friendship, I would do it. If he was already getting worse, I would cut him off. There are so many wonderful people in the world and so many potential friends that it is not necessary to hold on to everyone who was ever a friend. For the end of every relationship, you can create a new relationship instead, which will be different. I considered the friendships and relationships in my life, and I committed at that moment to observe them and do my best to ensure they were all getting better or, if need be, that I would walk away.

Sometimes it's important to notice how you let other people treat you, too. I have found in the past that I was too apologetic to certain people, and I've let others take advantage of me when I have been trying to be nice. Since I have made an effort to change this, I have found that they no longer treat me in the same way. It's funny, but we tend to teach people how to treat us. I realized that I had made mistakes and was human like everybody else, but I was no longer going to take the blame for everything anymore. I decided I had no more need to apologize for existing. Being nice is one thing, but it is also so important to stand up for yourself. I had given this advice out on so many occasions that I eventually had to put it into practice myself. You have to treat yourself as being as important and as valuable as others. That way you'll more likely attract people into your life and increase your chances of finding real love with them.

CHAPTER 42

The Art of Real Love

IT WAS THE most amazing experience. I had waited for it my whole life.

Imagine—you wake up beside the girl of your dreams, the love of your life; as you watch her sleeping, you adore her silently. You caress her face gently while she sleeps so beautifully there, and you can feel her heart beating so miraculously.

Imagine—you simply take the moment and gaze at her, inches from her face. You listen to her breathing softly while she exists in her own dream-world. You are feeling an overwhelming sense of love that fills your body, like constant explosions are taking place in your heart of absolute and complete ecstasy, joy, and bliss.

Imagine—you breathe in her breath and hold her so tightly that she feels like another part of you. You study her face so completely and simply appreciate such awesome beauty. You just enjoy the moment, wanting so desperately that it will never end, that you could just exist there forever.

Imagine—you smell her hair and inhale a fragrance of such potency that it melts your heart instantly. As she slowly awakens, you gain a glimpse of the most beautiful eyes you have ever seen, while you become hopelessly lost in them so deeply. You gently taste her lips, and she smiles deliciously in her half-awake slumber. You hear the words and sounds of love and capture that moment and complete yourself there in your heart forever. It's so hard to capture the true feeling of ecstasy that comes with moments like these.

There were only a couple of questions left for me to ask Richard, but they were the most important ones. You see, I had fallen for a girl. I couldn't stop thinking about her. When I made her smile, it made my entire day. One night, we went for drinks. I asked her out, and she said yes. I was in heaven. We began to date.

Think about love. It's the most desired thing throughout the world. Nobody can quantify or define it, yet we all know what it means. We all want love and to be loved. Most movies and pop songs are inspired by love, while two days in the year, in February and December, celebrate different forms of love.

There are many kinds of love. You can love as a lover. You can love as a friend. You can love as a mother or father. You can love as a child. You can love as a husband or wife, brother or sister. You can love as a soul mate or spiritual mate. You can love as a best friend, close friend, or secret admirer. You can love as a fan or performer. You can love as a grandparent or godparent, aunt or uncle, or as a cousin. You can love as an individual or as part of a group.

There is more than one way to love. You can love with a song or a poem or a hug or a kiss or an arm around a shoulder or a bunch of flowers. You can love with an e-mail or text or answering machine message. You can love with a word or a look or a smile. You can love with a silver ring or gold earrings or a diamond or a plane ticket to Paris. You can love with a tone of voice or a card or letter. You can love with a compliment or a joke, with a tease or a prayer. You can love with applause, a cheer, or a pint.

Love can make you feel on top of the world or like the whole world is on top of you. It can elate you and depress you. It can produce manic states of ecstasy and devastation. It can fill your soul with joy and break your heart in a million tiny pieces.

Relationships can seem complex sometimes. The chances of meeting someone who falls in love with you, and you with them, and both of you being single don't seem that high. The chances of you both feeling the same way, or better, when you get to know each other, can't be that high. The chances of you resisting the temptations of the other potential partners out there again can't be that high. Yet, all over the planet, there are so many people in relationships. There is no doubt that some settle and some are lucky enough to find one of their soul mates: someone whom they love and adore.

The mind games that often plague relationships involve the different expectations and rules we bring to them. We have certain preferences, beliefs, and understandings about things, and when our partners have different ideas than us, it can cause conflict. What is worse is that often such rules are unspoken, and we have to guess them. To make matters even worse than this, we have the unreliable state of neurochemistry affected by how we think toward a loved one, which changes quite often. We can also bring negative issues and problems from our past relationships into each new relationship.

You can best minimize the negative influences on your relationships by accepting the differences between you and your partner. You can make more of an effort to explain or convey your expectations and respect the other person's. You can become more aware of your own neurochemistry and control your behaviors as much as possible. You can pay attention to your behaviors in relation to when you are bringing your "issues" from your past into your new relationships.

Valentine's Day can be seen as a mass-marketing phenomenon designed to make more money from consumers or as a day when you get to express your love and have it expressed to you. It becomes a love disinhibitor, giving each partner an excuse to be romantic again—without needing a drink. For those in new relationships, the day often symbolizes a perfect day with your ideal mate. For those in long-term relationships, it exists as a well-needed excuse to spend more time with each other and attempt to recall the romance of times past.

Christmas is a time where love again takes a front seat. Sentimental seasonal movies focus enthusiastically on how important our families are and on the idea of being a good person. It is constructed as a time to share love with each other and enjoy spreading good feelings to each other.

When it comes to our special relationships, we are born into this life, and many of us find someone special with whom we want to spend our time. That person becomes our ideal. Sometimes we lose that person and sometimes we stay with him or her forever. Eventually, whatever happens, happens, and we move on or stick together.

In this culture, days like Valentine's Day, romantic movies, and songs can often create in people a relationship "need." It's like we fall in love with the idea of falling in love. Therefore, we meet someone, and that person becomes for us our ideal or our soul mate. Plato's dual-self idea is expressed in Hollywood over and over again. It is the idea that we were initially made of two souls when we were born and were separated and that we spend our lives searching for our "other half."

Some settle happily for a relationship; others hold out for a relationship with someone they fall madly for—some get it, some don't. All in all, there is suffering that goes with relationships. Attachment causes suffering. When you are attached to something, you will have to suffer when it eventually ends or there are problems in it, and invariably it always will and there always will be.

So what's the secret? What's the best way to look at relationships with others? What's the best way to think about love? Well, to me, the idea to be without attachment of any kind to anything at all is impractical—most important because then we become attached to being detached. Even some Buddhists who move away from the idea of attachments are attached to the idea of detachment!

The best thing to do is to realize that there will be wonderful times and times of suffering in all relationships and existence of love but that the wonderfulness is invariably more powerful. There are many dangers to watch out for in relationships.

I wanted to find some solutions to these dangers. I had made some mistakes with girlfriends before, and I wanted to make sure I learned from them. I had always given clients wonderful advice that worked really well for them in their own relationships, but here I was faced with a situation that I found hard to deal with objectively. I loved this girl so much, and I found it hard to think straight.

You see, when you fall in love with someone, you can often lose your sense of rationality. A combination of factors can serve to throw you into a quagmire of desperation, neediness, and pining. This only puts you into a worse situation whereby you present your worst self to the other person. This paradox goes with my phrase: if you want to get who you want, you need to let go of neediness.

We all do ridiculous things when we are in love. They are called cringe moments. But forgive yourself. Just put them down to being crazy for some moments; you no longer are crazy and don't think about them. You are human, and as long as you learn from your mistakes and control your feelings more powerfully in the future, you'll know what to do. I had my cringe moments. There was nothing I could do except make a commitment to be different in the future.

Finding your true love and holding on to him or her often seems so impossible given all the things that can go wrong, but the wonderful truth is that, as the saying goes, love usually finds a way.

A soul mate can be a friend with no romantic interest as well. It is, to me, someone with whom you connect on such a deep level that you feel like you can touch that person's soul and know his or her real self. So if you are in a relationship, hopefully you are with the person who is one of your soul mates. It's so important to make every day a reminder of just how lucky you are to be so close with someone whom you met randomly and connected with wonderfully. Every day must remind you to acknowledge the aliveness and joy that is part of falling in love and being in love.

Relationships need effort. Whatever state your relationship is in, let today be the spur that propels you to make your relationship better than ever. Focus on working with your partner to regularly enhance the quality of your time together. Be tolerant of each other's flaws. Forgive each other's little mistakes. Share your feelings in many different ways. Show your parner, tell your partner, and let your partner feel that you love him or her.

You go through this world and face many of your struggles on your own. But having a partner with you, a soul mate with you, is so invaluable, and if you are lucky enough to have found that person, then let yourself appreciate that and feel grateful for that, not every February 14 or every Christmas—but every single day.

Now even though we use the term, "relationships" are not things. They are processes that we do. We do the act of relating to each other. It is a skill.

As long as you remember it is something you are doing, you can begin to make a disciplined effort to do it more successfully. So what are the steps that we can take toward doing "relating" more effectively?

The first step is to recognize the difference between real love and other kinds of love. Love can be addictive and can make us crazy. Real love is different. Real love is about doing the act of loving the other person and being loved as much in return. It is about giving yourself to another from a place of not needing to but simply wanting to more than anything in the world. It's about unconditionally committing yourself to making someone's life become happier with you in it.

Back in the car, on my way up to Richard's house, I had been listening to a radio program on the local station, and they began talking about love and the neurochemistry of love. I had always been fascinated by this, and as they began to make connections between love and obsessive-compulsive disorder, I became intrigued. As I approached the important topic of love with Richard, I used this program as an example.

OF: Richard, on my way over to you here, I heard a scientist talk on a radio program about the similarities between love and obsessive-compulsive disorder. What do you think about the connection?

RB: Well, my definition of love is a lot different from that. I've been in love with the same person for almost thirty years, but it doesn't make me obsessive and compulsive. It makes me care. It makes me more rigorous about certain things. It makes me more loyal, but I think what that's all about is more along the lines of infatuation or lust.

OF: So, is that idea of OCD and love being connected more about the initial feeling?

RB: Yeah, that's more about when you give people a taste of endorphins. It's the "first one's free" concept. You know? "Here, smoke this. Well, now, the next one you have to pay for." This concept of love is that the longer you're in love, the less you can feel it, and that it doesn't get stronger; it gets weaker, and that's wrong. That's not what love is; that's what lust is, and that's the difference between addiction and friendship.

I liked his answer. It finally put the picture together for me. You see, I have had the experience quite often of falling for someone, but I began to realize that I didn't actually fall in love with them; I fell in love with the idea of falling in love. Our culture through the media and movies and books, and so on, has constructed one of the ultimate forms of happiness as being the notion of finding your soul mate and falling in love and living happily ever after. Since way before the time of Shakespeare, this has been a constant search humans have gone through. When we find it everywhere dominating our thoughts and preventing us from seeing things in a useful and intelligent light, we can know that it's most probably an addiction.

The trick is to appreciate it as an addiction and begin to understand that it comes from us using our imagination to create ideas and images of us being in love. We actively use our brains to fall in love. We make images of what it would be like to perfectly exist with this person, and we imagine how wonderful it is to be with them. I have thought I was in love many times, but with Richard's description, I could see how I had been creating an addiction in my mind of the idea of love.

I asked Richard another question. I wanted more clarity.

> OF: So how can you tell when you are in love?
>
> RB: You know when you're in love. Trust me; the world stands still. If you feel you're more of a person when you're with someone than when you're away from them, then you're addicted to them. If you feel happier when you're with someone because you enjoy being with them more than you enjoy being away from them, then you're in love.

I had definitely been addicted many times before. It was being with someone who made me feel like a better person. Love, on the other hand, I had rarely experienced until I met this girl. I had watched Richard with Paula and Paula with Richard. Their relationship is certainly one to model. What impressed me, as much as any of Richard's genius or ability to affect a brain so marvelously through language and his state, was his absolute love and commitment to his wife and hers to him. I thought about Paula. She is such a beautiful person. She is the kind of person who just seemed to bring out the best in people.

Richard's adventures had led him through so many experiences, and yet through it all I could see the love he and Paula shared for each other was amazing. It was almost like you could feel it being near them. He went nowhere without her, and they took care of each other. If there were such a thing as soul mates, they were a perfect example. From this perspective, I quizzed Richard over relationship advice.

> OF: You have been together with Paula for so long. . . .

Richard interrupted me immediately.

> RB: It doesn't seem like long to me. It only seems that way to you. It's the most important part of our life because everything before that seemed like it went on forever.

Pure glamour—Richard and his gorgeous wife, Paula.

I smiled. He was speaking from his heart.

OF: Well, in the time you have been with Paula, I've noticed you are so perfect for each other, and you seem to have such a wonderful relationship. What advice do you have for people in relationships?

RB: I would give the advice before you're a couple. The first piece of advice is to make sure that you get together with the right person, and the first thing to do is to be the right person to get together with so that you feel good for no reason inside yourself. Then you'll suddenly open your eyes, and you'll look around, and in all the chaos in the universe, you'll look at somebody, and you'll realize the two of you see each other, and everything else is in chaos. When you get together with that person, remember in each moment you have got all the time in the world, and there's nothing more important than how you feel in the now.

OF: How can people make sure their relationships work out?

RB: Relationships either improve on their own or they don't. It either gets better or it gets worse, and as long as you know that's how it's going to be, then even if you have a bad patch, and it goes on a day or two, you keep in mind that everybody goes through bad patches.

I've gotten grumpy for a month at a time, but Polly never thought that it was going to mean that we were going to break up or that life was going to end. She just said, "Well, he's going through a bad patch," and just waited. "Things run hot; things run cold. Things get better; things get worse," she would say, but, over the long run, then even a dent like that is just a little notch out of a really big journey.

Most people will never know the kind of intimacy that we've had because most people never give themselves a chance. They make a deal about everything; they're too busy talking about things. Polly and I never talk about anything bad that happened a long time ago because it's not important. We remember the good things; we associate with the good things, and the trick is to make pictures associated with all the good things that happened, and if you think of something bad, disassociate and burn it.

Richard kept making things so simple. As I struggled with such simplicity, I realized that was really what it was about. There is this myth that exists in some self-help ideologies that you always have to express what you are thinking about to the other person. Instead, Richard's suggestions made much more sense. To focus on improving the relationship, it's essential to do things that will improve the relationship.

You have to be able to accept the imperfections of others. You have to be able to accept that your relationship will change. You have to be able to remember that you have the power to ensure it improves positively and stop being annoyed by some of the things that the other person does. If they didn't do those little things, they wouldn't be the people we love.

When we marry, we do so "for better or for worse" and never for perfection. If you can accept there will be tough times and resolve, no matter what occurs, you will always remember how much you love each other, you'll find happiness will become a long-term part of your relationship. We only get a certain amount of time to spend on this earth with our loved ones. While we have these moments, it's so important to make them count and enjoy them as much as possible.

Mentioning bad times will not make things better. Focusing on feeling good with each other and becoming more intimate with one another will make your relationship better. Constantly worrying about the state of your relationship will not make your relationship easier. Accepting that things will not always be perfect will make it easier. Being needy and dependent on others won't help your relationship. Being happy with yourself and being the kind of person you want to be will help your relationship. It's that simple. My friend Gillian once summed it up very basically for me when I asked her the secret of her wonderful relationship with her partner, Brian. She simply replied, "We really make an effort to treat each other as well as we can." So, I considered, it's about being nice to each other. Isn't that why you got together in the first place? That is real love. It made sense. I had that answer.

We finished the recorded conversation before I got to ask my most important question. That night, before I went to sleep, I sat on my bed and replayed some of the tapes of the conversations I had with Richard. Things began to become clearer and clearer for me. I thought back to what had been at the forefront of my mind, and I soon realized that I no longer needed my final and most important question answered. I had an epiphany that gave me an amazing a sense of freedom and clarity.

You see, I began to think of this girl that I had fallen head over heels in love with. I thought of my feelings for her. I had really connected with her wonderfully. The chemistry was so strong between us. There were so many synchronicities that seemed to connect us together. I had waited all my life for this—she was everything I had ever desired. There were so many things right about it that it just couldn't be wrong. I knew her so well, and she knew me, almost instantly. Even when I went away on my travels, we kept in close touch, talking hours at a time by phone. Wherever I went, my journeys were full of dreams and thoughts about my future with her. It was literally painful not to be with her. I loved her so much and knew that nothing would come between us. I had found my dream partner. I was so happy. I promised myself it would last forever.

CHAPTER 43

Sometimes Things Just Don't Work Out

I WAS WRONG.

When I arrived back, this girl I adored broke up with me. My heart broke. I was devastated. I never saw it coming. For a while, I tried to suffocate the pain by drowning it in drink. While working as much as ever, I went out every night. Everything reminded me of her. My ego felt battered. Nothing mattered in my life. My feelings ranged from devastation to hate, anger, and insecurity. Outside, I held it together for the most part, but alone, I often lost it, sick to my stomach. It was only a few months, I kept reasoning with myself. How could such a short time mean so much to me?

Before the breakup, when I was away, I did my best to stay as positive as I possibly could and told her how terribly I missed her. I sent her songs I composed. Every stupid act I could have done, I did. Little sleep, lack of contact, a few drinks, and the mind can go crazy. When she broke up with me, I let myself go and embarrassed myself by revealing every thought and feeling I had. It was pathetic. With her, I had developed a habit of rambling about my thoughts constantly, overanalyzing everything.

I had had relationships end before, but this time the pain of rejection stung as if for the first time. She was pretty cold in the way she put things when she broke up with me. I did what I could to respond with maturity, but inside, my heart shattered. I wished her well and said my good-byes to her. Deep down, I had felt something wasn't right all along, but I had denied it over and over again. I loved her so much. Now my instincts had been proven right.

When your heart breaks, you just have to take time to get over it. Getting over it means being able to look down at it from a higher plane, a higher mode of thinking. You have to accept the mistakes and the cringeworthy experiences and accept that, for a short time, you were crazy. Love can make you crazy for a while. The art is to make sure you learn from each mistake. Feeling bad about them continuously doesn't help you learn.

A week after our relationship had ended, I was out on yet another night in the city. Eventually, left on my own, I finished my drink and walked outside the bar and got straight into the first taxi I saw. At first, I made the usual small talk with the driver. Somehow, and I can't remember how, girlfriends and partners came up, and out of the blue, the driver began recounting his own state of woe. He had been left by his wife of twenty-eight years just three months earlier. He was madly in love with her, and she left him for another man. He painfully recounted how he adored her and tried to provide everything he could for her, and out of nowhere, she just left him for an ex-lover of thirty years ago.

For whatever reason, even before I became a psychologist, when people meet me they feel like they can share anything with me. We parked outside my house—it was about 2:30 AM, and he turned off the engine. He began pouring his heart out to me. He showed me the words he had written to his wife and asked my suggestions on it. For the next two hours, I talked with him about the true nature of love, rejection, hurt, loss, separation, and relationships. While my words seemed to help this man heal, I felt my own heart benefiting, too.

His wife had cheated on him and left him for another man. That was the ultimate blow to his ego. There are many reasons people cheat. Generally, they do it because they feel attracted to someone and their guard is down. Maybe it's down because they are drunk; maybe because they are in a relationship they are unhappy with; maybe because they are just sexed up and don't care as long as their partner never finds out; maybe because they have fallen in love. Maybe it's all of the above.

It's also very obvious why people hurt. The ultimate rejection comes from knowing that you were left or cheated on for someone else. You were not "good enough," and your partner went to someone "better." What's crucial to realize, and what I explained to the taxi driver in great depth, is that, again, everything can be explained better chemically. Her brain was chemically attracted to someone else, and she changed her perception of him as a result. This made it possible in her mind for her to do what she did.

When you love a person so deeply and it ends, the feeling of heartbreak is one of the most painful feelings we, as humans, can experience. The other person learned to see you really, truly, deeply. He or she got to see you at your best and at your worst. The ultimate evaluation seems to be of your partner's validation of your worth, as he or she seems to be the only person who really knew you. The reality is, however, that nothing could be further from the truth.

You see, when you fall in love with someone, you go into an altered state in which the person becomes your ideal mate. When you do this, your partner's flaws become acceptable and often "cute," but it is not your worth as a person that is in question when you someone breaks up with you.

Falling in love with someone can affect your judgment on that person's good and bad points. Falling out of love can also affect your judgment on those good and bad points. The process of falling in love is when you intensify the good things about another in your mind and disassociate yourself from the bad points. Falling out of love is the exact opposite. It is when you intensify the bad things and dissociate yourself from the good points.

Once you realize that a person's rejection or deciding to break up is really a reflection of the way that person's internal chemistry is being activated, you can let go of much of the hurt that comes with such an event. You are not being rejected because you are you or because your partner is who he or she is, it is out of your partner's distorted way of seeing you. For whatever reason, that person is not in love anymore and is no longer seeing you in the same way that he or she used to. Although people can fall back in love, there is no point expecting this to happen. There is a life to be lived and many more people to meet out there.

So often, if two people break up as a result of falling out of love, it is not a judgment on the value or attractiveness or goodness of a person. Instead, it is more of a reflection of the altered state of mind of the person falling out of love. It is crucial to accept this. People will sometimes say that they were never attracted to their ex. The truth is that the majority of time they were, but when they go through that threshold and fall out of love, they no longer find that person attractive. From that perspective, to be consistent, they more than likely changed their beliefs about what had happened.

You'll always have radically different memories of relationships from the other person for the simple fact that a psychological law known as the hindsight bias effect exists. We alter our beliefs about how we felt or experienced an event based upon what we learn after having had the experience. Many people try to convince themselves that it wasn't love, despite the fact they professed it during the relationship many times. But how could it have been? The way they feel is so different to the way they felt, and it's hard to believe that they did feel like that once.

I had a client who came in and said that he never had a good experience in his life. He claimed that there was never a time when he felt happy. After challenging him on this, I asked him about a few events in his life, and he replied, "Yes, at the time they 'seemed' good, but looking back on them now, I realize I didn't really feel happy." This is an example of how people can distort their experience when they look back at it. The key is to reflect on what you felt the experience was like and accept that it was true for you.

Now if you can realize that how you think it was, wasn't how it was, and how the other person thinks it was, wasn't how it was—then you can get freedom. You can get freedom, because you can realize that there were moments when you loved your partner and your partner loved you, and now you are both different and feel different than you did then—if that works better for you.

I spoke with a friend of mine recently, and we talked about old memories from past relationships. What struck me was that she never really felt that bad when she remembered back to the times she was in the relationships. I was curious about this, as most people tend to feel heartbroken again when they remember past relationships. What I discovered was that there was a wonderful secret that she used to remain positive and happy about the experiences. When she thought about the good and bad times, she always thought about the good times at the end and, therefore, was always happy when she finished thinking about the relationship. Thus, when you are nostalgically remembering past times, simply remember the best times at the end, and it will be so much easier and better to do.

That way, there will never be a desire to wipe your memory of anyone or anything. I went through my phase of being angry and furious with my ex-girlfriend, but that didn't help. She had not meant to do any harm; she was suffering herself and acting from what she felt, and unfortunately it affected me. Breakups are never easy, and often hurtful words can be expressed from negative feelings of hurt. Often people say things that they don't mean. We are all just human.

It's important that you begin to accept the good with the bad and remember the good after the bad and know that the wonderfulness of the special moments make life worth living. No pain can ever tarnish those moments. Moving on involves accepting that that person was right for you then, and you for them, but then is not now. Now is the time to get back to awaiting the next potential love of your life.

There's no accounting for the matters of the heart. Many of us spend our lives loving the idea of "true love," and when we feel we have finally gotten it, it takes us by the hand and leads us into mountains and valleys of intense emotion. We often transform those we meet into "the one" simply because we crave real love. The feeling of love can also become too intense and can sometimes seem like neediness. Often, the worst thing you can do in the initial stages of a relationship is to express this neediness.

In the taxi driver's state of pain, his letter was an effort to convey how bad he felt and how his wife had destroyed his life. I chatted to him about doing what was useful instead of doing what he felt like doing. The state of hurt, betrayal, and devastation he was in was affecting his judgment, and he wasn't seeing how letting her know how hurt he was put him into a position of weakness and made him look pathetic.

Often when we feel angry, we let this anger invade our relationships. When we feel frustrated, we can let this frustration out on others. When we feel needy, we reveal this neediness to others. Why? There are many reasons, but they aren't even relevant. What is relevant is that this is what we do, and this can destroy our relationships, but we can change this around. It's about separating your feelings from your actions and basing your actions on that question, "What is the most useful thing to do now?" That must be done regardless of what you are feeling at that moment.

You must realize that your feelings distort your thoughts and the chemical storm inside your mind will last like a storm lasts, but it will also end like a storm ends. While it's going on, you've simply got to be as smart as you can. If you are, then when it comes to an end, you'll be free and ready to move on wonderfully. The taxi driver smiled. I knew I had gotten through to him.

Often, when you break up with someone or you lose somebody, you have so many questions that you feel a deep need to have answered. I had questions. Why had she changed her mind so suddenly? When did she go through threshold? What made her go through threshold? Did I do something I didn't know about? Was there someone else? Did she even like me at all? Was I paying for her past hurts? Why did she say so many hurtful things? Why? Why? Why?

The answers never came. One day I was chatting with a friend, and he suggested that sometimes there are no perfect answers, at least none that I will ever get. Sometimes people just change and act differently. You won't always be able to find out why. Hence, I wrote out every question I had and let them be. I decided I would know the answers when I died. That was it. What I didn't realize at the time was that there would be a point at which I didn't care anymore. There would be a time when I would remember the good side of this person and the connection of love we once had and just appreciate that.

To me, it's important to recognize that such breakups can provide growth and strength. The heart heals itself every day. The heart never really breaks; it just feels that way. What happens is that the love you feel is substituted for a mixture of loss, anger, regret, and other ugly feelings. It's not that you lose your spirit, even if it feels that way. It's that these feelings zap your energy for a time. When you can learn to love yourself more and truly feel great, it won't prevent you from feeling heartbroken, but it will ensure you bounce back from it better. There are people who let heartbreak break their spirits. They become cynical and find it impossible to let themselves fall that deeply for anyone ever again. It's crucial that you resolve never to let this happen to you. You must keep the belief and faith that an ideal mate is still out there for you, whoever they are.

I recently saw the movie *Eternal Sunshine of the Spotless Mind*. A brilliant film, it highlighted a fascinating moral question: if you could wipe a person from your memory, would you? I considered what it would be like to wipe my ex-girlfriend from my memory—never to have met her, never to have known her, never to remember her. I wouldn't know of the pain, the heartbreak, and the sad memories of no longer being with her. At the same time, I began to realize that despite the pain, the memories of the good times far outweighed the pain. I agreed with Tennyson when he declared, "'Tis better to have loved and lost/ Than never to have loved at all."

It was not about forgetting, it was about letting the pain go and the hurt heal. Hurt is inevitable when a relationship ends. Sometimes it can be pretty bad. This is true of all close relationships. However, I believe there is someone out there for everyone. We don't always find that person, but when something goes wrong, it's important that we get over it as quickly and as thoroughly as possible by getting out into the world and realizing the "plenty more fish in the sea" cliché has much truth in it. As Richard had said to me, "Your girlfriend leaves you, and it seems like your life is over, and everything is the end of the universe, but if you could float twenty-five years down the line, some people won't even be able to remember the name of the girl."

When we can realize this through the tears, anger, and pain, it enables us to open up the possibility of hope once more. Heartbreak is just a terrible, terrible winter in life, and after winter eventually the spring always follows. Once we know that, we can grit our teeth and do our best to learn and become better through this tough time.

When a relationship ends, there often can be such bad feelings associated with the ex-partner. The people we love can hurt us when we let them, and when people are very close, words can produce massive pain. Even the best of us can feel cut to the core when we are attacked by someone we love. It's often better to cut off all contact with the person and just move on.

Sometimes, however, getting back in contact with someone you were in love with once can work. Change is inevitable. All we can do is control the change as best we can. A connection can remain strong, yet different. Hearts do heal.

This girl had entered my life for a reason, but no matter how much I thought she was "the one," she wasn't, and I had to accept that. Now, when you can realize that that person was right for you for the time you were with him or her, and that you were right for that person, you get the freedom to realize that it's time to move on. Maybe the next person you connect with will be "the one" you have been looking for to spend your life with, or maybe it'll just be someone who is right for you for a time.

Either way, sometimes things just don't work out, and the only thing that you can be certain of is that there will be other people in your life to love and to be loved by. You can learn from every relationship. Although you cannot always make things work out, no matter how hard you try, you can learn from every relationship and become better at relating the next time.

What is essential is that you realize that you never "need" anyone. You can survive happily on your own. I had known this before my heartbreak, but it was only after the experience that I began to really feel it deeply. Heartbreak takes time to heal, and it's important to let yourself grow as much as possible from it. For no matter how painful it can be, the power of love in your life can help you overcome suffering eventually.

CHAPTER 44

All You Need Is Love

BILL HICKS, THE FAMOUS American comedian and philosopher, once said that we have two choices. We have the choice to see the world through the eyes of fear or through the eyes of love. As I began to reflect on everything Richard had been saying and everything in my own life, I began to understand things in a way I never had before.

You see, everyone has to deal with tough times. It is through these times that we reveal our true character. Most of us have experienced heartbreak, loneliness, and hurt in relationships. The key is to stop yourself from letting these tough times impact negatively on your future. The world is full of goodness and evil, happiness and sadness, depending on how we decide to look at it. When you can remember what is truly important—connecting with people and loving them for who they are—you can find salvation from the bitterness that eats up so many people.

This is not just about romantic relationships either. Hurt can be healed with family members or friends, but first we must let go of our stubbornness. Stubbornness often gets in the way of true happiness. When we connect with other people and we meet some who we love to be with, it's imperative that we take such opportunities and forgive ourselves and others. By forgiving, I mean that we forget about it and harbor no ill feelings toward them. We can remember the acts, and learn from them, but not let them dominate our thoughts.

We only get a short time on this planet, and many of us waste so much of it dealing in stubbornness and harboring anger and resentment. Meanwhile, the loved ones in our lives suffer as we do, while we forget our own flawed nature as human beings.

A friend of mine once shared with me a very poignant quotation from Marianne Williamson, "Please share with me, but try not to attack or judge me for these wounds I carry. And I will try my best to do the same for you. . . . Forgive me, if you can, and I vow to try to forgive you." I began to understand just how valuable this was. No matter what people say and do or what you have said and done yourself, the past is the past. Learn from it, but never let it dominate your life. Hurt comes to us all. It is in rising up while looking out to the future that we grow larger and stronger than we can possibly imagine. No matter what!

We all have emotional wounds, and we often bring these wounds to each relationship we have. Sometimes we treat people badly because we are taking out our wounds on them. It's important that we realize this and stop—and also accept that sometimes people will do this to us. As Richard had explained, sometimes it is necessary to detach yourself from people in your life. If they make it easy for you to feel bad or have let you down a number of times, then these are good reasons to do so. There are more than enough people out there who are good and worthwhile.

We have edges and limits in our relationships with people, and when something doesn't work out, it doesn't work out. What's necessary is that you understand that it is never just them; it is you, too. Not in a bad way— you may have done nothing much wrong, but it means you are not for them because they have reached a threshold in their mind where all of a sudden, or over time, they have changed how they feel. At that point, your failings or flaws won't be tolerated by them anymore.

As Richard had said, it's important that you "realize the time you spent with those people wasn't a lie; it's just that they changed." Regardless of what is said in haste, the time you spent together is valuable and real and true. It existed, and you existed, and they existed, and for some moments, it's probable that they adored you and you adored them, and for those moments, you had that kind of love between you. When they expressed how much they loved you, it was most likely true for them then. They did—then. Nobody can ever take that away from you.

The key is to make the most of every relationship that you enjoy while you are in it. The trick is to allow yourself to fully experience "relating" to other people. You don't have to constantly tell them how wonderful everything is, but instead, just make the time with them quality time. All too often, people allow the fear of rejection, embarrassment, and awkwardness to get in the way of their relationships.

In Ireland we wait for drink to do its duty of removing inhibitions so that we can tell people how we truly feel, but it's never quite the same. I feel very lucky because I have been able to say what I wanted to say without the aid of alcohol. I did so because I was willing to take the risk. I have told my mother and father how I feel. I have told my mother how I love and adore her more than life itself and that she continues to give me life even now so many years after giving birth to me. I have told my father that he is my idol and hero and that I love him and look up to him more than he will ever know. I have told my family and friends how much I love them. Now I tell them in print. I tell them in words that will last for eternity.

I was once told that relationships can be healing environments or emotional torture chambers. I believe they can also be environments that not only heal us but also improve us. Those who we love and who love us, regardless of how long or short it lasts, are our soul mates. If, when we die, we are reincarnated over and over again, then I believe they have been with us before in every lifetime in some form. We have only a few soul mates, and what's important is to appreciate and feel grateful that you have met some of yours and rejoice in the fact that for a time you adored them and they adored you—that you experienced love for at least a moment.

If you are lucky enough to have found someone you see yourself staying with for your lifetime, appreciate that person. Avoid the common mistake so many make by taking a loved one for granted. There are so many people who haven't found a person to love and be loved by, or have, but it hasn't worked out. Let each and every moment you spend with your loved one be special and wonderful. Let yourself express how you feel from time to time.

Let yourself always remember what is truly important is not the small things we bicker about but the fact that, one day, you laid your eyes on your partner and and your partner on you, and there was a flash of magic. Let the thought of this magic bring you ever closer to your partner, so that you can know what it's like to enjoy and revel in true intimacy. It's also good to remember, as Richard explained, that there will be good and bad times, and it is important to ride out the bad times by recognizing why you are with this person in the first place.

Connecting intimately with a soul mate is such a wonderful experience, and it is important to appreciate it as often as you can by making the most of it.

If you are single, it's important to be happy with that, too. We can't predict the future. I have already met so many truly special people, and I am very sure I will meet more. That "special person" will come along for me, or for all I know might have come along already and we haven't connected yet. Regardless, all you can do is be as happy as you can be and be who you want to be and feel as good as you want to feel and ensure that you make whatever special people come into your life as happy as possible. Life brings unpredictability with it. That's the way I like things. Whoever she is, I'll find her, and if not, I'm meant for something else.

People sometimes wonder if I am destroying the whole spirit of love by attempting to explain it. I think that, on the contrary, by understanding love in this way, it helps us to love more and hurt less. Some people settle for someone who doesn't treat them well and end up "surviving" for most of their lives. Some people settle for someone who is wealthy or attractive but that with whom they have little connection or for whom they don't have deep feelings. Some people refuse to settle and keep hopeful that they will meet their love through destiny.

I know so many people out there who are not satisfied in their romantic relationships but who are used to it and are terrified to be on their own again. The sad truth is that they are not free. They are trapped by their own fears. Great relationships exist out there, but we have to raise our standards and look for them. Every one has to make their own choices and live with them.

When you can get to the point where you don't mind being single, then you are in the perfect state for a relationship. That's one of the crazy paradoxes of life. Loving freedom is about welcoming people into your life and loving the people in your life. It is about realizing that it is "all about chemistry" and that the magic of love can overcome all boundaries and can free us toward living in complete happiness and bliss.

To awaken beside the love of your life and feel wonderful because of it, or to awaken on your own but to feel brilliant because of all the people you have in your life who care for you and love you dearly; to realize how many people exist in the world and how many potential friends there are out there; to spend quality time with your family and friends and enjoy every moment you can with them—that is to know the art of loving freedom.

Life is just many moments that go by. Whatever hardships and breakups you have been through, I always believe that things work out for the best. The fairy tale is that, one day, you meet someone and something clicks. As Richard said: "You'll suddenly open your eyes, and you'll look around, and in all the chaos in the universe, you'll look at somebody, and you'll realize the two of you see each other, and everything else is in chaos."

It is only then that you will truly look back and realize that all the hardships and heartbreak you have experienced have been there only for a time so that this moment could happen for you in the best possible way and that they were all simply lessons. Everyone is here to teach us a lesson and give us an experience. People will come in and out of your life, and when one person leaves, you must accept the lesson and growth experience that they gave you. If you can learn to treat yourself and others well and make yourself and others feel good, then you will find life will present you with opportunities and the fairy tale may well come true. It's a fairy tale worth believing in, and if you are lucky enough to experience it, it is so important that you make every single moment of the time you do have together count.

Just as there are people in your life with whom you'll find pain, there are people in your life who are like angels. Some time after the heartbreak of mine, I met another girl. She was like a beautiful angel, and through the time I spent with her, I realized that I didn't have to have all the answers. I just needed to live as well as I could, as fully as I could. She showed me what pure love was about: loving a person for who they are and not from some addiction to love. When you open yourself up, you will find someone you can love and who will love you truly for who you are. Since then, we have both moved on, but we were so much better for the experience of having been together.

Not everything will work out, because often life isn't fair, but we have to take all we can from every moment. We have to feel grateful that there are angels in our lives who care for us and for the time we have with them, who bring us smiles, happiness, and a warm feeling of love.

The media suggests that there are many people we cannot trust or who are out for themselves. Their portrayal of human beings is less than flattering. They are probably right quite often. There are many people who are selfish and negative in what they say and do. There are many people we know who have hurt us terribly in the past, and there are many who will do so in the future. However, there are also many people who are fair, honorable, compassionate, and loving. It's not always expressed that well, but when you look deeply within most people, you will find a powerful sense of love. It comes out when they come face-to-face with a child or a baby. It arises in the spirit of Christmas and on special occasions. It comes to fruition when tragedies and crises occur. The paradox is that the evidence of evil in the world is always followed by evidence of goodness.

We must find a way to let go of the pain, heartbreak, hurt, and regret and instead allow ourselves to love the magic of life. Deep behind the masks of society, many good people exist, and when we can break through the social chains of fear, we can see through the eyes of love and understand how love really is all that we need.

As I sat on my bed, listening to the tapes, everything that Richard had been saying all along about relationships and heartbreak started to make sense. A tear rolled down my cheek as I thought about all the people I loved so dearly in my life. I thought about my ex, my family, my friends, and all the angels in my life. I began to feel a great sense of delight and awe at how lucky I truly was. I felt a wonderful sense of compassion for everyone. I felt so free from the bitterness, anger, hurt, jealousy, and pain I had felt for so long. I saw everything differently. I was ready to truly make life wonderful. I smiled and closed my eyes and entered a deep sleep full of enchanting and wonderful dreams. I would be going home tomorrow.

Loving Freedom Exercises

1. Write down all the people you know and evaluate your relationships.

   Note whom you have to contact and when.

   Then note when you are going to contact everyone else on the list and how often.

   Set a regular time to contact each person. Some you may only need to be in touch with once a year, others once a week.

   Get into the habit of dropping a line to each of them.

2. Find out everybody's birthday and make an action plan to contact them.

3. In looking for a relationship, what kind of person are you looking for and what kind of person would you have to be to get that person? Make a list of those qualities.

4. Meet at least one new person every time you go out. Simply chat.
5. Give compliments to some people with no expectation of anything in return.
6. Practice using different tones of voice, accents, rhythms of speech, gestures, and expressions.
7. Practice using all the senses when you describe your experiences or tell stories.
8. Do nice things randomly for friends and loved ones.
9. Recall the nicest memories you have had with loved ones.
10. Recall the lessons you have learned from each person in your life.
11. Write out your questions, feelings, and thoughts about things that are on your mind and describe the most useful way of thinking about them.
12. Let go of all the bitterness and negative feelings toward others.

CHAPTER 45

Random Ramblings 5:
Trance Ending

I HAVE OFTEN BEEN asked to help people learn how to go into an altered state. I have been in so many altered states since I first began to learn NLP. Many of my trances, and the altered states I create with people, have been heavily influenced by Richard. So in helping people go into altered states, I often will use the teachings and understandings that I have integrated at a deep level.

One of the simplest ways to do this is to find time when you can be by yourself and simply relax while sitting or lying down. Once you are in a place where you can relax comfortably, it's usually helpful to close your eyes. Then you can do certain things that will help you to fully relax.

Obviously, while you are reading this book, it would be ridiculous to close your eyes. Instead, you can keep your eyes open and simply read yourself into a relaxed state. You see, you are not alone while you are reading, as your mind keeps alive the words of the author. A big problem that people frequently have is that they feel lonely. It's amazing when you think about all the millions of people who are out there waiting to find somebody who let hesitation stop them. What's wonderful is that when you stop hesitating, being scared, thinking too much about it, and taking everything so seriously, you can create good feelings inside of you and just go for it—just like you can drift into a comfortable state of mind while you relax.

First, you can begin to notice the sounds around you. For example, here and now, you can hear sounds that surround you that you weren't aware of until you read these words and realized that . . . the very sound of your inner voice reading these words is a sound . . . which isn't the same as the sounds outside . . . yet you can hear it like you can hear the sounds that you can name . . . and those that you haven't named . . . and you can remember that it's not always possible to put a name or label on your experience . . . especially because it's your experience . . . and that label will give you a different experience from someone else . . . no matter how similar your experience seems.

So with this in mind . . . you can allow your body . . . to notice . . . with every deep breath . . . you can find yourself taking . . . how easy it is to relax. . . . Your focus can begin to . . . become aware of the different parts of your body . . . for example . . . how relaxed your head is . . . relaxing comfortably . . . as you read this book . . . and your eyes . . . as they scan each letter so quickly and effortlessly . . . and how well each word brings with it new meaning . . . so that while your body rests here . . . your imagination is led by the pages . . . whether they bring you to India . . . or Ireland . . . America . . . or anywhere . . . everywhere . . . . your mind traveling while your body rests deeply comfortable.

Meanwhile . . . as you allow yourself just to slip off and enjoy the wonderful experience of daydreaming in an altered state . . . you can find yourself becoming even more powerfully relaxed and at ease. It's like when you were young . . . and fascinated with the world . . . and you had so many questions . . . and anything was possible . . . and everything was so much fun . . . and you made adventures from the stones on the road. . . . You learned many different things . . . and you did so, so easily . . . so quickly . . . so thoroughly . . . so enjoyably. . . . You learned through experiencing . . . through absorbing . . . through integrating . . . through stories . . . stories about adventures . . . stories told about fairy tales . . . tales about the structure of magic . . . stories about frogs that became princes . . . princesses who went through "tranceformations" . . . pigs who began using their brain for a change . . . so that houses wouldn't be blown down . . . stories that showed magic in action . . . when you had time for a change . . . adventures of anybody and everybody you could dream of . . . with far away lands . . .that were closer than you thought . . . and dreamlands that captivated you . . . in the most delightful ways.

Now, you can realize . . . through your real eyes that see things clearly . . . that the real lies that have held you back . . . have been the chains of limiting beliefs . . . negative ways of thinking and feeling . . . and your unconscious . . . which is close enough to hear and respond . . . knows that the teachings and understandings . . . that you received here . . . will begin to integrate themselves . . . inside of your life . . . so you'll find yourself . . . absorbing all the positive messages . . . conscious and unconscious . . . you received through our ideas here . . . and you'll discover how wonderful . . . the world really is . . . as you change your habitual ways of thinking . . . and feeling and realize . . . how much fun there is to have . . . in the world and asking . . . how much pleasure you can stand.

Inside your mind . . . as you relax into this state . . . deeply . . . you can simply enjoy . . . how it feels to be alive and to know . . . as the universe spins and turns . . . and the world spins and turns inside it . . . with all this spinning going on . . . it feels like we are just still . . . here and now . . . because we are. . . . As the world spins . . . and time goes by . . . each star seems so far away . . . and yet each star shines . . . as darkness falls . . . and we reach for the stars . . . yet through millions of miles . . . through space in time . . . the world millions of years ago . . . when we all originated . . . we came from one moment . . . and many moments went by . . . many moments moved on . . . and we can see the stars that exist . . . many millions of years in the future . . . contemplating how . . . as Richard explained to me once . . . we are all made of stardust . . . stardust that makes us up . . . and when we realize this we can realize our potential . . . deep inside . . . the magic that exists in each and every one of us.

You can notice . . . that what you thought was right . . . may not be . . . and what you thought wasn't right . . . may be left . . . as a better idea to ponder . . . because the more you try and stop yourself . . . from preventing the fact that . . . what it was that you were thinking about . . . when you did feel bad . . . your remembering to forget . . . the more you'll be delighted in understanding . . .

that you are forgetting to remember . . . bad feelings . . . and remembering to remember . . . good feelings . . . so that you can remember not to forget . . . to remember how wonderful . . . life can become when you aren't . . . doing what isn't good for you . . . and when you instead . . . remember the simple message . . . that my friend . . . the Indian guru said to me. . . . It all comes down to . . . deciding to . . . "be ever blissful."

Because, before you continue to enjoy . . . knowing that this is something . . . that you can already enjoy doing . . . you can begin to start to allow yourself . . . to realize that whether everything becomes clear immediately . . . or whether you understand it all after a few moments . . . either way, you can relax in knowing that the first thing you will wonderfully experience . . . while you develop more positive feelings . . . will be the sensation of understanding and becoming more aware of . . . how quickly and how easily you are finding yourself . . . loving the comfortable fluidity . . . of the best kinds of feelings . . . seeping inside every part of you as . . . fortunately . . . this is simply a natural . . . and obvious part of existing . . . and unconsciously taking ideas . . . that naturally change your mind.

Once you do this, and then allow yourself to return to full awareness, you can feel as Richard describes "an unexplainable sense of well-being." Trance ending is about connecting with an altered state where you can feel yourself as a real part of the universe and you can begin to practice relaxation, meditation, allowing yourself to simply drift into a state of daydreaming and inner peace.

PART VI

The Art of
Spiritual Freedom

CHAPTER 46

Free the World

THREE MONTHS LATER, I was back again with Richard. This time we were in a beautiful place called Puerto Vallarta, a seaside resort in Mexico. Richard had been telling me how wonderful it was. I had to go there. He described it like paradise, and to be fair, he was pretty accurate. We sat down at a table in the empty hotel bar. It was about 3:30 on a Thursday afternoon. Richard had been teaching a course for the previous few days, but this was a day off.

The gorgeous smell of the food that had been served for lunch still wafted from the kitchen. Very soft music could be heard in the background, and we could hear the sounds of people playing and swimming on the beach nearby. The sky was powerfully blue, and the sun shone down with great intensity. We were in the shade just indoors, and we looked through the veranda at the gorgeous ocean.

Since our last conversation, transformational changes had been happening for me. I was no longer ever lonely, really, and I finally felt completely over my ex-girlfriend. I realized just how much even failed relationships were potential growth experiences. I was seeing different people, but I was carefree about everything. I had met so many friends I hadn't seen in so long. I was going out lots and really enjoying myself. My state of mind was constantly good for no reason, and I noticed, as a result, just like Richard had said, that people were more and more attracted to me.

I felt remarkably good most of the time, and I felt so close to what I believed freedom actually felt like. My experiences on my world tour finally made so much sense. However, I still had some more questions that I wanted to ask Richard. Underlying all the lives on the planet are our reasons to live. People need a purpose to exist, a purpose to live. I wanted to uncover from Richard how important spirituality really is and what his perspective was on living a spiritually fulfilling life. How could personal freedom extend to worldwide freedom, and how could we see an end to slavery, ignorance, fear, and hate on this planet? A big question I knew, but I was sure that I would gain some wonderful insights that would at least help me make my own difference to the world. The least I would learn was about better ways to become more spiritual.

CHAPTER 47

Windows on Spirituality

I REMEMBERED MY experiences months earlier. During my travels throughout the world, from India and Nepal to Tibet and Thailand, from Italy and Ireland to the United States and Mexico, I had been exposed to many different perspectives on religion and spirituality. I had met various popular gurus and had become good friends with people from all kinds of religions. I remembered the seminar I went to with the Dalai Lama. All of these adventures had given me a different perspective on spirituality and religions. I was brought up a good Catholic boy in a suburb of Dublin, but now I had learned so much more about the beliefs that exist worldwide.

Perhaps one of the most important dimensions in many people's lives is their spirituality. By spirituality, I mean a person's beliefs about the universe, whether or not the entity called God exists, and if so, what form it takes. I am talking about how people believe they fit into the universe and, in essence, why they are here. It is about their connection to other human beings and how this connection affects the world around them. I had recounted my experiences at length to Richard and Paula. They were, after all, the main reason I had gone to such places as India. The stories they had shared about their time over there had intrigued me. Now I wanted to know more about Richard's perspective on spirituality.

OF: Richard, I want to talk to you about spirituality. How can people become more spiritual?

RB: Well, I think the misconception is that people who do a little yoga think they're more spiritual than other people. Everybody lives in the world, which is spiritual. In fact, we don't live in the world or on the world, we are the world. We are the same stuff that all the rest of the universe is made up of, so it's inescapable. The more you isolate yourself mentally and run little, tiny loops that make you think that it's only this and it's only that, there's only this God and there's only that God, and there's only patriotism, and all of these things that disconnect you, the more you miss the point.

People spend so much more time inside than they ever used to that they don't realize we are not "in" nature, we "are" nature, and that people need to go outside and look at the sky. Instead of thinking of it as a place where planes flop around, start to realize that, since the beginning of time, people have looked out and gazed at the stars. The more we learn about how immense the universe is, the more we look through the Hubble telescope and see the birth of galaxies, the more we see that they look exactly like the birth of a child. I mean it's absolutely mesmerizing. People can begin to take stock of this.

I think that religion can be either good or bad for people, and it's good for people when it opens them up so that they feel like they're a part of the grander scheme of things, which is nature. When I say "nature," I'm talking on the big scale. I'm talking about the big U, the universe. To me, the more that people get in touch with their own force of nature, the more they are going to get out of little thought patterns and begin to feel more strongly about everything. They'll feel love more deeply. They'll feel curiosity to the point where they'll do more things.

I've brought things back from India, Nepal, and Tibet and wandered around South America and hung out with American Indians and sat cross-legged until my knees felt like they were going to fall off for one reason only: so that I could get the same results as them. I did it to ensure that, instead of people getting therapy, they get to make changes in their lives today. People used to have to sit and wait for the garden to grow to eat, but now people's lives are busier than ever; they are busy all day from morning till night. They're lucky if they have an hour to sit around with their kids.

They need to be able to change their state faster, and not through years and years of meditation. They need to be able to get there now. They need to be able to get the same things they would get in traveling up to Tibet to participate in rituals and they need to be able to get it today. I think it's immense when we get rid of the gibberish that's around it and realize that all of the great shamans and all of the great religious leaders have just put people in touch with the forces of nature and with the power of believing.

It was apparent that Richard had learned much from the various religions and spiritual leaders he had met. I agreed with his idea that we need to get more in touch with nature and understanding first that we are a part of it already. Far too often, the busy, working world lets us get caught up in the unnatural cycle of technology. With advancements in what we *can* do, we have gradually created more things *to* do. With every new invention, we are being given less time and taken farther away from the natural world. We take our lives for granted, and we fail to provide enough time to exist and simply be in the world.

It's so important to get back to our roots and appreciate once more the immense fascination of the universe. It's essential to realize that the world is such a miracle and that so many miracles occur in it every day. It's necessary to understand how our beliefs can restrict us from experiencing spiritual delight should we take them too seriously.

What we can conclude is that spirituality must be looked at from a point of view that enables us to understand that it is unimportant which religion we follow or which rituals we perform. Rather, it is through our intention and our efforts to take time to appreciate and feel gratitude for the world that we can more closely connect with who we really are.

OF: With all the various religious leaders out there, what suggestions do you have for enhancing our sense of spirituality?

RB: Proceed with great caution. These people have been great hypnotists for many centuries. Most of these cults are very good at getting people to become followers, and the best way to get out of that is to make your own relationship with your own deities before you start, and make sure you give yourself your own posthypnotic suggestions. In this life, you are going to become a leader not a follower so that when you go, you go to find out what they are doing, not to follow them. Don't drink any tea. Don't swallow anything. Drink nothing, because some of these cults drug people. Bigger religions don't need to do this, but they still indoctrinate people. That's part of the whole concept of religion.

Gurus have followers. People have said to me, "Are you a guru?" I'm not, because I'm not that social. I don't want people to follow me. I don't want a commune, and I don't want huge groups of followers. I want educated people who guide their own lives and do their own things, and so I can't complain about the fact that there are people who have taken my work and are doing different things with it, and I think that's good.

Some people work in education, some people in architecture. There are lots of scientists who use my work as the foundation to overcome difficulties in science, because the same meta-model that works to expand people's understanding of their personal lives works with problems in science and in business. Problems are the same, because these difficulties don't exist devoid of human beings. They don't exist in the universe at large. They exist in our perceptions and understandings of how to manipulate the universe.

Our belief in things is what makes them real, and once we find out how to alter our belief, we will find things in the universe, and we will find out that the universe has limitless power. Instead of worrying about running out of energy, there'll be energy in the small piece of dark light. The physicists believe now that all the laws of thermodynamics are absolutely wrong—I fought for years to try to prove that. It started with the law of entropy—that everything's getting more random—and I thought, "Why are all the toasters appearing on planet earth?"

There must be a force that they're not taking into account, and that force, of course, is consciousness. The more we develop consciousness as a living species, the more we'll be able to control our destiny and the destiny of everything in the universe with whatever else is conscious, because I've got a feeling that consciousness is a lot more common than most people would ever imagine.

People say, "Do you believe in UFOs?" and I say, "No, because I believe we've identified them quite well." They're just FOs now. To me, I don't worry about spacemen. I worry about planet earth. The search for intelligent life on *this* planet is still underway, and the nice thing is evolution isn't over. I don't think evolution works the way people tend to think it does. I think it all progresses much faster and that our consciousness influences genetics just like we can influence the course of how the physical universe changes by our ability to affect it. As we go into space to do things, we'll discover that going across space is the slow way; there's some way to go through it. This is not a problem with the universe. It's a problem with how we perceive the universe, and when we perceive the universe differently transteleportation will be a piece of cake.

The idea that our perceptions of the universe are mostly responsible for our limitations was initially difficult for me to take onboard. Then, as I began to research and study some of the greatest accomplishments and discoveries in science, I realized that it was a change in perception or "paradigm shift" that enabled the discoverer to achieve these results. The more we learn about the universe, the more we realize how wrong we were, and we continuously gain new understandings and insights about how things work. Just when we think we know it all, we find out we actually know very little.

This reminded me that the more we learn and the more we develop new ways of thinking about the same things, the more intelligent we get. Gaining different perceptions on the world is not just useful because it gives us more choices; it is useful because it makes us smarter. When you can see things in a different way, you can understand more about it, and it helps you overcome problems that once seemed insolvable.

Over and over again, Richard's words repeated themselves inside my head: "Problems . . . don't exist devoid of human beings. They don't exist in the universe at large. They exist in our perceptions and understandings of how to manipulate the universe. . . . Our belief in things is what makes them real."

I began to understand what I had always known unconsciously. In the case of every client I had worked with successfully, I had helped them take care of the problems that existed in the way they were thinking. Problems didn't exist in their lives, because it is only by representing something as a problem that it becomes a problem. Otherwise, it's just an event or experience. When you can help people to change their beliefs and perceive their world more usefully, problems are dealt with, and they gain the freedom of peace of mind.

I began to recall the various spiritual perspectives I had learned about, and I realized one thing: they all emphasize the role of a higher being— be it God or Buddha, Allah or Krishna, Jehovah or Jesus, Shiva or the universe or nature itself. This higher being must be respected and thanked for good things.

When we can learn to do this and appreciate our universe for all the wonderfulness in it, we can live a happy, spiritual existence without the endless suffering and repetitive rituals.

The more we learn about the universe, the more we realize how little we really know about it. What is so critical is that we allow ourselves to tolerate this state of "not knowing." Otherwise, we can find ourselves caught in a belief system that restricts us and limits us. Having the best spiritual perspective is about having the best spiritual perspective *for you*. We are all unique, and therefore, it's essential that we enjoy our own ways of experiencing the universe and appreciate that other people are different.

There is a tremendous liberation in all of this. When you can appreciate your own and others' perspectives, you can discover how to feel extremely centered and spiritually content. You can feel this way because you have realized that the "truth" is that there is no truth; there are only perceptions. Many authors describe us as spiritual beings having a human experience. If this suits you better than an alternative, then believe it. Personally, I like the idea that we are spiritual and human, emotional and rational, intelligent and kind, all at the same time. How you live depends on which reality or perspective you decide to experience the world from. The perspective I choose enables me to embrace the full potential or infinite wisdom that exists in me and enjoy the idea that I will continue to learn more about myself every day.

The Dalai Lama says that the most important part of religion is to be kind and compassionate toward our fellow human beings. Compassion, for him, is really the center of humanity. Whoever or whatever we believe, we must get to a stage where we accept everyone's unique right to believe in their own ideas. I began to think about the prejudices that existed in the world.

OF: What about all the prejudices in the world?

RB: I think it's important to overcome the prejudice on this planet.

I have friends of every race, every color, and every religion. I'm the Jewish guy who gave away the bride at a Muslim wedding. There are no limits to whom I'll hang out with, yet I've been places where people hate me just for my religion, and I don't even practice being a Jew. I was just born one. I can't help it.

It's not like it's stamped on my forehead or anything, but you know, just the fact that people know is such a major deal to them. There are people who hate Indians and Pakistanis and those who hate Mexicans and call them wetbacks but you know, we all bleed red. There's only 3 percent difference between us and the chimpanzees.

We're 95 percent the same as squirrels, for heaven's sake. So the difference between us as human beings is primarily in how we live and how we act. It's crazy to think of all the human beings I've met on this planet. Most human beings will only meet 40,000 people. I, on the other hand, have spoken to millions and millions of people—and I haven't said the same thing each time. I've also listened to people, and I've met the great minds of the last century. I met Fritz Perls, Virginia Satir, Abraham Maslow, Moshe Feldenkrais, and the top physicists on the planet. All of these people that are real creators; they all lived spiritually in their own way. Virginia talked about spirituality in a different way than Maslow, and he did in a different way than Moshe Feldenkrais, but they were all great healers. Every one of them knew and believed in human beings and found healing where no one else could.

When the truth becomes illuminated to us, if that ever happens, we could be like the woman who mistook her cookies for those of the man she sat beside in the airport. Then all the wars, arguments, debates, and disagreements would be over one big mistake. Instead, we have to accept that we can't be too sure about anything. We can only believe or not believe. If people believe they are spiritual beings or human beings, I accept that, and they are not wrong. Like eating an ice cream, sometimes you like one kind of ice cream, and sometimes you like another. Different people like different ice creams. Is there one *true* ice cream? No, not that we know of. So instead, why not choose the most delicious? Why not choose spiritual delight?

OF: So religion is like ice cream.

I blurted it out. I had forgotten that these were all thoughts inside my head. Richard smiled and looked at me as if I had twenty heads.

RB: What? Owen, come back to earth. Come back to planet earth. It is safe now.

OF: I mean, in so far as you get to choose whatever ice cream you like, and respect other people's choice in ice cream, too.

Richard laughed.

RB: Yes, Owen, it's exactly like ice cream.

CHAPTER 48

The Freedom to Grow

IT WAS ANOTHER TOUGH DAY. The heat and humidity were so high. I had spent all morning dropping off resumes and filling out applications. That evening, I went to work at 5:00 PM and was sent home at 7:00 for failing to reach my quota. It was telemarketing, a rough business in New York. I never did reach my quota—until I abandoned the script. One day I began to do it off the cuff, and in two days, I had beaten the company record for the most sales. This didn't last long. I was told to go back to the script. There was no place for flexibility, no matter how successful I was. That day, after work, I went up to the top of the World Trade Center and had a drink. It was July. I was living in New York City.

I found myself living alone for much of my time there. I had managed to get a place out in Brooklyn. I met up with a friend of mine. We had a great night on the town. We sang karaoke in what had been the highest bar in the world back then, the top of the World Trade Center. I often wonder how many people I spent time with that night were there on the fateful day in 2001. It's so sad.

That night, pretty late, I got the subway back home. As I walked back through the derelict streets in the heart of Brooklyn, my heart began to race. I heard the sound of the latest rap artists blaring out in a tiny playground that I would soon be walking through. A car parked there played the music, and about twelve or thirteen guys about my own age were hanging out around the car. I couldn't turn back, as I had no where else to go. I continued to walk.

You see, I was the only white guy in the area, as far as I could tell. In all the shops around and every time I got on the buses, I rarely, if ever, saw another white person. Not that it bothered me—for the most part, the people of the neighborhood treated me far better than some of the white people I'd met in Manhattan. As I walked along the street, however, I was becoming more and more scared. I had seen all the movies. As a simple Irish guy, New York was a culture shock for me. I had always felt safe back in Dublin, and that I could take care of myself, but this was not Dublin. I began to replay images from the movie *Boyz n the Hood*. I entered the playground and tried to avoid all eye contact. They all turned, and I could feel them staring as I walked passed. Then one of them called out to me.

Richard's humming brought me back to our conversation. I asked him my next question.

OF: One of the most amazing things that I've found in my life is the speed with which I've grown, emotionally, mentally, and spiritually. Each year has brought so many challenges, so many events, and so many experiences. I've found myself dealing with the toughest things and coming through them a different person. As a teenager, I was so down, and yet I grew up so quickly. How can we help teenagers grow more, emotionally, and feel better about life?

RB: Teenagers aren't ready to be happy until they grow up and get their chemicals in order. Teenagers have to go through chaos. This I think is genetically predetermined to get people out of the house and out into their own lives. I think the trouble with teenagers is that they don't have long enough timelines. They haven't been alive long enough to project into the future far enough, so they don't think that things will hurt them. "Even if I become a heroin addict, what difference is it going to make? Nobody cares anyway." They don't think about being alive for fifty years!

None of us, when we were fifteen, thought that we'd ever live to be fifty. It's just not how it works, and you need to extend your life and look at the people around you and notice who is really happy and who isn't. Is the guy sitting in the gutter addicted to heroin happy? They may tell you, "Man, this is the best rush you'll ever get," but it's the best ten seconds that will ruin the rest of your life. So big deal. Do you want a whole life or a good ten seconds?

You've got to make that judgment. You've got to have a good enough decision strategy to say, "Look, I'm going to do the things I need to do." People say you have to go to college. No, you don't—but it's a good idea. Even though I went to college and I studied all these things I never used, going to college was a good idea because I went to a different place. I met different people. I learned about things that I would have never learned about. Many of the things I learned at college, I don't care about and will never use, but I got used to learning things for no reason other than to know about them, and I think that's good. That's why I think that it's important for young people to go to different places. I always took my children to foreign countries, and it's one of the best things that happened to them, because they met people from other cultures. They saw things they never would have seen, and even if you're not rich, I think it's important that you hop in a car, and you travel to whatever country or whatever county or whatever city lines and go into restaurants that have different ethnic food, if that's what it takes.

If you can't go to India, go to an Indian restaurant, but don't just have dinner. Talk to the people from India. If you go into a Mexican food restaurant, talk to the people from Mexico. Ask what it's like. Meet the children. Listen to their language. You know people are terrified of Muslims, and they don't know anything about them. Hang out with them for a while. They have very strict rules about what it is to be a Muslim—and it doesn't include killing people. Muslims are not violent people, and yet they are portrayed as being violent. They have some rituals I would never participate in and beliefs I would never share, but they're very, very ethical and have very strict rules. The Koran is very, very specific about not hurting people and property, even in wartime.

True freedom, it became clear to me, was not just about having the freedom to be able to feel good and think cleverly. It was also about the freedom to enjoy growing through different experiences. We must begin to appreciate difference and learn as much as we can by experiencing as much as we can. Experience, good and bad, is truly the best teacher. While we exist on this planet, we need to reach out and connect more with life, with places, with people.

When we do this, as Richard explains, we discover that those we feared, we had no reason to fear. We realize the universal similarity between all human beings. We learn more accurate perceptions of the world, and we grow more spiritually, emotionally, and mentally.

I grew so much as I experienced those four months in New York. As I walked passed the guys in the small playground, I heard one of them shout out to me, "Hey, what's up white boy? You gonna be the next Neo? Is this *The Matrix*?" I turned nervously and looked over at the face I guessed the voice was coming from. "Yeah, sure am. I think it is," I smiled back. He smiled back at me as the others began to laugh. "Damn boy, you gotta watch yourself out this time of night. Nothing but ill-thinking ganstas hanging out here, boy." I nodded and smiled and kept walking. I made it home. I found out the following week that this particular "gansta" lived in my apartment building when I bumped into him in the elevator. His name was Troy. We became friends. Experiences like my time in New York helped me grow massively. As I did, I began to get to know more of who I was. I realized that "who I was" changed from day to day. I decided I would ask Richard about this.

CHAPTER 49

How to Find Yourself

DURING MY TRAVELS in India, I began to realize that the vast majority of westerners who traveled there did so with one main objective on their mind: they traveled from temple to temple and guru to guru in an effort to "find themselves." This always seemed strange to me, but I had seen quite a lot of clients who failed to know "who they were" and longed for some self-insight. I guessed this was a similar experience. I talked to Richard about those I had met who were attempting to find themselves.

OF: When I was in India, I met a lot of people traveling around there searching for themselves. Have you any advice for people who feel lost in life and want to find themselves?

RB: I had a friend who did that. He told me he was looking for himself, and he was on his way to India, and I tried to explain to him that he was right here, but he didn't listen to me, and he was gone for three years.

What people have to realize is that it's not that they're going to find who they are. It's that you will become who you are. If there are negative things about yourself, you have to learn to stop doing them and do something else. It's to develop new rigorous habits of thought, and this is what most religions teach you how to do. This is true especially for the ones that are more spiritual in nature.

Some of them, of course, are just really good marketing schemes. I come from the United States. Religion there has almost nothing to do with spirituality other than a little faith healing here and there. You bring a person in front of 100,000 people in a stadium, and it's a lot easier to do faith healing because they are in such an altered state, because they are in a situation they've never been in. Now when you go to India, you are in a situation that you've never been in, and people are highly affected by being in some places. To me, you can highly affect people if you go in and create dramatic internal states, and realize that there are certain simple rules.

All of the chanting in all of the religions seems to focus on vowels, for example. That's why there's a difference between vowels and consonants. In Hebrew, the word for *letter* is "vibration." To say something vibrates and to say it's a letter is exactly the same thing. To be able to change the internal tone and the vibration of your internal voices, to change your own brainwave patterns so that they vibrate differently means that you'll see and hear and feel and act differently.

The reason I've focused so much on hypnosis in the thirty years that I've worked is not just because people need to relax. They need to do more than relax. They need to be able to go into states in which they have tremendous energy, yet they feel tremendous comfort and vibrate with their environment in a way in which they get things done. Manifesting, to me, is the most important thing that human beings do. Psychology was doing badly when I came along, because it wasn't manifesting results. It was locking people away, giving them names for their problems, and criticizing them, but it wasn't making it so that their fears disappeared. It didn't give them the feeling of success. It didn't give them the feeling that they could do things in their lives, the feeling that they had control.

Now, you can turn your control over to a guru and let him order your life, and you'll be at peace as long as the ashram has enough money for you to survive, but to me, that's really different from the true spiritual leaders who are the ones who are not going to somebody else's ashram. They're the ones setting up their own. To make your ashram only your house with your children and your relatives and your next-door neighbor, to me, this is what people need to do.

They need to make their life the temple. They need to make their life the church so that they begin to live in accordance with a set of principles that let them vibrate so that they feel like they are doing the right thing. They need to have their own moral code, and this stuff about people becoming suicide bombers so they can have a good afterlife is too big a gamble for those of us who have been in near-death and postdeath experiences.

We don't all report the same things, and the best way to really feel good and spiritual about yourself is to do the things that will enable you to live in harmony. One of those things is to have a sense of adventure. Try a little yoga. Try a little chanting. Try a little trance. Go and hang out with some people who do different things. Me, I'm not a joiner; I don't like to join cults or join things because I think you can get enough from small doses of things that you can make something of your own.

OF: So avoid the gurus then?

RB: Yeah. As I said, they once called me a guru in the newspaper, and I became furious, and I told them I'm not sociable enough to be a guru. I don't want people following me. I don't mind if they visit me from time to time, but I'm just not the kind of guy that wants a thousand people around me day and night. I don't want followers. I want to produce leaders, and I've heard such things from people who say how they want to produce leaders and a lot of people that come out of their seminars are waiting desperately for the next fire-walk rather than thinking about how they can change the fears in their own lives.

I'd like to see people generalize, and this is why I'd like them to overcome the fears they actually have, because not many of us find a fire in our backyard we need to walk across. I want to find them the toughest thing in their life and have them conquer it so that they realize that once they do that, they can do so much more. I always tell them ahead of time, "Look, if it's a fear of heights, if it's a fear of this, then think what else you can do once you have done this."

I just did a personal change workshop, and there was this lovely man in there, big guy with huge muscles who obviously works out all the time. He looked like he could crush steal marbles in his hand. His muscles were glistening, and when I was asking people what they wanted and had them turn in their little pieces of paper, it just said on his: "fear of heights." So I looked at him and said, "So you want a fear of heights? That's pretty easy. I'll have to take you upstairs and scare the shit out of you." He said, "That won't be necessary. I'm already afraid of heights." I carried on, "Well, what is it that you want? Do you want to stand next to the ledge and feel comfortable and fall off? What do you actually want?"

Most people are so busy avoiding things that they're not thinking about what's going to help them. He said, "Well, I want to overcome this fear because then I'll believe I can do anything in my life." I said, "Well that's the best reason for doing anything," and so I used the techniques that we use. I had him take his fear and spin it back the other way. I know enough about fear that most people who have a fear of heights also have a short motivation strategy. They see themselves getting out of bed, and they get up.

They walk near the edge of a building and see themselves falling off and they feel like they are going to. For a lot of people who have a fear of heights, this is very, very common. Therefore, I made it so that, when he went near the edge, he would feel different. I said, "As soon you get close to the edge, see yourself standing back two feet and being comfortable," and suddenly he was. It wasn't that there was something wrong with him. It's just that people don't really stop and think about what they're doing with their brain.

Of course, if you see yourself falling off a building and feel like you're falling, you're going to be afraid, but we're not taught to use our brains as if they're capable of the spiritual event of manifesting, because at the moment he realized that and he made something new in his mind, he engaged in the act of creation, and it is the most spiritual act there is.

Every religion on the face of the earth has a story about the universe beginning. All of this something came from nothing and that's the biggest miracle of all. So, if you can take the *mischegas* inside somebody's head and get them to engage in the act of creation to create a new thought, to create a new feeling that no one ever had, this is, to me, the most spiritual thing of all because once they do it once and once they realize how it's done they can take any bad feeling and spin it in the opposite direction. They can take away any set of pictures that make you feel bad and make pictures that make you feel good. They can begin to see the world in a different way.

When I began to think about what "finding yourself" really meant, I started to understand that the very concept presupposes that people are lost. I began contemplating whether or not they were actually "lost" or if it just felt that way. What soon became apparent was that it wasn't about them being lost. As Richard had pointed out, it is more about people becoming who they are. When someone feels lost, it is simply because they act and think and feel in so many different ways.

As human beings, we have a need for consistency. But in different situations our feelings, thoughts, actions, and behaviors are different, and we find it harder to define ourselves. In the modern world, as flexibility becomes a necessary skill and we become bombarded with mass amounts of information, it becomes more challenging to know who we really are.

Besides, just as we are discovering in the advances in quantum physics, as soon as we think we know what is "really going on," we discover that we may be wrong. Our perceptions of ourselves are no different. Hence, the way we think and feel about ourselves or see ourselves is constantly changing. So there is no real way to find out who we really are because the subjective nature of thought prevents us from doing that.

All we can do instead is attempt to understand ourselves, not as a fixed entity but as a creature of potential. If we can focus on everything that we can become at our very best—we can begin to find a self that is consistent and constant. You see, if we can think of ourselves as brilliant selves who don't always think, feel, act, or behave in that way, we can gain a new way of finding ourselves.

We can realize that whenever we think, feel, act, and behave at our best, we are getting closer to our real selves. Whenever we do not, we are simply making mistakes we can learn from. Sometimes it's important for us to get lost in our experiences, so we are focused on what we are doing rather than on ourselves doing it. That way we can more fully enjoy each moment and make them worthwhile.

OF: What about prayer, Richard? What do you think about the power of prayer?

RB: Well, prayer is the name of a meditative state. Some people think that prayer is only used to ask God for things. I know people in the United States who pray for parking spaces. It seems to me the Almighty Being—if you believe there's only one in the universe, the whole universe at large—probably doesn't have time to stop and think about parking spaces.

I don't think of deities as being a request center. I think that real spiritual people access powerful states. When I saw the mullah at that Muslim wedding putting those services on, he went into a deep altered state. The man had a power that you could feel that affected everyone in the room much more strongly, but still, everybody in the room affects everybody else to some degree.

Gregory Bateson once said that he was looking at the mantelpiece and, "In one sense that mantelpiece knows me and one billionth of an awareness of me knowing it and everything affects everything." I believe that everything's alive in it's own way, including ideas, and that you need to be able to give birth to ideas, and call it spiritual or not, that will influence everything around you in a way where people take more control. The operative word for me is "freedom." Freedom is everything, and love is all the rest.

Studies have shown that, regardless of what kind of prayer from what kind of religion is practiced, prayer has an impact on things like healing. This seemed to be true regardless of whether or not people knew they were being prayed for. In these studies, those who didn't know that they were being prayed for still found they were helped by prayer more than in the control groups, which removed any possible explanation using the placebo effect. What Richard explained was that prayer enables you to enter an altered state where you can get access to a universal energy. Christians call it God, shamans call it nature, Hindus can call it Shiva, and Muslims call it Allah. Regardless, the principle is the same.

It is about, as Richard says, doing the things that help us go into altered states and engage in spiritual practices that enable us to develop the confidence to turn fears around and appreciate the differences that exist in the world and learn from them. It's about discovering your own unique spiritual take on things and learning from different religions—whatever helps you feel better and connect more with what's truly important. That's taking a step closer toward spiritual enlightenment. Otherwise, we rely on the gurus. I had some experience with gurus while I was in India, and I didn't believe this was the most useful option.

CHAPTER 50

The Attraction of Gurus

IT WAS SUNDAY MORNING, about 4:00 AM. I was still half-asleep. I had to get up. The day before I had conducted a daylong workshop on NLP and happiness and then an evening workshop on NLP applied to business. I was pretty tired and had only got a few hours sleep. In about six hours' time, I was to present an advanced NLP workshop to over 200 people. The driver came on time to take me out to the ashram, which was about an hour's drive away.

As ever, there was traffic on the road as the morning got brighter. The guru I was about to experience was very popular. I was open-minded about him, but I knew I would have to keep my opinions to myself. When people follow gurus, it often brings rigidity, fanaticism, and stupidity. I entered the ashram and discovered thousands of people there all dressed in the same color. I felt a sense of eeriness as I took my place. I had been given a special VIP pass from a woman who went to one of the workshops I taught.

I sat in the lotus position, on the ground with my legs crossed underneath me. I was really uncomfortable and extremely tired. As I waited for hours in the same position, I noticed all around me thousands of people all repeating prayer after prayer. I was the only one dressed differently. I had a brown shirt and sandals and green trousers. I was also the only non-Indian I could see anywhere close. I stood out from everyone else, obviously. There were people of all ages praying up to the statues on the stage in front.

Eventually, after much of nothing, he arrived. He arrived in a chariot carried by two devotees on either side. He got down and began to walk slowly up and down the aisles smiling, waving, and blessing people. He took many envelopes from people on either side. I wondered if there were letters in them or donations. He continued down until, eventually, he stopped at the man in front of me. After a brief few words, he moved on, and I caught his eye.

This guru was about two feet away, and we began to stare each other down. It wasn't that I was trying to, I was just tired and found myself looking straight at him with a blank expression on my face. As we continued to stare, a silence fell over the audience. His expression changed from one of love and peace to what seemed one of anger and disgust. Not a word was said. The seconds ticked away, each one seeming longer, but I would not draw my face away. I'm not sure why, but we kept it up.

I'm not sure, even now, what made him stop and look at me. Maybe I was the first person he had come across in a while who didn't feel he was a higher being than me. I didn't intend to give him any "bad" looks; I just wasn't seeing him as a god.

While I was in India, I was introduced to a number of other well-known gurus. I met the spiritual teacher Sri Sri Ravi Shankar who is behind one of the most popular forms of yoga around the world today. We got on pretty well, and we chatted about NLP and yoga for a while. I got a nice energy from him. Similarly, I met a guru who Richard had met when he was in India, and it was great to talk to him, too. We exchanged stories and discussed different perspectives on life. I learned so much from them.

Best of all, I was introduced to a young guru named Sri Nithyananda Swamigal. He had been discovered when he helped a prominent businessman to overcome cancer. These healing qualities were soon made common knowledge. He was the fastest "up-and-coming" guru in India and had the backing of some well-known businessmen. He was close in age to me, and when we met, we discovered we had much in common. He had heard of NLP, and we discussed how our approaches were similar. Both were about helping people to quiet their minds from negative thinking and to focus on going into happier states. At one stage, a huge portrait of him fell suddenly toward where he was sitting. In an instant, I caught it, surprising myself in a flash. Without having flinched, he turned, smiled, and said, "Thank you. I see NLP also gives you lightening-quick reflexes."

We chatted for over an hour, and he began to do some energy work with me. I had experienced energy work before, but never even close to being as powerful as this. As we chatted, I asked him to sum up his main philosophy in one sentence, and he replied, "Be ever blissful." He looked at me when he said this, and I could feel a remarkable energy coming from his eyes to mine. I began to get what Richard always calls an "unexplainable sense of well-being." I began to see things a lot more simply, and everything Richard had taught me about going into powerful, positive, happy states made sense again.

Some of the secrets I have learned from these gurus have made a huge difference in my life. I met others on my travels, including a number of holy men as I trekked through the Himalayas. What interested me most was that every guru I met spoke highly of the others. They all seemed to have figured out that it was so important to appreciate other people's sense of spirituality. I realized that most of these Indian gurus and Tibetan lamas were simply good teachers and that it was the "dependence" on them that was a bad thing.

Unfortunately, people often rely on gurus to help them achieve spiritual enlightenment. The gurus become not only the "teacher" but also the "god." This was especially true in India. I was not under the illusion that the religions we had back home were much different. We, too, have such notions, such as papal infallibility. In every religion, I realized, there always seems to be someone who is a leader, and unfortunately, it is a case of relying totally on that leader being a good person, much like totalitarian regimes. Since I did my master's thesis on the "guru factor," I was still curious about Richard's thoughts on them.

OF: Why do you think there are so many people attracted to gurus in India?

RB: Well, in India, to get an education is the most important thing you can do. In India, it's much different. It's not like the Hare Krishna people in the United States, where they are trying to sell incense at the airport. They are trying to teach people principles that they can live by and have freedom. Poverty is the most limiting thing that there is on the earth. When people live in poverty, it's very hard for them to have freedom, and if they can go and listen to someone talk who teaches them how to overcome wanting things that they'll never have and still feel good, then that's great.

The most amazing thing about India is that people live in abject poverty and don't have low self-esteem. This impressed me. I went over to people's houses where they had no electricity. They had dirt floors. They didn't have any furniture. They had a couple of chairs that they took out of the wall. They rolled out mats. They worked twenty hours a day, and yet they had no low self-esteem. They were proud of where they lived. They knew that, where I came from, I had a lot more money and was a famous person. But they wanted their children to hear me talk, even if they didn't speak the same language; they figured the vibrations would seep in.

When you were there, I know people came up and asked you to bless their children, to bless them, and really what they want is a little bit of the flame that burns around each of us. Just like some people give you the creeps when you stand next to them, people want to feel anybody who's got great teaching power.

In India, they teach people how to take a little piece of that flame for themselves. There are spiritual leaders I've seen standing with lines of a thousand people. They walk up, and each one of them takes a bit of his flame, and he blesses them, and they walk off. It's what they do all day long. Some of them don't even utter a word, but they're in such a pleasant state that they know how to share the state.

One of the guys I met, when I walked up to him, looked at me and went into such a pleasant state that he dragged me right with him, and it felt wonderful. I learned in India how to do that with people, and you can take them. That's where I can look at people, and they'll go into a trance. I can take angry people and make them happy. It's the most important thing that I have learned. Real spirituality is realizing that, when you vibrate real joy, the people around you will begin to do the same.

Again, Richard's words resonated in my head: "Real spirituality is realizing that, when you vibrate real joy, the people around you will begin to do the same."

Real joy—Richard laughing.

I began to understand that, again, all of this came back to feeling good and sharing this with those around me. It was difficult to believe that this simple principle was what everything kept coming back to, but I had yet another example, and I began to wonder what it would be like if my entire focus switched to this one simple principle.

I was also interested in what Richard had talked about regarding that "fire" or "energy." Some Indians had, indeed, come up and asked me to bless their children. I was taken back by it, but I put myself into a powerful meditative and positive state, and I blessed them with my best thoughts as I put my hand on their head and thumb on their forehead. I wanted to know more about this fire.

OF: By fire, do you mean energy or charisma?

RB: Well, charisma can also be when people are around people, because most people try and emulate others. The advertising agencies understand this. Eighty percent of the population is trying to be like somebody else because we learn by imitating adults. Our whole life, we're imitating things to learn them. Sometimes that goes overboard. People look at some of these gurus and say, "If I was just like him, then I'd be happy. If I was just like so-and-so, then I'd be happy."

It doesn't surprise me that young people get into this stuff. They follow these people. They hang on every word, but they're not being like them. They're listening to what they're saying, and they're being obedient. They're not really emulating. The trouble is that when they stop becoming like the person that they think this person is, and then start doing what the person says, they're not doing what humans do best, which is to learn.

OF: On this point of emulation, I feel it's important for people to remember that, to teach people things that are supposed to make them happier and better, it is not about being perfect yourself. It's like the Dalai Lama says, being spiritual is not about being Buddhist or Christian or whatever; it's about being good and treating people well and living well. He is truly wise.

Richard agreed wholeheartedly.

RB: Yeah, he's truly a wonderful man.

OF: Many of these other gurus or speakers seem to present an image, and this image is used to inspire people. So the problem still exists of people wanting to emulate them. They inspire others in a worthwhile way, but often these gurus don't walk their talk, which I think is a problem.

Richard again agreed.

RB: Some people are too busy to be happy themselves. This happens to a lot of people, they talk a good game, but they don't actually apply it. I've been married for so many years, and a lot of people talk about having relationships, but they just can't do it. If you are having a relationship with the wrong person, then you really need to find the right person—but there are some people who live in misery instead.

There are some people who have jobs they absolutely hate, but they don't believe that they can change their lives and start doing something that they'd rather do. I've seen hundreds of thousands of people change their lives in so many ways over the years that every fiber of my soul believes in miracles. I've seen people overcome fatal diseases. I've seen people switch from having prestigious jobs where they were running corporations to become a school janitor and be happy for the first time in their lives.

It was very true. What Richard was talking about was so important. In modern society, many people do jobs that provide them with a lot of status but little happiness. He was emphasizing the importance of walking your talk and enjoying your life. So many people talk about it, but it's essential to do it. What's critical is that people begin to believe in themselves and their ability to turn their lives around.

I realized something about the guru I stared at, as he kept my gaze and his expression worsened—with the negative vibes I was getting from him, at the same time there were thousands around me who adored him. He eventually turned and walked to the other side of the crowd, and I noticed many negative stares coming my way from the white-dressed devotees. They had seen him frown at me, and they, too, frowned intensely at me for "showing disrespect." They worshipped him and were happy because of it. It made me wonder. He provides much happiness to many and is seen as a god by them. If only they could realize that the real spirit of God exists in them and in their connection to the universe. Then it suddenly occurred to me that that was just my perception.

The most useful way of thinking about all this seemed to be in realizing that we are responsible for the experiences of our lives. Again, not to blame for the bad ones, but we are the source. This enables us to control the way we deal with everything. With this control, we can make our lives a heaven. We must hold the power of the spirit inside ourselves. We must take responsibility for our lives and connection with the universe ourselves. We must be the owners of our own enlightenment. Robert Anton Wilson mentions the idea of us all being our own popes. Really it's about having your own sense of spirituality that's right for you, not because of what someone tells you but because of what you feel about it, yourself. Once we find ourselves connecting spiritually to the world, we can look at making a positive impact on it. I once thought that was impossible. There are so many problems in the world. Richard soon explained to me, however, that, while there was no point in taking on the world, I *could* take the world on.

CHAPTER 51

Feeling Helpless in the Modern World

IT BECAME PRETTY OBVIOUS that Richard believed that one person could make a difference to the world. My thoughts wandered back to poverty-stricken places in India. It had affected me deeply. I looked around and my heart broke for the thousands of people I saw living in small tents on the side of the road. I felt such a sense of helplessness with all the children coming up to me begging. I wondered what Richard had to say about this.

OF: Richard, when I went through the streets of India, and I walked along the road through shanty towns, I felt so helpless because I could not help the people living there at all. So much poverty and so much sickness—how can we deal with this sense of helplessness?

RB: Well, keep in mind the following thing. If a kid has enough strength to pull at your shirt, he's not starving to death. A lot of it's a con job to start with. When you go to India, you learn that where the real needy are is outside the temples. You go outside the temples, and if you give them any money, they'll go buy food. They'll split it up and share it with each other. The people on the streets begging for money are professionals. This is what they do for a living, and you can't be fooled by things. You have to see things for what they really are.

You want to see poverty, go to Africa. I mean India is poor compared to where we live, but these kids have enough strength to run down the street. There are places where that is not true. You have to keep in mind that you can only change things one person at a time. You can change opinions through the media, but when it comes down to changing people, still every person has to change. They need to challenge themselves and make some friends of different races, colors, and creeds.

A Christian, who wants to be a good Christian, should make a Muslim friend and not try to convert him from being a Muslim but learn about his religion and learn how to respect it. I think that this is one of the worst things that happens. Everybody is trying to convert everybody else to their ideas. It's like if I can't convince you, then I am wrong. This universe is vast enough for more ideas than we could ever generate on this planet, and to me, it's the challenge of human beings to realize that what they really need to do is to face up to difference and just say, "It's different"—not to have to change it, not have to join it, just to know what it is.

You ask most people and they will agree. When I was in Ireland, there weren't that many Jewish people there, and it was really funny because people asked me questions. They were very confused. One guy asked me a question. He's thirty years old, and he says, "Is it true that Jews don't believe in Jesus?" and I said, "Well we're still waiting for the Messiah, you know; we heard about him, but we're not buying into it." There are certain things that were supposed to happen when the Messiah comes, and they didn't happen when Jesus came, so we pretty much figured out it wasn't him. But it doesn't mean he shouldn't believe in it. I mean, they don't even teach people enough about other religions to be respectful of them.

They asked me how could I celebrate Christmas, and I said, "Well, we don't celebrate Christmas." We get the day off 'cause everybody else does, and I'm willing to take any day off. I like it. In Ireland and the United Kingdom, they have holidays they call bank holidays. When I first heard about this, I said, "Well, what exactly is it celebrating?" because in the United States we always make up an excuse: "It's Abraham Lincoln's birthday," even though we move it around, "It's the day the war ended." We always have some excuse, "It's the day trade unions became legalized."

OF: Well, the way the world's leaders are acting at present, it looks like with the rate of wars being started, soon every day would be a day off!

RB: Well, yeah, I don't see these leaders getting to the end of any wars. They are very good at starting them, I have to admit. They're really cleaning up the messes that have been left by people behind them. The people of the planet tried. I mean the "autonomy of nations" is nice, but we shouldn't allow nations to practice absolute inhumanity, and the reason we know that some of these countries have all those nasty weapons is that we have the receipts from selling them.

That's not a joke. How we knew the Iraqis had any bombs is because we sold them all to them, and the Germans sold them chemical war plant equipment. We need to internationally stop making land mines and stop making ways to kill each other.

Of course, you know, it's like a bunch of teenagers running around slaughtering each other in African nations and calling themselves rebels.

I mean, excuse me, but until we give people some better way to live, that's what they are going to do. I personally believe that Iraq is going to be better in the end. It's going to take twenty years, but twenty years from now, every child in that country is going to stand a better chance. Every kid is going to school in Afghanistan, and that wasn't the case before. At the same time, I'm against bombing people from the sky and things like that because, if I were president, I would legalize assassination and put a large price on these people's heads and kill them all and take the risk that they would hire someone to kill me.

That's why we passed a law in the United States that said that you are not allowed to assassinate heads of state. It was passed so that other people would stop killing our presidents. Jesus Christ, Ronald Regan got shot, and he didn't even know. Now that is not being terribly in touch with your own feelings. To me, I think that it's very important that people realize that there are horrible things all over this country.

I mean, in the United States, when I went into mental hospitals, I was absolutely appalled. The people were treated even worse than in prisons. They gave them electric shock treatment and horrendous stuff. It's so easy to become immune, and I think Hollywood people better get on the stick and do something. To me, the media better stop focusing on all the stuff in Los Angeles. The first place they go to for news is where any gun is shot. It doesn't matter what happens. There could be wonderful things happening, but the news is based on what brings in good ratings, and they've made it so that people almost expect murder to occur all over the place.

You know, when they do a report on the news, the first thing that they tell you is how many people were killed in Iraq today. They don't tell you how many schools were opened. They don't tell you how many people that had been locked away in prison for nothing more than their political ideals were freed. They don't tell you how many people haven't been buried in a mass grave in Bosnia this month.

So many people die in wars all over the planet. Let me be very simplistic. They die because there are many people who are scared of other people who are different from them. We have developed a world where differences seem dangerous, and sameness seems essential. Thus, we develop weapons to destroy those who are not like us or to "defend" ourselves from those who are not like us. In our civilized world, we have just gotten better at killing people. Our evolutionary forces suggest that only the strong survive. My question is why can't we all be strong and help each other survive? Competition to cooperation. Again, I hear the cries of "pointless idealism," but I believe in the possibility of making the world a better place.

I have heard many intelligent social commentators, from journalists to comedians, academics to book authors, discussing the causes of many of the world's problems. I have heard blame being cast the way of the political system, the media, or politicians. I have heard blame being cast the way of the environmental circumstances on the planet or the human race as a whole.

It has always struck me as pointless to complain about things and ascribe blame. Surely the aim is to get people to become aware of the problem and then to try to fix it. Blaming and complaining sometimes achieve these ends, but often they don't. Instead, I believe that we must develop intelligent understandings about how things are and how we want them to be. That way, we can best create new solutions to the problems that exist. Instead of focusing on who is to blame and why things aren't working, we must instead focus on what we can do and how things can work. Our focus determines our results. This we can alter.

As Richard says, however, it's about changing people slowly, starting with yourself. It's about getting people to appreciate and respect the differences between them and beginning to get the media to focus on the good things that happen and not just the bad. It's the old idea that you always get more of what you focus on in life. So as the world focuses on all the tragedies, we wonder why more seem to occur. We must begin to open our eyes to the good in the world. Then, maybe, one day we will all wake up and start figuring out these simple things. Of course, we will endure our own tragedies in life, and there is no quick-fix solutions to them. I hoped, however, to gain some of Richard's advice on them.

CHAPTER 52

On Pain of Death:
The Tough Things in Life

THE HARDEST AND toughest experience in life beyond a shadow of a doubt is losing someone you love. Grieving for someone you loved with all your heart is truly the most agonizing event we ever have to face. Unfortunately, we all have to face it. I brought this situation up with Richard.

OF: Richard, have you any words of advice for people going through the grieving process? What can they do?

RB: Get on with your life . . . as fast as you can. The faster you get from feeling bad to getting on, the sooner you stop looking at the past and start looking at the future, the sooner you're going to get something good going on. I mean, sure, it's hard to get over the death of someone you've loved for thirty years, but the truth is that you're never going to get over it, so you better get on with your life anyway and make it a fact.

Some things are just facts. You know, some terrible things have happened to me, and they're just facts. I wish they didn't happen to me, but I can wish in one hand and shit in the other and, if I slap myself in the face, guess which one sticks. I used to tell my clients that for years, and they used to take it as a metaphor, and I used to say, "Look, we can do this for real, because I'm doing it to you verbally. You're doing it to yourself physically." You know, you're taking shit and hitting yourself in the face with it every day and then wondering why your life stinks.

I mean if your child dies, you are going to feel bad. I just recently worked with a woman whose sixteen-year-old son had died. Okay, that's when you feel bad, but it's now been three years, and every moment of every day she feels bad. That's too much. There's a point at which her pictures should have flipped, and she should be associating with this fact because I asked her, "Would you rather if he had never lived? Would you rather have those sixteen years, or would you rather he never existed?"

She answered, "Well, he was the most important thing in my life." And I said, "Good. That doesn't have to change, but what you have to change is that you have to see what you saw in every good memory, and then with the bad memory of the time when he dies, you have to see yourself in it and push it off in the distance so that you can appreciate the time you had with him."

Everybody on this planet is going to have to accept that the people they know die, and you have to decide that you're better off for the good times that you have with them or whether you are going to lock yourself in the closet and never meet anyone again. I know it sounds ridiculous, but that's because it is.

I always said that there were never any NLP techniques that would immediately and successfully deal with three things in life. Those three things are: serious illnesses, the end of a relationship, and death of a loved one. Although I had worked with people and have seen people who overcame serious illness through using their minds with NLP and hypnosis, I am talking about dealing with these illnesses when your loved ones are suffering. As Richard said, it's not about getting over someone who has died. It's about feeling grateful for the times you had with that person, remembering the best experiences you shared, and asking yourself what that person would want you to be feeling now.

My personal beliefs are that my loved ones who have died are out there somewhere waiting for me. They are there to give me advice when I need it and to listen to me when I need someone to talk to. I like the idea of something like heaven, personally. That's only my personal belief, and I think that the key is for people to allow themselves to believe in whatever afterlife comforts them the most.

Many people don't stop to take the time to let those whom they love or have loved know how they feel or felt. Soon we will all be in a grave or out in the stratosphere and our opportunities will have passed us by. When we are alive and with our loved ones, this is the chance we get, and yet we waste much time clinically responding to the world as if we are in the center of it, arguing over ridiculous things and getting annoyed about nothing. Meanwhile, the clock ticks. We must remember this always. We must remember that we have limited time and in the time we have, we must take every opportunity to show our love in whatever form it takes. We must let bitterness fade, and in place of it show compassion and all the love we can muster.

When we lose a love, life can be so cruel. When we lose a friend, life can be so awful. Death takes our friends and true loves away, but as Morrie Schwartz once said, "Death ends a life, not a relationship." Over the past few years, a few of my relatives and friends have passed away. I still think of them every day. I ask them questions. They are still as wonderful and as close to me as they ever were.

A very good friend of mine died a while ago out of the blue. Her husband and soul mate, also a dear friend, talked about her and how much he missed her. He described how important it was to enjoy every single moment you have because, at any moment, you could be robbed in the same way he felt he had been. Every part of me broke down into tears, and my heart was more deeply affected and more deeply inspired from his words than from anything else I had ever experienced. I can't explain it, but since that day my life has been profoundly different.

Every morning I wake up, and I am focused on making each second count. I finally got the epiphany that I needed—the epiphany of realizing life is far shorter than we imagine, and in this blinking of an eye, we have to make it worth something. There is so much to do, so many people to love, so many good times to have, so many moments to cherish. And we can do this—or we can waste our lives. It is our choice and we must make it.

We cannot eliminate grief. Time will heal eventually, but while it does its work, we must focus on getting on and doing things that make our lives and the lives of the loved ones we have left better. I learned from my experiences and from Richard one hugely important lesson about grief—make every moment count; you don't have nearly as much time as you think.

At any second, your loved ones can be stolen away from you. Far too often we spend our time with them arguing about silly little things instead of enjoying each and every moment. Take each second and feel grateful for it. Time will go by, and things will change. While you have such beauty in your life, it is crucial to take the time to truly appreciate it and live every second fully.

In life, we never know what is around the corner. It's important to be ready for whatever comes our way. I was about to learn more about how to do this more successfully.

CHAPTER 53

How to Deal with Change in the World

WHEN I WAS TREKKING back down Everest, my ankle gave way. It was agonizing as my hiking boot scrapped against my shinbone. I tried to walk down, but I could not manage even a few steps. There was still a long way to go before we were back at the airport where we could get a flight to Kathmandu, and I knew I was in trouble. I was concerned, yet I kept focusing on what I needed to do. Chabbi seemed to be unsure, too, and as much as he helped me, we could not get down the rest of the trek like that.

Life is like that. You never know what challenges you are going to have to face. With dramatic changes affecting us continuously, it occurred to me that a key part of staying centered in the modern world is gaining the ability to deal successfully with change. I wanted to ask Richard for some advice in coping with change.

OF: I've been reading Robert Anton Wilson lately, and he discussed the idea of remembering our beliefs and realities often change from time to time. What do you think about this idea that we can never be sure about anything because everything changes over time?

RB: Well, Robert is a man of very strong beliefs and very strong morals. He's also probably the smartest person I've ever met in my life. What he's talking about is the Heisenberg uncertainty principle. Even the rules of physics are changing. It used to be that, whenever you passed electricity through a wire, it had to give part of it off as heat, and they absolutely believed that formula, but it turns out that when you reach a certain temperature, the formulas change so that there are more variables. People always think, "There are three variables," "There are five variables," and yet, there are an infinite number of variables.

So our universe is constantly changing every moment, and we cannot understand everything about it at the same time. Instead, depending on what we "tune in" to, we will only experience a part of it through our own nervous system. As the rate of information available in the world is expanding and doubling every year, many people find it challenging to face such rapid change. When the world is changing so dramatically so quickly, it can often be hard to predict the future and predict how to handle the future most usefully. Whereas once careers lasted a lifetime, now most people will have many different careers during their lives.

OF: So with that in mind, how can we best cope with change in the most effective way?

RB: Most spiritual teachers teach you one thing, which is to not have negative feelings but to change them. Whether you have to take hours to meditate it away or whether you go through yoga positions or whatever, it all boils down to the same thing: learning to take feelings that are a reaction and doing things with them. Even Dianetics and Scientology talk about being able to make it so that your immediate reaction to things is something that you can change.

Now my approach to it is spinning feelings backwards. When you have feelings you don't like, you spin them backwards in your body and put yourself back in the same situation so that you don't limit what situations and what people you can be with. Instead of limiting your universe based on your bad feelings, you learn to just make it so that the feelings just relax, because you have to understand these are just chemical reactions inside of us.

These are not real things, and if you learn to change the chemical reactions in your body, so you can be around people, things will feel different than they were. The reason white supremacists are so messed up is that they haven't been around black people. They haven't sat and had dinner with them. They can't. That's why their internal states goes wild, yet if they could learn to take the feelings and spin them backwards and relax and sit down and meet people, then they would hate no longer.

Hate is based on ignorance, ignorance is based on fear, and the fear is based on bad chemical reactions in your body. So to me, it's all a much simpler phenomenon than most people think. That's why my seminars are so integrated compared to most people's. If you go to a seminar I hold, there are people of every race, color, religion, and creed, laughing about jokes about everything. Most of the jokes that I tell are not just about religion; they're about me because I think if you can't take your own worst parts and make it so that you can laugh at them, you are going to be at the mercy of them.

If you are afraid of heights and if you don't know how to sort it out, then you should get a professional who does. I've trained a hundred thousand people. In fact, I've trained probably a lot more than that by now, but in every country on the face of the earth, there are people who should be able to teach you how to get rid of a fear. If not, buy a copy of *Frogs into Princes*. You'll have to buy a used one 'cause it's out of print right now, but I'll bring it back into print eventually.

If not, get books like *Using Your Brain for a Change*. Also, you don't even need my books. My stuff has been stolen and written about by many people, and the reason I invented these techniques is that they do the same things that spiritual leaders do. They teach you how to do the most spiritual thing of all, which is to change one thing into something else. The universe is in a constant state of flux. Energy converts from one form to another. You burn wood, and it turns into a gas. It's the same with consciousness—the elements of it are all there in one form or another, but they transform.

We're just a part of consciousness. We don't have a separate consciousness, and our consciousness affects the people around us, and whether we say anything or not, the vibrations are there. Learning to be in a good state is a responsibility. Even in a country with all the chaos and poverty of India, people are a lot more relaxed. I think we need to do it and be civilized. When they asked Gandhi about Western civilization, he said, "I think it's a lovely idea. I think you should try it."

It is our responsibility to use our own response ability. What much of this book has been about has been the importance of getting into a good state and managing your state regardless of what occurs. In the face of change, if you can learn to adopt and adapt your own positive state and react usefully to what happens, you'll find yourself dealing with everything in a wonderful way. If you can focus on just your state, then when the unexpected arises, you'll be in a position to deal with it all brilliantly.

I pulled off the painful boot and put on one of my white sneakers that I had carefully tucked away in my haversack. I proceeded to limp down the tallest and most well-known mountain in the world. As I did so, I fell a couple of times, but I managed it. The trek down was not all downhill. It was full of ups and downs, and I knew that for every descent, there would be most probably a climb. Eventually, we made it down. I remember on my way down, as the sherpas who lived along the trek passed us by, they laughed and sniggered at my odd shoes. It's funny. It doesn't matter whether it's in the heart of Dublin city past a group of teenagers or up in the hills of eastern Nepal, people will still find another person's mishap hilarious.

As I told you, life for me often seems chaotic. I usually experience one adventure after another. I have never told anybody about some of the experiences I went through on that mountain and on that trip, but many of them served to change my life forever. Life is filled with synchronicities or coincidences. All in all, though, I always manage to deal with things successfully because I have learned how to take things in stride. The trick is to manage your state and use your brain effectively. Regardless of what happens, you can always sort it out. Taking life in stride is being prepared for uncertainty and relishing it. This is what makes life so interesting, so wonderful. I knew that from this state it was also possible to change the world.

CHAPTER 54

How to Change the World

I HAD ONE FINAL QUESTION.

OF: So how can we make the moments of this world more special and more wonderful? How can we change the world in a positive way?

RB: Become a television producer. If you have control over the media, you can influence a larger number of people. As I mentioned before, *All in the Family* probably did more to put an end to racism than anything else. All the marches, all the other stuff helped, but you know, Archie Bunker making a fool of himself as a racist led to fewer people treating black people badly—more than anything else, and I mean categorically, across the board. When I was young I stayed in hotels where they wouldn't take phone reservations because it might be a black person disguising his or her voice.

I remember hearing about stuff like that. I remember my mother walking out of a hotel we were supposed to stay in when she found out they wouldn't let black people stay there; she was utterly offended. It's funny, Jewish people know a lot more about racism than most people. We've been experiencing it longer, but I would never have thought that things would change as much as they have in my lifetime.

I would never have thought that schools would be as integrated as they are. Some schools are more integrated than others, but you know, the world's whole boundaries are breaking down. This whole thing in Europe I find really interesting. This is going to change everything because just like Louisiana is different from California, it's still part of the same country. They're still on the same side, and now Europe wants to be on the same side.

What I think will be really interesting is that if this European Union keeps growing, pretty soon it will all just be one planet. I think everybody ultimately knows that's gonna happen. I think it's in every science fiction movie, and when that happens, we'll get rid of the borders, because they won't serve a purpose anymore. That's based on the scarcity model.

People ask me about the different NLP trainings out there. People need to move away from scarcity. Instead of saying we have one pie, and we can divide it up, what we really need to do is to create more pies. Everybody should really go through twenty-five practitioners. I mean, I went through thousands and thousands of hours of tape of everybody I could find, and some people were better than others, and so they were the ones I focused on. Some people teach people better than others. I think the wider variety of information you're exposed to, and the more you pursue, the better it is. Instead of trying to categorize everything to be the same, try to find what's unique and get the extra piece.

It would be a very dangerous idea to give me control of a media company, because I would definitely use it to influence people in a positive way. I would influence people so that they couldn't feel bad about things. I'd start with children, teaching them not to be afraid so much but to be curious and to appreciate the difference between things so that if they looked at a different religion, they didn't feel like they had to become a part of it or that they had to hate it. This is one of the problems with human beings. They don't realize that you don't "have" to do anything.

If something's totally different, you can say, "Oh, well that's interesting," and check it out, but you don't have to accept it wholeheartedly. You don't have to become a Hindu to look at Hindu temples. When I was in India, I went through lots of these Hindu temples, and when I came out of them, there'd be thousands of people coming in.

The thing that amazes me most of all is that these Indians would come up to me and my wife and thank us for visiting their temple because they didn't see us purely as tourists. They were just shocked that we walked up the hill for five hours into the mountain where most westerners never went unless they became devotees of the gurus. We came in just to say hello, because we appreciated it. They were beautiful temples. They were beautiful people. I couldn't live like that, but I still appreciate the fact that others can.

It's just that simple. Today, a lot of people are mad at Muslims. I think it's the Muslim teachers we should be mad at. There's nothing in the Koran that's nearly as horrible as what is being taught. The Koran is quite clear: you don't hurt innocent people and you don't ruin property. You're not supposed to do these things, you know, but it is possible to justify everything, especially for religious fanatics. Whether they're Christian fanatics, NLP fanatics, est fanatics—they're still the same. They say, "If you don't agree with me, you're bad." They don't appreciate differences. It's the same sort of thing that you saw in every high school, just on a bigger scale. People are trying to be one up because they think that, if they push other people down, they will feel better, but it doesn't work that way. They have to keep doing it more. I think peace comes when you build lots more McDonald's in Moscow. It's then that the United States is a lot less likely to nuke Moscow, as we have all our investments there. If we have lots of politicians living in Moscow—

American politicians and lots of embassies, lots of missions—we're not likely to drop a bomb there.

The biggest problem I find is that when people isolate themselves and make themselves ignorant, because ignorance leads to fear, fear to anger, and anger to violence, which leads to more ignorance. This cycle is part of what's perpetuated. The fact that the Muslim society and the West cut themselves off so much from each other is ridiculous. I don't believe that you should have governments run by religions. I think that's a bad thing; I think there should always be freedom of everything.

To change the world, Richard was proposing the idea of education and integration—to educate people about different religions, ideologies, creeds, and perspectives; to integrate people from all kinds of backgrounds. Freedom lies in the void between fanaticism and apathy. It lies in the notions of tolerance and acceptance. To educate and integrate the world, we need to spread these ideas throughout the world. The media provides us with one way to do that.

The key to all of this is to begin with yourself. When we start changing ourselves and making ourselves happier, more productive, better, and more effective, we can make the world better, too. When we start becoming wealthier and richer, healthier and fitter, more relaxed and confident, we can make the world richer and filled with more peace, too. When you turn your own life around, you can turn the world around. It begins one person at a time. It begins with you. As you improve, those around you will be affected by that energy and "fire" that exists, and you will discover how wonderful it can be to start the process of change throughout the planet.

We have to accept that change is always possible, because it's always happening, and that we can affect it. We have to recognize that changing the world means never giving up no matter what. We have to learn how we can change our feelings and the feelings of the people we know, so they can start feeling better, happier, and smarter and that life can become wonderful for everyone.

It's about cleaning up the inside of your mind so that your thoughts are more useful and so that you manifest good things and good ideas. Changing the world is possible only when you know that you can. Engaging in practices like meditation, self-hypnosis, yoga, or prayer helps you clear your mind and focus it on good things. I remember learning yoga from a friend of mine, Michael Connolly, in his classes down in Waterford. Besides making it fun to do, Michael explained how it was just another way to go into the most useful altered states. From these states, you can better manifest a happier world.

What is great at the moment is to see celebrities such as Bono and Bob Geldolf using their influence and celebrity status to promote help for the third world. I remember being at a U2 concert as Bono described the plan to "make poverty history." It is wonderful to see someone taking such a stand for such a great cause. Now, although we don't have the same opportunities to make such an impact, we can join with such missions and do whatever we can to improve the quality of the world for every human being on it. The best way to influence others is through your own actions, and when you take good actions, you inspire good actions.

OF: Richard, thank you so much. It feels like I've got a solution to the world's problems.

In his usual literal style, Richard cleared this up for me.

RB: I didn't know the world had problems—the sucker just spins a thousand miles an hour round and round and round, and nobody flies off, except every once in a while.

I smiled. I looked out the window to the deep-blue ocean and saw the sparkling brightness that rested beautifully on the water. Richard looked out as well. Then there was a silence, and in that silence I realized something: we were sitting in a hotel in paradise, and the real paradise was not the lovely world outside, it was contained in the wisdom of choosing your own personal freedom.

Spiritual Freedom Exercises

1. Write down all the merits of reincarnation as an explanation of where we are going after death and all the merits of heaven as where we are going after death. Compare the two.

    You can also include whatever your own perspective is and find arguments in favor of all three.

2. Describe a spiritual experience you have had and how it has affected you.

3. Learn as much as you can about all the different religions.

4. Travel to and talk with people from as many different countries as you can.

5. If you were God, and you were giving the human you a reason to be, what meaning would you give yourself?

6. Every day, make some contribution to the welfare of the world in some way.

7. Be aware of your actions and attempt to always do the right thing for the right reasons.

CHAPTER 55

Random Ramblings 6: A Spiritual Experience

PEOPLE ALWAYS ASK ME what the most spiritual experience I have ever had was. I think back to all the amazing temples I visited in Tibet. I think about the seminar I went to with the amazing Dalai Lama. I think about the revered gurus and lamas I got to meet and was blessed by in the temples. I think of some of the weddings I've been to as two souls united themselves forever. There were so many spiritual experiences where I felt a real connection with God—however, one stands out above the others.

The heat had been dramatically intense all day. I stood there with 80,000 people that I didn't know, all of us there for the same reason. The gentle wind was starting to blow as it neared eight o'clock in the evening. We had come a long way, and it was soon about to begin. The excitement filled every human as far as I could see. We all wore our colors, ready to make our offerings of support. We were ready for the hymns we would sing, together, many thousands of us. I was there with a friend. We looked at each other. We were in heaven.

The place was Seville. The stadium was El Estadio Olympico. It was a warm May evening in 2003. It had been a gorgeously sunny day in Spain. The Scottish soccer team Glasgow Celtic was playing FC Porto in the UEFA Cup final. Now I know some reading this might feel disgusted by the thought of soccer being a spiritual experience, but please read on. Let me explain.

The hours leading up to the match had been a real carnival. The 75,000 Celtic fans who had come over for the game crowded in the city of Seville and took it over. Every bar was packed as far as the eye could see with green and white (the Celtic colors). That day I and my friend Ruairi had a few cervezas and met many fans who had come from Scotland and Ireland for the game. Many did not have tickets, but that didn't matter. They were there to show their support.

We mixed with the Porto fans, wishing them luck, and despite the language barrier we made friends with them. Everyone was ecstatic and full of joy. The police all seemed to be enjoying the festivities, as there was no trouble, just lots of people singing and dancing in the streets. The police were okay with that. That day many of us had sat in the waterfall in the main square, singing, getting wet, and decorating the statue with scarves and hats. It was wonderful.

That evening we arrived at the stadium, and as the match was about to begin, the songs began. At one stage, we, along with every one of the 50,000 Celtic fans in the stadium, all held up our scarves as we sang in unison. It was absolutely breathtaking. As I surveyed the stadium, there was green, white, and orange throughout. It was a sight to behold, one that I will never forget.

It was the most exciting event I can ever remember. Our opponents, FC Porto, scored first. It was gut-wrenching, but we took solace in the fact that there was still plenty of time to go. Then, just after halftime, our own hero, Henrik Larsson, playing absolutely brilliantly, got a goal back. Minutes later, our hearts sank again, as Porto scored once more. Then, like clockwork, Henrik scored a fantastic goal and leveled things again. Everyone's emotions were manic. Their goals felt like spikes to the heart; our goals felt like immense pleasure, bliss, and relief all rolled into one. Each time we scored, we lost all control and moved about kissing and hugging each other.

The game went into extra time, and in the torturous, dying minutes, tragedy crushed us. After chances at both ends, Porto scored, and a minute

Seville: The view that warmed my heart.

later the match ended. We were devastated. The months of hope and watching our team overcome the odds to win their right to be in a European final for the first time in over thirty years—and we lost. However, as I looked out at the eleven green and white shirts on the field and realized how they had fought their hearts out for this, I began to feel a deep sense of pride all over. They all sat and lay dejected across the field, inconsolable, with their hearts broken.

At that moment, something amazing happened. I stood up along with every one of the 50,000 Celtic supporters at the stadium. It's like we all had a psychic connection. We began to sing to them, "We are Celtic supporters, faithful through and through, over and over, we will follow you." In the most heartbreaking of moments, so many people were inspired by the hearts of our heroes. I have never felt prouder to be a human being. All you could see was a stadium of green and white scarves held proudly in the air. All you could hear were the thousands of us singing the team's praises while the victory cry of the other team faded into the abyss. I can't quite describe the overwhelming feelings that I felt that evening, but even now, the thought of it brings chills up and down my spine.

So much war, fighting, ignorance, hate exists in this world. Even in sports, humans can show themselves at their worst. Yet, in this very moment, I felt a wonderful sense of love for all my fellow humans. It was not about soccer in that moment. It was not about a final. It was not about winning or losing or even taking part. It was a feeling of absolute love and pride in the human race. As I sang my heart out, shivers ran up and down my spine. I have never felt closer to God.

You see, people don't realize that it's not about how many prayers you say. (Incidentally at that match I guarantee you there were more prayers said than had been said in any mass anywhere on the planet!) It's not about you trying to come across to others as holier than thou. It's not about following rigid rules and procedures and trying to force or convince everyone else to do the same. It's about something far more liberating than that.

I recently heard a program on the radio where people called in and told of moments in their lives when they cried tears of joy. Most of the guys who called admitted crying tears of joy over a soccer match. How can a game where twenty-two guys run to kick a small leather circular object around a field produce such intense emotion for those who ordinarily don't show it? Maybe it's because, in a way, football is a spiritual experience for many.

I remember people calling into this program, and one man recalled a soccer match in the 2002 summer World Cup when Ireland played Spain and Robbie Keane scored a penalty in the last minute after we had fought so hard and deserved it. He described crying at this moment, and as he described it, I remembered it vividly, chills went up my spine, and I welled up—so intense and yet without the restrictive moralistic doctrines of most religions. To many, soccer is a religion and certainly provides many experiences of bliss and suffering. The god in the game is in moments like I experienced that day in Seville—love for people.

To me, spirituality is made up of five things:

- It's about being happy with yourself and your place in this world.
- It's about loving others, treating them well, and doing the right things for the right reasons.
- It's about being grateful for all you have, all that you've done, and all the people in your life.
- It's about practicing entering altered states through rituals, prayers, or practices that enable you to connect with a greater force than yourself to make the world a better place.
- It's about respecting others in their beliefs and practices and accepting and embracing the way they are different to you.

When you can find yourself being happier and discover that you don't need any external guru to lead you to enlightenment, you can focus on reveling in what you have and what you can learn from everything. You can begin to try lots of different things and discover powerful ways of connecting at a deeper level with yourself.

In spiritual moments, sometimes it seems impossible to describe how joyful and blissful we feel.

All we can do is experience these moments and remember our experience of them so that it expands our ability to feel even better than before.

In that stadium that day, I had an epiphany moment of what true joy was all about. I experienced absolute love for the human race with no misgivings. I felt it in that moment with so many others. Whether you believe that god is Buddha, Jesus, Allah, Shiva, or whoever, regardless, you can live a spiritually enlightened life, once you accept that it's okay to differ from others. The feeling of absolute love for your fellow human beings is one of the most spiritual acts you can perform. And one summer evening in Seville, I felt closer to God and heaven than I ever had. I understood what a spiritual experience felt like.

Conclusion:
The Source of Human Joy

Every so often, a moment can just grab you and show you an inevitable truth.
In life, all we have are moments.
We can all be free in these moments.
We can all love in these moments.
It's just a choice.
Between fear and strength.
Between surrender and determination.
Between the chains of the free and the freedom of love.
It's about making every single moment count.
Only then can freedom and love be one again.

It was one of the greatest stories ever. They were free, and they were happy. They didn't need a reason. Life was simply wonderful. They had all they needed, and they made their lives wonderful. Most moments of every day, they were encouraged and treated brilliantly by their teachers. They were praised constantly and told they were really good people.

They were free from all fears and worried about nothing at all. They were heroes in their own right and given so many supportive messages that they became very secure and sure of themselves and what they could do. They connected with others around them and made fantastic new friends. Nobody could push their buttons. They were just happy. Some wanted to live life wildly. Some carried on enjoying every normal moment. Everyone was free to some extent, some more free than others.

They were constantly reassured about and learned from what they did. They were made to feel good each time they made a mistake because they knew they were learning. They were inspired to go for everything that they ever wanted. They grew more hopeful every day. They were proud of themselves and of each other and they expressed this. Meanwhile their teachers made things better, and they wondered how much better life could be. They were on top of everything they did and had to do. They loved life and spending time with each other.

They often had moments that were tough, but they knew they'd get over them and be better people for it. Deep down they knew they would have to learn valuable lessons from these moments. They were happy regardless. Their health improved from the good treatment and disciplines they engaged in. They slept soundly every night. Their lives had wonderful meaning. They walked around feeling really happy, relaxed, confident, centered, and clearheaded about everything. They enjoyed their freedom.

So, who were they? Who were their teachers?

They were the human race. Their teachers were their minds.

In this book, you have learned habitual ways of thinking, feeling, and behaving. Many of these habits can free you to experience happiness, love, self-confidence, motivation, courage, strength, and delight. These, in turn, affect your health, your relationships, and your life.

The source of human joy lies within you. It always has, and it always will. It lies within the way you use your brain and the way you control the way you think. It lies within the way you create powerful positive changes in yourself and others. It lies within your ability to control the way you feel about yourself, your life, and your problems. It lies within your ability to connect with and be loving to other people. It lies within your ability to become spiritually enlightened and loving toward the universe and all the diversity that exists in it.

These five abilities represent the five levels of freedom that, once achieved, will enable you to live and experience a joy-filled life. Beware, for the chains of the free are never far away. They always linger somewhere, around many corners in the future. What is imperative is that you are aware of this and you ensure that, when such chains reappear, you will remain free in every sense of the word. It requires discipline, it requires effort, it requires determination. In committing to these three qualities, however, the rewards are wonderful.

But remember that your moments can be robbed at any time. The more time you spend in the chains of the free, the more you spend locked up in regret, fear, sadness, anger, and apathy, the more you'll rob yourself. Take this moment now. Make it count. Really make it count. Take your life by the scruff of your neck and make it count. Make it worthwhile. Take your dreams and go for them. Take your freedom. It is right there. Become free. Free from all the negativity. Free from all the bad feelings and habits. Become free to use the ideas you've learned and manifest them in your life.

Live free. Learn the lessons of life. Connect with as many people as you can. Experience the true highs and deal with the true lows of life. Let yourself roam free in a world full of love. At some point in the past, you were put on this earth. At some point in the future, you will die. While you are here, make it count. Live. Really live. Escape from the chains of sorrow and fear. Say good-bye to your captors and give yourself a wonderful life full of true happiness, true freedom, and true love. They are all out there for you no matter how things seem from time to time. They are out there and are meant for you. As a human, you are capable of amazing feats. Your brain is the greatest miracle of all and can do wonders when you use it well. Always remember that.

> *"The things you have learned here are only the beginning.*
> *The real laboratory is when you leave."*
>
> —RICHARD BANDLER

By the time I stood on that stage in India on July 5, 2003, I had already recorded some of my conversations with Richard. I had learned so many things, but as I experienced my world tour, I began to understand what Richard was really talking about. This whole thing about change and happiness, having good relationships and becoming more enlightened spiritually—all of it was so much simpler than I really believed.

I attempted to convey all I could to the crowd of people who had come to see me, to ensure they, like the gentlemen who had come over a thousand miles to see me, would get ideas that could transform their lives. I spoke my heart out. Afterward, hundreds of people came up to me, thanking me profusely. They thanked me for all the workshops I was doing for free in India and all the good I would be doing. I smiled and had pictures taken with them. I gave them and their children the blessings they asked for. I turned around to my group of friends that looked after me, Jan, Van, Dan, Sajani, and so many others who had welcomed me with open arms. I smiled. I thought of home and I realized how special life really is and how wonderful the universe can be. I wondered what took me so long to really see it.

You see, that was a highlight of my life, but I realized that there are so many highlights. I have gone from watching Richard on stage inspire me greatly to cotraining with him and Brian only a few years later. I have gone from seeing that things will never be as they were but will always change, and as long as I'm ready I can influence them well. I've turned my life around, and I've dealt with some hardships, and there will be more to come, but through them all will be lessons; through them all, I will grow. I will love and lose. I will decide and choose. Maybe life will bring material riches and maybe not. Maybe life will bring my love to me, whoever she is. Maybe life will allow me to connect with millions of people. Maybe not. I don't know how long I have left on this planet, but however long it is, I do know I will make it count. I know with certainty that I will live well.

Richard has helped me to discern that what life is really about are the moments, and the moments in between the moments. That is what gives life breath. It is about ensuring that you treat each moment as sacred and special. It's about wasting precious few on feeling bad and arguing, and investing so many more into experiencing joy and love, freedom and bliss. I went from being depressed to loving life, from being fearful to enjoying adventure and living life to the full, from being unsure of myself to finding and becoming the person I want to be more and more every day. You can do it all, too. It is possible. I have proved that. And as a friend of mine once said, "You can't argue with the experience."

In all the things I've done, places I've been, achievements I've obtained, I owe an awful lot to my friend and mentor Dr. Richard Bandler. His genius enables me to have the wisdom to make a difference. I always had heart. He has given me a mission upon which to focus that heart. There is no better person to lead us into a heaven on earth. This better world is possible when we can learn lessons from his words and allow his ideas to manifest freedom and love in our own lives. I am very proud to have had the opportunity to help him share his gift to the world.

I remember my final conversation with Richard for this book; it was about changing the world. He had taught all day and was visibly tired, yet when it came to sharing what was in his head with me, he spoke at an incessantly rapid pace. He switched from story to story, in his own unique way expressing how we could change the world, and not for the first time, I really appreciated the fact I was two steps away from an exceptional human being.

I recalled that the moment of epiphany in the boat in Fiji did change how I thought about my life. I remember eventually arriving at the bigger boat and getting on board only to spend the next hour being sick. My heart raced for the next few hours as I began to make my way home. I didn't know it then, but I was to eventually return to bad news and heartbreak with the breakup of my relationship. However, my life continued to change as it always does, and I continued to learn as I always do. Life is unpredictable, and once more, I turned my life around. No matter what happens, you can always do this. When you know this, no amount of pain, no amount of heartbreak, no amount of suffering can break you. You can deal with anything.

Once upon a time in my life, I was really miserable with everything, but I found the strength to make a promise to myself. My promise was to live, really live, and to find out how wonderful life can be. I am still finding out, but I had no idea it could be this good. Through the philosophies, attitudes, ideas, and suggestions brought together in this book, I have discovered that life can be beautiful. I have never felt as free as I do today.

The main secret through all my experiences and conversations with Richard was that all bad feelings come from bad chemistry, and when you can realize this, then instead of blaming the world and feeling bad about your circumstances, you can remember it's only because of your brain chemistry, and you can change your brain chemistry by changing the way you think.

When I looked out from my apartment window as the storm graced the world, I realized how much beauty there was in even the darkest of weather. I understood for once that I could do nothing about it, simply experience it and let it be. As I felt the wet wind on my face, I simply enjoyed it—that miracle of being alive—and smiled brightly to myself.

This can be the book to turn your life around. Will you let it? It shows you how you can be happier. It explains how you can be smarter. It gives you a way in which you can be freer. It teaches you how you can give and receive more love. It is a book of the truth about the real lies that we can realize no longer matter. It contains only words, but words can have magic inside them. Words are ideas. Ideas create realities. Choose to create your own reality. You have that choice.

What are you going to do with that choice? Many people I know settle. They settle in unfulfilling relationships; they settle in unhappy jobs. They settle in unhealthy lifestyles. They settle in sadness, misery, pain, and fear. Will you settle? Or will you act? Will you act and choose to live this day as if it were the most important day of your life? This week, the most important week? This year, the most important year? ACT. We have only a short time here. Make it count.

Choose to smile. Choose to laugh. Choose to relate. Choose to embrace. Choose to be happy. Choose to never give up. Choose to set goals. Choose to believe in yourself. Choose to believe what's useful. Choose to focus on good things and good thoughts. Choose to deal with the tough times and difficult people with grace. Choose to connect with the universe. Choose to do the exercises in this book. Choose to live free. Choose to love. May you make those choices now, and may you discover a wonderful life and an amazing future full of love and happiness.

As I thanked Richard, I asked him of his hopes for the future.

RB: What would I like the future to be like? I'd like peace on earth and goodwill to all people and for karma to come along a little bit faster and to have free television once again!

I smiled, pressed the stop button on the recorder and ejected the tape for the final time. I had learned about personal freedom from one of the greatest geniuses of our era. It had been a thrilling few years. At the same time, I couldn't help but feel that my adventures in personal freedom had only just begun.

The end of this book
. . . the start of your freedom?

Glossary

Below is a list of some of the main processes related to NLP that are discussed in this book.

Anchoring The process of associating an internal response with an external trigger, so that the response can be reaccessed.

Auditory Relating to the sense of hearing.

Behavior The specific actions we take.

Calibration The process of learning to read another person's unconscious, nonverbal responses by observing another's behavior and the relation of their behavior with their internal response.

Congruence When a person's beliefs, state, and behavior are all fully oriented toward securing a desired outcome.

Conscious mind The part of your mind that is working when you are alert and aware. It is your critical faculty and your source of reason and logic. It seems to run constantly all day while you are awake, and its focus is always on particular thoughts. It is mainly controlled by the automatic processes of the unconscious mind.

Criteria The values a person uses to make decisions.

Design Human Engineering A technology and evolutionary tool created by Dr. Bandler in the late 1980s–early 1990s that focuses on using more of our brain to do more than was previously possible.

Gustatory Relating to the sense of taste.

Hypnosis An application of NLP as well as a field in its own right. Hypnosis is the process of guiding a person into a state in which they have more direct access to their unconscious mind, which is where powerful changes can be made, deliberately, through the use of suggestion.

Kinesthetic Related to body sensations.

Meta-model A model developed by Richard Bandler and John Grinder that suggests questions that enable people to specify information, clarify information, and open up and enrich the model of a person's world.

Metaphor Stories and analogies.

Meta-program A learned process for sorting and organizing information and internal strategies.

Milton Model A model developed by Richard Bandler and John Grinder on the patterns of hypnotic techniques used by Milton H. Erickson, the clinical hypnotherapist, and other masters of persuasion.

Neuro-Hypnotic Repatterning A technology that uses the hypnotic process to restructure people at the level of cortical pathways.

Neuro-Linguistic Programming An attitude, methodology, and technology that teaches people how to improve the quality of their lives. It is an educational tool that teaches people how to communicate more effectively with themselves and with others. It is designed to help people to have personal freedom in the way they think, feel, and behave.

Rapport The existence of trust and harmony in a relationship.

Representational Systems The five systems that we take information in from the world. Through these systems (our five senses) we create a representation of the information we take in.

State The total ongoing mental, emotional, and physical conditions of a person at a given moment of time.

Strategy A set of mental and behavioral steps to achieve an outcome.

Submodalities The sensory qualities of the representations we create through our representational systems.

Trance A state commonly experienced as a result of hypnosis. It is also a state of mind that is characterized by a focus of thought. We live in many different trances depending on what our mind is absorbed in at any given moment (television, driving, eating, etc.).

Unconscious Installation The process of installing skills, ideas, and suggestions inside people through communicating with their unconscious minds.

Unconscious Mind The part of your mind that is working all the time. It is what produces your dreams and regulates your bodily functions, such as your heartbeat, breathing, and habitual patterns of behavior. It contains all your memories, wisdom, and perception. It runs the automatic programs of thinking and behaving and therefore is the best place to make changes permanent.

Visual Relating to the sense of sight.

Well-formed Outcomes Goals that are set according to well-formed conditions. These conditions are that the goals must be positive, specific, sensory-based, ecological, and maintainable by the individual themselves.

Recommended Reading

Books

Bandler, Richard. *Get the Life You Want.* Deerfield Beach, FL: Health Communications, Inc., 2008.

———. *Richard Bandler's Guide to Trance-formation.* Deerfield Beach, FL: Health Communications, Inc., 2008.

———. *The Adventures of Anybody.* Capitola, CA: Meta Publications, 1993.

———. *Magic in Action.* Capitola, CA: Meta Publications, 1985.

———. *Time for a Change* Capitola, CA: Meta Publications, 1993.

———. *Using Your Brain for a Change.* Durango, CO: Real People Press, 1985.

Bandler, Richard, Judith Delozier, and John Grinder. *Patterns of the Hypnotic Techniques of Milton H. Erickson,* Volume 2. Capitola, CA: Meta Publications, 1977.

Bandler, Richard, and John Grinder. *Frogs into Princes.* Capitola, CA: Real People Press, 1979.

———. *Patterns of the Hypnotic Techniques of Milton H. Erickson,* Volume 1. Capitola, CA: Meta Publications, 1975.

———. *The Structure of Magic.* Capitola, CA: Meta Publications, 1975.

———. *The Structure of Magic.* Volume 2. Capitola, CA: Meta Publications, 1975.

———. *Trance-formations.* Durango, CO: Real People Press, 1980.

Bandler, Richard, and John LaValle. *Persuasion Engineering.* Capitola, CA: Meta Publications, 1996).

Bandler, Richard, and Will McDonald. *An Insiders' Guide to Submodalities.* Capitola, CA: Meta Publications, 1989).

Fitzpatrick, Owen. *Not Enough Hours: The Secret to Making Every Second Count.* Dublin, Ireland: Poolbeg Press, Ltd., 2009).

Farrelly, Frank, and Jeffery Brandsma, *Provocative Therapy.* Capitola, CA: Meta Publications, 1974).

Guerrero, Gabriel, *Deep Transformation.* Transformation Profunda. Khaos, 2002.

347

Guerrero, Gabriel. *Design Your Destiny*. Disenando tu Destino: Khaos, 2004.

McKenna, Paul. *Change your Life in Seven Days*. New York, NY: Bantam, 2005.

Wilson, Robert Anton. *Prometheus Rising*. Flagstaff, AZ: New Falcon Press, 1983.

————. *Quantum Psychology*. Flagstaff, AZ: New Falcon Press, 1990.

Not Yet Published
Fitzpatrick, Owen. *The Charisma Code*. (Forthcoming 2010).

DVD and CD Products

Bandler, Richard. *The Art and Science of Nested Loops* (DVD).

————. *DHE 2000* (CD).

————. *Persuasion Engineering* (DVD).

————. *Personal Enhancement Series* (CD).

————. *T-Break (Hypnosis* (CD, 2008).

LaValle, John. *NLP Practitioner Set* (CD).

These and many more DVDs and CDs, both hypnotic and from seminars Richard does, are available from the NLP Store. Richard is regarded by many as the best hypnotist in the world, so his DVDs and CDs are invaluable. Available from www.nlpstore.com.

Bandler, Richard. *Adventures in Neuro-Hypnotic Repatterning* (DVD set and PAL-version videos, 2002).

————. *Thirty Years of NLP: How to Live a Happy Life* (DVD set, 2003).

These and other products by Richard Bandler are available from Matrix Essential Training Alliance, www.meta-nlp.co.uk; email: enquiries@meta-nlp.co.uk; phone +44 (0)1749 871126; fax +44 (0)1749 870714.

Colbert, Brian. *The Rest of Your Life* (Hypnosis CD, 2002).

————. *Happy Dayz* (DVD set, 2007).

————. *Trancetripping* (Hypnosis CD, 2006).

————. *T-Break* (Hypnosis CD, 2008).

Fitzpatrick, Owen. *Lovin Your Life* (Hypnosis CD, 2004).

————. *Adventures in Charisma* (DVD set, 2008).

These and other CDs and DVDs available from www.nlp.ie.

Websites

www.richardbandler.com

www.nlp.ie

www.owenfitzpatrick.com

www.myownaffirmations.com

www.mysteriouspublications.com

www.NLPInstitutes.com

www.NLPTrainers.com

www.NLPLinks.com

www.purenlp.com

www.paulmckenna.com

www.neuroing.com

www.meta-nlp.co.uk

www.rawilson.com

www.lifevision.se

Recommended Training

Dr. Richard Bandler

Whether you learn NLP, DHE, NHR, hypnosis, shamanic states, or another exciting seminar with Richard, you will experience a true genius at work. Hilarious, fascinating, and one of the most creative people around, Richard performs his teaching like an art form at its best. You might have heard about him and read about him, but it is only in training with him that you get a really good example of a master at work. If you are like most people who have seen him, it will transform your life. If you are interested in learning how to have more personal freedom and interested in learning NLP from the creative genius Dr. Richard Bandler, check out www.richardbandler.com for information on training in England, Scotland, America, Mexico, and Europe.

IRISH INSTITUTE OF NLP

Owen Fitzpatrick and Brian Colbert cofounded the Irish Institute of NLP in 2001.

Brian Colbert is one of the top Licensed Master Trainers of NLP there is. His *Shoot from the Hyp* hypnosis CDs are some of the biggest sellers in the hypnotherapy and self-improvement market, and for good reason.

Owen and Brian are known for their remarkable ability to work seamlessly and hilariously together. Their unique training style reveals their great friendship and complementary skills, and they are known for their infamous and masterful, "Double Induction." Since they founded the Institute they have taught NLP training in Ireland and Scotland. They provide regular NLP Evenings, Life-Enhancement Weekends, Art of Charisma Workshops, NLP Practitioners, NLP Business Practitioners, NLP Master Practitioners, and NLP Coaching Programs. They also host events and cotrain with guests, such as Richard Bandler and John LaValle. They also do corporate consulting and present in-house training to the corporate sector in the areas of communication, sales, motivation, stress management, creativity, and business applications of NLP.

To learn NLP effectively, or to make your life and business better, visit the website today.

Irish Institute of NLP
84 Sundrive Road
Kimmage
Dublin 12
Ireland
phone: +353 (1) 490 2923
website: www.nlp.ie
e-mail: info@nlp.ie

The Society of Neuro-Linguistic Programming
Richard Bandler Licensing Agreement

The Society of Neuro-Linguistic Programming™ is set up for the purpose of exerting quality control over those training programs, services, and materials claiming to represent the model of Neuro-Linguistic Programming™ (NLP™). The seal below indicates Society Certification and is usually advertised by Society approved trainers. When you purchase NLP™ products and seminars, ask to see this seal. This is your guarantee of quality.

It is common experience for many people, when they are introduced to NLP™ and first begin to learn the technology, to be cautious and concerned with the possible uses and misuses.

As a protection for you and for those around you, the Society of NLP™ now requires participants to sign a licensing agreement that guarantees that those certified in this technology will use it with the highest integrity. It is also a way to insure that all the trainings you attend are of the highest quality and that your trainers are updated and current with the constant evolution of the field of Neuro-Linguistic Programming™ and Design Human Engineering™, etc.

For a list of recommendations, go to:

www.NLPInstitutes.com
www.NLPTrainers.com
www.NLPLinks.com

The Society of NLP
NLP™ Seminars Group International
PO Box 424
Hopatcong, NJ 07843
USA
Tel: (973) 770-3600
Website: www.purenlp.com

RICHARD BANDLER
The Father and Cocreator of NLP

GET THE LIFE YOU WANT

The Secrets to Quick and Lasting Life Change with Neuro-Linguistic Programming

Foreword by
PAUL McKENNA, Ph.D.
host of The Learning Channel's
I Can Make You Thin

Code 7760 • Hardcover • $19.95

Get the Life You Want is Richard Bandler at his best, sharing his remarkable insights, his controversial signature wit, and more than thirty-five time-tested NLP techniques that will bring about quick and lasting change in every area of your life, from breaking free of toxic or non-productive relationships, to delivering business presentations without a knot in your stomach, to quitting smoking for good.

By the father and cocreator of NLP,
NEURO-LINGUISTIC PROGRAMMING

RICHARD BANDLER'S
GUIDE to
TRANCE-
formation

HOW TO HARNESS THE POWER OF
HYPNOSIS TO IGNITE EFFORTLESS
AND LASTING CHANGE

Code 7779 • Paperback • $15.95

Richard Bandler shows how anyone can reset and
reprogram their problem behaviors to reach desired
alternatives with lasting and life-altering results.

the Vigorous Mind

Cross-Train Your Brain to Break Through Mental, Emotional, and Professional Boundaries

Discover the Power of *Kaizen* and
● expand your world ● explore your talents
● energize your life

INGRID E. CUMMINGS

Code 6985 • Paperback • $14.95

In The Vigorous Mind, professional 'Renaissance woman' Ingrid Cummings offers a soc criticism and inspiring self-improvement program that details the antidote to mental undernourishment, unfulfilling careers, untapped talents, and unexplained boredom. Through the techniques and insights in The Vigorous Mind, you will build a more complex, interconnected brain and replace indifference with cognitive reengagement, sense of optimistic gratification, and a full-to-the-brim life lived without regret.